Cohabitation Nation

Cohabitation Nation

Gender, Class, and the Remaking
of Relationships

Sharon Sassler and
Amanda Jayne Miller

UNIVERSITY OF CALIFORNIA PRESS

University of California Press, one of the most distinguished university presses in the United States, enriches lives around the world by advancing scholarship in the humanities, social sciences, and natural sciences. Its activities are supported by the UC Press Foundation and by philanthropic contributions from individuals and institutions. For more information, visit www.ucpress.edu.

University of California Press
Oakland, California

Library of Congress Cataloging-in-Publication Data

Names: Sassler, Sharon, author. | Miller, Amanda Jayne, 1979– author.
Title: Cohabitation nation : gender, class, and the remaking of relationships / Sharon Sassler and Amanda Jayne Miller.
Description: Oakland, California : University of California Press, [2017] | Includes bibliographical references and index. |
Identifiers: LCCN 2017009019 (print) | LCCN 2017012984 (ebook) | ISBN 9780520962101 (epub and ePDF) | ISBN 9780520286979 (cloth : alk. paper) | ISBN 9780520286986 (pbk : alk. paper)
Subjects: LCSH: Unmarried couples—United States—Interviews.
Classification: LCC HQ803.5 (ebook) | LCC HQ803.5 .S27 2017 (print) | DDC 306.84/10973—dc23
LC record available at https://lccn.loc.gov/2017009019

Manufactured in the United States of America

25 24 23 22 21 20 19 18 17
10 9 8 7 6 5 4 3 2 1

Contents

Tables and Figures

Acknowledgments

Many individuals and organizations made our collaboration possible, and we would like to express our thanks to them. Our greatest debt is to the Columbus couples who shared their relationship stories with us, opening up their lives and describing in such rich detail their joys, frustrations, and dreams for the future. We also want to acknowledge the assistance of Sarah Favinger, our third interviewer, who helped make this endeavor possible when one of us had other obligations. Finally, both Sharon Sassler and Amanda Miller were beneficiaries of various awards from The Ohio State University, from the Seed Grant that provided start-up money for this project, to several research fellowships that supported Amanda during the interview, transcribing, and analysis phases.

We are also grateful to Naomi Schneider for pushing us gently along, understanding when being too "popular" was beyond our limits, and her helpful suggestions. During the course of writing, Suzanne Nichols also provided very helpful suggestions and encouragement. We also owe a debt of gratitude to Paula England for her extremely cogent and careful reading of our initial draft.

We both are indebted to mentors, colleagues, and students, who helped make the research process meaningful and rich.

SHARON SASSLER

I would like to acknowledge Fran and Calvin Goldscheider, who have long served as role models in life, as well as in academia. Despite having numerous students, Fran was an exemplary advisor and dissertation chair, always generous with helpful comments, gently directing me toward new studies to enrich my work and never complaining that I had difficulty mastering when to use possessive apostrophes. Her work continues to influence my research in ways large and small, as well as how I approach teaching. Calvin, my master's thesis advisor, challenged me to think comparatively when I first arrived at Brown University, provided me with a rigorous background in my second area of interest, race and ethnicity, and pushed me to improve my arguments and written work. I look forward to many more years of intellectual and personal engagement with them. My colleagues from graduate school days at Brown, especially Ann Biddlecom, have long provided nourishment of all kinds as we pursue our various professional paths, and I cherish our gatherings at various meetings.

Several people played important encouraging roles when I initially embarked on this qualitative project. First, I would like to thank the cohabitors I interviewed in New York City when I began this project in 2000, several of whom still keep in touch with updates on their relationships, moves, careers, and families. Verta Taylor, who at the time was a professor at Ohio State, gave me the soundest of advice as I mulled whether to embark on qualitative research, including her admonition "not to give up my day job" and put aside quantitative work. Pamela Stone at Hunter College has been a constant source of wise counsel and guidance over the years, initially as my department chair and subsequently as someone who shared tips and strategies for morphing into a qualitative researcher, and advice on how to pick the best editor. Wendy Manning played a key role in encouraging me to "just go for it" and embark on a project that would ask flesh and blood people questions about how their relationships began and progressed. She continues to be the first source for new developments in cohabitation and other evolving relationship forms. Various cohabitation scholars, particularly Kara Joyner and Susan Brown and others at Bowling Green State University's Center for Family and Demographic Research and at the U.S. Census Bureau have also provided feedback and support for various components of this book. Jennifer Holland and Helga de Valk provided a welcoming environment in The Hague during the drafting of the earliest version of this book, as did many others at the Netherlands Interdisciplinary Demographic Institute.

Of course, an academic life is enriched by collaboration with smart, funny collaborators, and I have been blessed with many of these. Among those I am most indebted to for providing the best advice, picking up slack when I dropped the ball, celebrating successes, and making me laugh when I needed it are Kristi Williams, Jennifer Glass, and Yael Levitte. I have also been fortunate to work with an amazing group of former students and current collaborators, including Fenaba Addo, Katherine Michelmore, and Dela Kusi-Appouh. My colleagues at Cornell have also provided encouragement and support; I am particularly thankful to be in the same department as Kelly Musick, Laura Tach, Rachel Dunifon, Matt Hall, Maureen Waller, and Chris Wildeman, and for supportive campus demographers like Lindy Williams.

The opportunity to work with creative and talented graduate students is among the best perks of being a professor. I was particularly fortunate to have had the opportunity to work with Amanda Miller from the very beginning of her graduate school days at Ohio State. Without her hard work, willingness to invest so much sweat equity in a project initiated by a junior faculty with not much of an established track record, insight into the processes we were exploring, and amazing sense of balance and humor, we would never have completed this project. I have truly enjoyed our journey together, through several states (and countries) and schools as well as ranks. I look forward to working with and learning from her on many future projects.

Finally, I owe a huge debt to the men in my life, Dan and Ben. Dan opened my eyes to the myriad ways that social class differences are manifest in the United States. He introduced me to rural America and the Midwest, embraced my interests, and bears with me and our different work styles in our collaborations. He has even adopted some of the books' quotes as his own (particularly the one about taking out the trash). His ability to master so many new skills—including the art of moving repeatedly and becoming the best latke maker ever—has made the journey more fun, as have his quips that crack me up. Ben was born around the time this project began and has always been a part of it in some way. Whether reading together, walking to school and talking, or going on adventures, Ben constantly showed me the joys (and challenges!) of family. Both of my men have provided distraction and laughs when needed, as well as music, nourishment, and almost enough hugs.

AMANDA JAYNE MILLER

I would like to begin by thanking the late Stan Harris. Stan was my high school sociology and government teacher. When I enrolled in his class, I had no idea what sociology was; when I left his class, I couldn't imagine doing anything else. Each year, I volunteer for his favorite academic program, We the People: The Citizen and the Constitution, and every year, I am reminded what a huge impact he had on my life, both as a teacher and as a person. If we ever question how teachers matter, Stan is the perfect of example of someone who continues to influence me and many other of his former students to this day. I would also like to thank a former professor, C. Christi Baker, for teaching me how to interview while I was in my master's of social work program. It was Christi who first forced me to examine my presentation of self, and without her forthrightness (which always stemmed from a place of caring) I could not do this today.

I, too, would like to thank our colleagues from Ohio State who helped us arrive at this place. Betty Menaghan, Liana Sayer, and Kristi Williams helped me through my dissertation years, and the caring friendship of my fellow students provided inspiration for various chapters this book. You all are amazing, and I look forward to our "fancy dinners" each year at academic conventions to talk more about the wonderful things happening in your lives. I particularly want to thank Dan Carlson for his friendship, which both led to a brand new research stream and also helped provide some of the framework for the housework chapter of this book.

My colleagues at the University of Indianapolis also provide me with so much support. Thank you, especially, to my dean, Jen Drake, and department members Phylis Lan Lin, Tim Maher, Mary Moore, Jim Pennell, Bobby Potters, Kevin Whiteacre, and Dennis Williams for helping me always feel like I'm exactly where I'm meant to be as a teacher-scholar. And, there is no doubt that the heart our department, Gwen Thomas, has, without fail, always provided me with support in more ways than one.

Along the way, students Ilene Harrington, Tamara Green, Grishra Rawal, Ellison Darling, Elizabeth Horn, Heather Coyle, Brittany Sichting, and Ningning "Derek" Zhao provided invaluable support for this project. Students like you make my work such a pleasure.

Were it not for Sharon, I would not be writing this today. Our friendship was forged over a decade ago when she put out a call for interested student research assistants and I eagerly answered. She patiently taught me in the apprenticeship way of qualitative research, and we moved over time from teacher/student to mentor/mentee to friends. You have always gone above and beyond to support me professionally as well as personally. I could not ask for a better collaborator and look forward to what our next season of research and friendship brings us.

And now, more personally—I am lucky enough to have lifetime friends, many of whose names grace these pages as pseudonyms or who helped support me through various parts of the data collection and writing process. Thank you all for figuring out the appropriate way to ask "How is the book going?" to keep me motivated without pushing me on "Why isn't it done yet?" Your support and love, as well as the ways you model egalitarianism in friendships and your own relationships give me hope that equality for all is on the horizon.

Finally, for my family—the ones who show me, every day, that team work, a wicked sense of humor, and a good meal can get us through almost anything. For my parents, Rick and Pam Miller, my lifelong supporters; for my brother Josh, my first friend; and for my husband Jeremy, my everything. Thank you.

Cohabitation

Exploring Contemporary Courtship Trajectories

In the spring of 2013, various newspapers and magazines breathlessly declared that cohabitation was the "new normal."[1] Drawing from the 2006–2010 National Survey of Family Growth, these reports revealed that nearly half of women's first live-in unions with opposite sex partners—48%—were cohabitations rather than marriages. The NBC news story featured a blogger for *Glamour* magazine, who wrote about her experience moving in with her boyfriend and the couple's subsequent engagement. Commenting on the news story, family scholars discussed the growing acceptability of being in long-term committed relationships without being married. "The question becomes not who cohabits, but who doesn't," one prominent demographer of family change concluded.

The number of unmarried couples who live together in intimate unions has increased dramatically over the past few decades. As of 2010, 7.5 million heterosexual couples were living together without marriage. This was a big jump from the 5.5 million unmarried couples who lived together in 2000, and more than double the 3.2 million that were cohabiting in 1990.[2] These households are disproportionately young. As a result, the percentage of young adults who have lived with a romantic partner (or more than one) rose across the last quarter of the 20th century and continues to climb.[3] Furthermore, two-thirds of couples married since the beginning of the new century lived together before the wedding—suggesting that we have truly become a cohabitation nation.[4]

Glossed over in coverage of the new normal, however, are important social class differences in how romances progress. Less advantaged young adults are more likely to cohabit than their counterparts with college degrees and middle-class family upbringings. The outcomes of their relationships also differ. For college-educated cohabitors like the *Glamour* blogger, cohabitation frequently leads to marriage within a few years. For the less privileged, the sequence is more varied and often bumpier. These cohabitors face a much greater likelihood of having children, often unintentionally, breaking up before a wedding, or divorcing if they do tie the knot.

Describing the relationship patterns of the highly educated as the new normal ignores the challenges to forming stable and fulfilling intimate relationships that the less advantaged face. Compared to their college-educated counterparts, young adults with less schooling and from less advantaged families are taking longer to complete their educations, attain financial independence, find decent full-time jobs, and move out of the parental home.[5] While the highly educated have not been immune to the social and economic changes that have transformed American society over the past few decades, the growing divide in our country between the more and the less advantaged suggests a need to move beyond a narrow focus on the relationship pathways of the highly educated.

What our research discovered is that the very trajectories couples follow—the steps leading up to shared living, the reasons for moving in with a partner, and what happens once couples are sharing a home— are quite dissimilar. For example, young adults from less privileged family backgrounds move in together far more rapidly, often within a few months of meeting, than do those from middle-class backgrounds. Compared to their college-educated counterparts, their reasons for cohabiting more often hinge on economic need or lack of the financial wherewithal to rent an apartment, rather than simple convenience or to test the waters for marriage. Less advantaged young adults more often face barriers to accessing resources—such as family support, health care coverage for contraception, and economic opportunities—that can strengthen relationships. Social class also influences the ways that couples negotiate their relationships, from how housework gets done, to whether and when to become more serious, to what kind of contraception they use—if any.[6] Finally, gender roles—in particular, the ability of the female partner to have a say in how relationships progress or change—are enacted quite differently among more and less privileged couples. In other words, common presumptions about the new normal mask considerable social class variation in relationship progression.

The challenges faced by young adults as they form romantic relationships have intensified by the decade. Fewer Americans are getting married, and for many young adults the specter of divorce looms. Policy makers often tout marriage as a solution for all that ails us. Yet describing the relationship patterns of the highly educated as the new normal ignores the challenges to forming stable and fulfilling intimate relationships that the less advantaged face. A real understanding of the factors reshaping the American family requires a fuller awareness of not just how the highly educated meet, form intimate relationships, and ultimately marry, but also how young adults who are located at different spots on the advantage curve fare. Illuminating those differences is the mission of this book.

WHAT WE KNOW ABOUT RELATIONSHIP PROGRESSION

While our study set out to examine social class differences in how cohabiting relationships progressed, a great deal of existing research provided empirical and qualitative grounding for our agenda. The basic facts about contemporary union formation—what proportions of adults cohabit, how that varies by educational attainment or race, and shifts in the factors conditioning transitions from cohabitation into marriage—are well known.[7] Less well understood are whether attitudes about cohabitation as an alternative rather than a precursor to marriage differ by social class background, or if gender norms work in ways that differentiate behaviors and experiences. We summarize that background here, from time to time pointing out holes that invited our attention.

Is Everyone Doing It? A Snapshot of How Cohabitation Varies by Educational Attainment

As is the case with other new family behaviors—including bearing children outside of marriage, serial cohabitation, and multipartner fertility—highly educated young adults and those from families where parents also have educational credentials are considerably less likely to have cohabited as their first coresidential union than women and men with lower levels of educational attainment. Data from the National Survey of Family Growth provide a snapshot of these differences. One in five women (20.2%) aged 22 to 44 who had not completed high

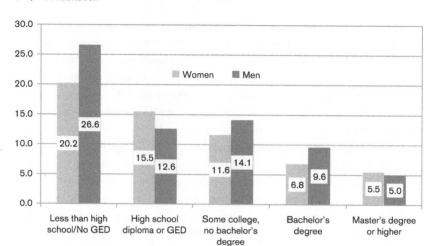

FIGURE 1. Percentage of Women and Men Age 22–44 Who Are Currently Cohabiting: United States, 2006–2010

school were cohabiting in 2010. So were 15.5% of women with a high school diploma or GED. But only 6.8% of women who had a bachelor's degree were cohabiting. Similar trends emerged for men, though college-educated men were more likely to be cohabiting than their female counterparts (see Figure 1).[8]

Focusing on who is cohabiting at one point in time understates the proportion that have *ever* lived with a partner, as many of these unions either break up or transition into marriage.[9] To get a better approximation of the prevalence of cohabitation and how it varies by educational attainment, demographers also look at those whose first union was cohabitation (rather than marriage). Even though the proportion of those who have cohabited has increased across all education levels over time (see Figure 2), women with a bachelor's degree are far less likely to have cohabited as their first union than women with more limited education. Between 1995 and 2006–2010, the proportion of women who first lived with their male partners grew by 38% among the college educated, compared with 59% among those with a high school diploma.[10] In the words of demographers Larry Bumpass, James Sweet, and Andrew Cherlin, "College graduates have been not the innovators in the spread of cohabitation, but rather the imitators."[11]

Also of note is the age at which people move in with a sexual partner. Women who do not pursue or complete a bachelor's education enter into cohabiting relationships at younger ages than those who obtain a

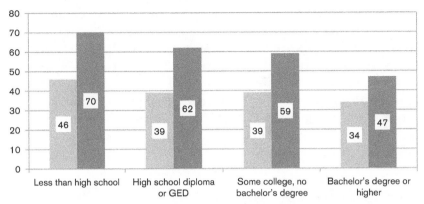

FIGURE 2. Percentage of Women Age 22–44 Whose First Union Was a Cohabitation, by Education: United States, 1995 and 2006–2010

college diploma. By age 25, almost two-thirds of women who received a high school diploma (or GED) but no more schooling (64%) had cohabited, compared with only 36% of women who had completed college.[12] What this means is that even when the most highly educated adults engage in the same behavior as their less educated counterparts, they do so differently. They are often older and have completed their schooling, or at least hold a degree that sets them on the road to the middle class. They may also be better established in the job market.

Finally, there are also sizable differences in what ensues once couples begin living together. Take the case of our happy cohabiting *Glamour* blogger, whose story begins this chapter. After dating for two years, she and her boyfriend moved in together. Before taking that step, she had plenty of time to determine how they got along, whether they were able to manage disagreements and finances, if she could tolerate how neat or messy he was, his willingness to compromise, if he wanted children or not, as well as whether he left the toilet seat up or put the cap back on the toothpaste. But in this day and age, relatively few sexually involved adults date for long before moving in together—in part because it's expensive to maintain two separate places.[13] Dating couples who are romantically and sexually involved for longer periods before cohabiting are better able to have serious conversations about the future than are couples who move in together early on.

All this leads—sometimes—to the grand finale for many relationships. Our *Glamour* blogger provides a neat and tidy ending to the story. A little over a year after moving in together, her partner proposed, and when she was interviewed for the NBC news story, they were planning their destination wedding in Aruba.[14] That is consistent with what we know from the national data: Cohabitors who have at least bachelor's degrees often transition into marriage within a few years of moving in with their first and only live-in partner.[15] But while living with a partner is now a normative step in the transition to adulthood, there are important social class differences in the timing, progression, and quality of cohabiting unions. What is it about social class that results in these differences?

The Importance of Social Class

Transformations in family formation processes have taken front stage in contemporary public policy debates in the United States. But much of that attention has focused on the child-bearing and union formation patterns of the most disadvantaged populations—those who have very limited educational attainment and have often grown up in poverty. Overlooked in this emphasis on low-income families is growing evidence of divergence in the life opportunities available for the moderately educated—a group that accounts for the majority of American adults. As of 2006, when we completed our interviews, 58% of Americans aged 25 and older had obtained a high school degree or pursued some postsecondary schooling but lacked a bachelor's degree. Only 28% of those in their mid-twenties or older had a college degree or more.[16]

This group was not always neglected by researchers. In the 1960s and 1970s scholars such as Mirra Komarovsky (1964, *Blue Collar Marriage*), Arthur B. Shostak (1969, *Blue-Collar Life*), Lillian Rubin (1976, *Worlds of Pain*), and Chaya Piotrkowski (1979, *Work and the Family System*) focused their attention on the family lives of the group that accounted for the bulk of American families. Many of these studies utilized qualitative approaches to better understand the ways that families who were described as "working class" made sense of the challenges of modernization, consumerism, and changing gender roles. Between the 1960s and the latter half of the 20th century, however, the working class went missing from scholarly analysis.

In his 2014 book, *Labor's Love Lost*, the distinguished family sociologist Andrew Cherlin chronicled the fall of the working-class family, which had been classified largely on the basis of the types of jobs that men held—in industrial factories manufacturing goods, driving trucks, or working in construction. Such jobs, while perhaps not particularly satisfying or stimulating, were relatively stable, paid decently, and often were unionized. Furthermore, they were readily available for men with only a high school degree or even less. But in today's society, according to Cherlin, the challenges facing young adults who lack a bachelor's degree is that "they cannot *become* working class."[17] Good working-class jobs are hard to find. Workers are no longer needed in large numbers to man (literally) large plants that pump out steel or manufacture cars; technological advances have made these jobs obsolete or companies have transported them overseas. The labor market has hollowed out for those with only moderate levels of schooling, and the jobs of the past have been replaced by low-skilled service positions. The lack of skills required for many service jobs means that employers are not interested in training and retaining workers, often preferring to just replace them. As a result, the economic floor has become far less stable among the less educated, particularly less educated men.

The need to focus on this group has again burst into the foreground. In several books, Cherlin and others have highlighted the need to turn the spotlight on the sizable proportion of the American population that is neither the most disadvantaged (the very poor) nor the most advantaged, but rather the large group that lacks the educational credentials needed to place them firmly in the middle class.[18] The message of these books was somewhat overshadowed by the attention paid to Charles Murray's (2012) *Coming Apart: The State of White America, 1960–2010*. Murray attributed the divergence between what he termed the "college-educated elite" and those with less education to a shift away from traditional values such as marriage, religion, industriousness, and morality. Murray's work extends the libertarian and conservative perspectives attributing behavioral manifestations of inequality to individual values rather than to the structural factors contributing to wage declines, marital delay, and rising levels of personal debt. In Murray's view, economic insecurity does not result in changes in family-building behavior.[19] Rather, desires for short-term gratification, weak wills, and inadequate parental guidance have caused the economic crises rocking today's less educated adults.

Unfortunately, Murray fails to test his own assertion that "culture" causes a growing proportion of whites to make morally bad decisions regarding their lives, such as cohabiting (and bearing children within cohabiting unions) rather than marrying. Despite the dramatic historical shifts that have seriously diminished the economic prospects of today's moderately educated men and women, the closest Murray comes to testing his theory is to cite unemployment over time and to assert that plenty of jobs are available. His book does not acknowledge that though Americans without college degrees still aspire to be a part of the middle class, attaining this goal has become increasingly difficult. In fact, the prospects for these men and women, whom we term "the service class" as many worked in service jobs in retail, telemarketing, and food production, are often considerably worse than they were for the working class of previous generations.

In the past few decades, demand for low-skilled labor has steadily decreased, while demand for (and supply of) higher-educated labor has risen.[20] In 2006, when we concluded our interviews, high school graduates 25 years and older were more than twice as likely to be unemployed compared with college graduates, who also had shorter spells of unemployment and tended to earn substantially more for their labor.[21] This was the case for both men and women.

Youth with college degrees and those with only a high school diploma or some postsecondary schooling hold similar views regarding the desirability of marriage, the acceptability of premarital cohabitation, and the challenges facing marriage.[22] But cohabitation has increased the most among those with less than a bachelor's degree. Other factors have also aligned to distinguish the family formation behaviors of the more and less educated. College-educated cohabitors are far less likely to bear children within their informal unions than are less educated cohabitors, though they presumably have a similar risk of conception.[23] Furthermore, the divorce rates of the highly educated have declined, whereas the marriages of couples with lower levels of education continue to dissolve at high rates.[24] The conditions encouraging getting and staying married appear stronger among the college educated than they are for the less educated.

But just what *are* the conditions that encourage marriage among those already living together? Most Americans assert that the bedrock of marriage is love and commitment. When asked about their *own* private relationships, most individuals do not believe that marriage will improve their level of financial attainment.[25] Rather, most strongly believe in the importance of being "financially established" *prior* to getting wed, which is also a long-standing trope in literature.[26] In fact, wealth is an important predictor of first marriage.[27] Many cohabitors say they will not wed until they have a good job and some money in the bank.[28] It should not be surprising, then, that abundant evidence finds men's odds of marrying increase among those who have completed their schooling and obtained a good job. Earnings and educational attainment also predict transitions into marriage among recent cohorts of women.[29]

Less well understood is why the decision-making processes of couples with resources differ in so many ways from those of couples who are more economically challenged. Many politicians and social commentators view marriage as a means of reducing poverty in the United States.[30] But evidence that exchanging rings somehow leads disadvantaged men or women to earn more is thin, at best. While married men, on average, have higher earnings than unmarried men, much of this differential is due to selection—their desirable characteristics make them both readier for marriage *and* more marriageable to prospective spouses.[31] And increasingly, women are also positively selected into marriage, as those with college degrees and presumably more earning power are now more likely to be married than are less educated women. As a result, marriage has been transformed from a normative rite of passage for the majority into the equivalent of a luxury good attainable mostly by the privileged—leaving many of the less advantaged working toward a goal that seems increasingly out of their reach.[32]

He Said, She Said: Why Gender Still Matters

It is not just social class that impacts couples' lives. In her classic book, *The Future of Marriage,* Jessie Bernard argued that marriage differed for men and women. In her words, there were "his" and "her" marriages. According to her thesis, men benefit more from their marriage than do women because they have more power, control, and freedom, all explicitly supported by the very institution of marriage and buttressed by existing gender roles.[33] While marriages in the latter quarter of the 20th century and the early years of the 21st have become more egalitarian, it is still the case that when it comes to power, money, and prestige, men continue to hold the dominant hand in American society.

Whether that remains the case, or to the same extent, among cohabiting couples is more debatable. Cohabitors differ from married couples in many ways, including the ways they enact gender roles. Whether this is because marriage is selective of the most educated, due to the relative resources partners bring to their relationships, or because cohabitors and marrieds already hold different views regarding normative gender roles is hard to ascertain. Scholars who examine couples often focus on how gender is enacted in either paid work arrangements or the division of domestic labor. We also explore a third dimension—relationship progression—where both paid work and reproductive labor may feature in negotiating power.

Women account for about half of the paid labor force and have greatly narrowed the gap in earnings with men. But men continue to earn more than women, at all education levels. The proportion of women who out-earn their male partners has increased in recent decades. But the dominant pattern among couples is for the male to earn more than his female partner and for this gap to increase when couples bear children.[34]

In 2006 the median earnings for female high school graduates employed full-time year round was $27,240, a full $10,000 lower than wages for similar men and also only about half what women with a college degree or more earned (their median yearly income was $50,400).[35] Gender disparities in earnings, and changes in returns to education over time, have exacerbated the difficulties facing the less educated. While men still out-earn women, women have fared better than men with respect to earnings growth over time at all levels of education. Between 1979 and 2006, men with only a high school degree or some postsecondary school actually experienced a decline in inflation-adjusted earnings.[36] Over the same period, women's inflation-adjusted earnings grew, though the largest returns to education were experienced by female college graduates, whose inflation-adjusted earnings rose by 33.5% over that time period, compared with college-educated men, whose inflation-adjusted earnings grew by 18.4%.[37] These shifts have dramatically decreased the earnings gaps between men and women with only moderate levels of education, and at a far faster rate than attitudes toward gender roles have changed.[38]

Cohabiting couples demonstrate greater similarity in earnings than do married couples. So it makes sense to ask whether partners who hold more of a desired attribute—such as earning more, or having more schooling, a better job, or even being more attractive—have greater decision-making power within the relationship, what sociologists often refer to as a "relative resources" perspective.[39] The evidence suggests that this does not hold true. Even if cohabiting women earn a larger proportion of the couples' combined earnings, they still remain disadvantaged when it comes to their negotiating power relative to men.

Much more evidence, in fact, points to cultural attitudes about gender and gender roles as the primary organizing principle within American households. Normative gender roles assigning to men the dominant role of family provider and to women the primary homemaker and nurturer role persist even if she is working for pay as well, notwithstanding several decades of progressive policies, consciousness raising, and changing relations between men and women.[40] Gender theory explains these findings by noting that gender is a primary stratifier in society, one that trumps other resources. Gender is performed by individuals on a routine basis and reinforced by interactions with others. It is not created anew in each interaction but is instead shaped and constrained by the larger social structure.[41]

Cultural ideas about men's and women's roles help determine which gendered paths individuals can walk and how comfortable they are in those paths. Men in the United States have the right to be stay-at-home fathers, for example, but face challenges in integrating their roles with their individual views of self and often lack peer and communal supports—as evidenced by the fact that as of 2011, only 3.4% of all stay-at-home parents were fathers. Women, too, face individual, interactional, and institutional challenges in breaking culturally gendered norms. Those who wish to propose to their partners, for example, must first see themselves as "that kind of woman." They then must ensure that their partners will accept this reversal of tradition when the big moment comes. Finally, few cultural classics feature young women proposing to their Prince Charming. Traditional models, however, abound. Early socialization in normative gender practices include Disney classics like *Snow White* and *The Little Mermaid,* where women wait passively for men to pursue them or make deep sacrifices for their true loves. Although no hard and fast rules or regulations prohibit American adults from bucking gender traditions, hidden constraints often discourage them from doing so.

To be sure, how gender roles are enacted within romantic relationships are more varied than in the past. This is especially evident among cohabitors. Survey results reveal that cohabitors adhere less strongly to traditional gender views regarding women's place in the home or men's role as providers.[42] But that does not mean that cohabiting couples are free from the expectations and norms of gender. It is much easier to express egalitarian views than it is to practice egalitarian behaviors.[43] Just as attitudes are not always congruent with behavior, behaviors often lie along a spectrum of more or less equal, rather than fitting neatly into categories of either "egalitarian" or "traditional." Furthermore, discussions of "service class" versus "middle class" and "men" versus "women" often miss the fact that men don't always have more power than women. Those who have a college degree are not all more privileged than their less educated peers. There are intersecting layers of dominance and oppression.[44] Simply put, an individual's place in the power hierarchy cannot be explained by examining their social class or their gender in a vacuum. Rather, both must be examined simultaneously. At the same time that all women are subjected to similar cultural norms based upon their gender, the experiences of less educated women are likely different from those of middle-class women because their social class status also shapes their expectations, power, and opportunities.

What Role Does Cohabitation Serve?

To understand why the relationship trajectories of more and less advantaged young adults have diverged so dramatically also requires an understanding of the role that cohabitation has served, both in the past and today. As a living arrangement, cohabitation as we know it has not been with us very long.[45] Early research on cohabitation as a new living arrangement often presumed that it was mainly used as a precursor for marriage.[46] In fact, the majority of cohabitors surveyed in the 1980s expressed the belief that they would marry their partners, and more than half of them subsequently did so.[47] As a result, studies often concluded that living together had become simply one more stage in relationship progression, a precursor to marriage.[48]

But others challenged that notion. Examining young cohabitors living together in the 1980s and earlier, several scholars argued that cohabitation instead served as an alternative to being single—better than living and paying rent alone. They pointed to the behaviors and expectations of cohabitors to support their case. Cohabitors were more like singles than marrieds in their near-term childbearing intentions, as well as in their likelihood of being enrolled in school, owning a home, and being financially dependent upon their parents. And while cohabitors interviewed in the 1970s and 1980s were more likely than singles to anticipate getting married, the majority of those living with a partner did not report plans to wed within the next year.[49] Cohabitors interviewed in later decades demonstrated similar behaviors; most indicated that when they moved in with their partners they had not yet discussed marriage. Such findings challenged the notion that cohabitation was a stepping-stone toward marriage, at least early in coresidence.[50]

A growing body of evidence supports the idea of cohabitation as an alternative lifestyle. The proportion of couples who live together for extended periods of time has increased over the decades in the United States, though stable long-lasting cohabiting relationships still account for a relatively small share of all cohabiting unions.[51] These couples may reject the institution of marriage as a patriarchal arrangement or irrelevant in modern society or eschew the involvement of the state in their intimate affairs.[52] Among the group to receive the most attention for not marrying is the growing proportion of couples who bear children within their cohabiting unions.

As of the early years of the 21st century, the majority of babies born to women under the age of 30 were to unmarried women, and over half of those new mothers were cohabiting.[53] Cohabitation increases the risk of childbearing, and various studies have reported that cohabiting women often report their pregnancies were unintended. But contemporary young adults frequently assert that becoming a parent is not a good enough reason to marry, though many believe that living together is optimal for the child.[54] As a result, once traditional patterns of family formation—embedded in the children's chant, "First comes love, then comes marriage, then comes baby in the baby carriage!"—are being challenged.

In fact, cohabitation may serve as any or all of these things—a precursor for marriage, an alternative to being single, or an alternative to marriage—at different points in the relationship. Some couples may initially move in without thinking about or discussing marriage, viewing living together as a way to share costs while still experiencing companionship, a kind of "marriage lite" with all of the fun but fewer of the role expectations. But with increasing time together they may come to believe that their partner is a "keeper" and that their relationship is marriage worthy. Others may move in with intentions to marry their partners but come to realize that they are not compatible or that they want dramatically different things. Still others may move in with intentions of jumping the broom, but over time wonder what difference it will make in their relationships or worry that they should not "fix something that ain't broke." Existing studies, based largely on cross-sectional surveys, cannot unpack how shared living can shift between these roles over time or identify what factors may increase the likelihood that a relationship that once was a better alternative to being single will transition into a precursor to marriage or an alternative to it.

The alternatives to marriage that have arisen over the past few decades—including cohabitation, childbearing within cohabiting unions, or remaining single—are in many ways the result of the changing economic situations facing today's young adults. Such changes may, in fact, alter young people's views about the institution of marriage, as culture interacts with structure to reorient the value system of a particular segment of the population. Young adults have high expectations that they will marry someday. Among unmarried young adults in their early twenties who were interviewed in the early years of the 21st century, 83% thought it was very important or important to be married someday.[55] Our study reveals how the issues and challenges that seem so personal—like the decision to move in with a new romantic partner within a few months, or a lapse in use of contraception, or continued deferral of formalizing a relationship—reflect larger social and economic forces that contribute to the growing gap in the well-being of young adults from more and less advantaged backgrounds.

WHAT WE SET OUT TO LEARN

To understand how the relationships of young adults from across the economic spectrum progressed in the early years of the 21st century, we spent over two years interviewing cohabiting couples living in Columbus, Ohio. Between the spring of 2004 and the summer of 2006 we interviewed over 130 cohabitors—white, black, Asian, Latino, and multiracial—to find out about their relationships. Our respondents were between the ages of 18 and 36, the prime family formation years when young adults make key decisions about work, marriage, and children. Given our interest in how social class mediated relationship behaviors, we worked to recruit a sample that was moderately educated—whom we subsequently refer to as the *service class*—as well as college educated, whom we term the *middle class*.

We asked our participants a wide array of nosy, personal questions—not only about the families they had grown up in and what they had anticipated in the way of families but also how they had met their partners and how their current relationships had unfolded. In particular, we focused on understanding why they had moved in with their partners, when this occurred, what they had expected the arrangement to be like, and whether it matched their expectations. To get a flavor of their day-to-day lives, we probed about who did what in the home, if they had discussed household chores and who would do them, how living together had affected their sex lives, and if they were ready to have children (or what they were doing to prevent that eventuality if they were not). These questions are listed in Appendix A.

Who Did We Interview?

Defining social class is, of course, a thorny conceptual and methodological issue. It is rarely captured by a single measure, whether educational attainment, occupation, or earnings. We focused on both education and occupation. For our moderately educated sample, we recruited at a local community college that offered a variety of two-year degree programs and also prepared students to pursue a four-year degree at a university.[56] Despite the recruiting locale, fewer than half of these respondents were students, and most attended school part time or intermittently while working at least part time. Because of the occupations held by these respondents, throughout our study we call them the *service class*.

The jobs held by the service-class women often involved taking care of others—as nannies or veterinarian's assistants, waitresses, or baristas—or providing office support as administrative assistants or bookkeepers. Service-class men's jobs tended to be oriented toward machines or data, with more of them working in some noncredentialed way with computers or as mortgage processors. Several of the men also held traditional working-class jobs that involved physical or "dirty" work, such as mechanics, dock loaders, carpenters, or postal workers. But these men were in the minority, and only two were working in these occupations full-time; the others either could get only part-time hours or had to combine their desired manual job with other service work, as waiters or kitchen staff, to accrue enough hours to make ends meet. Many of these moderately educated cohabitors described frequent job turnover and experienced the challenges of obtaining enough hours to pay the bills. Some were working toward getting the degree that would allow them to obtain jobs they found interesting. Others were still searching for what they described as their "dream job."

Our second group, whom we call our *middle-class* cohabitors, was also defined predominantly by their level of education; the majority of these couples consisted of two partners with at least bachelor's degrees. They were recruited via signs posted at high-end grocery stores, gourmet coffee shops, and restaurants, and, in two cases, through referrals. The cohabitors in our middle-class sample were generally in professional jobs that required academic credentials, as teachers, therapists, and social workers, as well as lawyers, professors, architects, and auditors. While their jobs were also somewhat gendered, in that the men were far more likely than the women to be employed as computer programmers or in information technology, women also held jobs that required intensive work with data, as auditors or scientists. A handful of respondents in this group did not work in professions that would place them firmly in the middle class, even though they held college degrees; such respondents tended to have recently obtained their degrees in an arts-related discipline and combined their interest (e.g., photography or art) with food service (waitressing, pizza delivery) or worked providing specialized services to those who could afford them (as a pastry chef or tennis professional). A more detailed discussion of our recruitment methods, sample information, and analytic approach is available in Appendix B.

We interviewed a total of 30 couples (60 individual cohabitors) in the service-class group and another 31 couples (62 individuals) in the middle-class group. Because we were interested in how respondents perceived their own relationships, we interviewed both members of the couple separately but simultaneously. We hoped that this would better get at the "his" and "hers" story of cohabitation.

What are our couples like? Our sample of middle-class couples were slightly older than the service-class couples, but the latter were more likely to have children, either shared or from a prior relationship. The largest number of service-class couples had obtained some postsecondary schooling, typically at the community college level, whereas among the middle class not quite half had obtained a master's degree. Reflecting these educational disparities, income levels are quite a bit higher among the middle-class sample, with an average couple-level income of $67,672 versus $38,971 for the service class. Women in the service-class group were somewhat more likely than their middle-class counterparts to be bringing home the majority (60% or more) of their household income, suggesting some potential avenues for discord. Additional descriptive results about the entire sample are presented in Table 1, and details about each couple's specific characteristics are provided in Tables A1 and A2, in Appendix C.

One major distinction between the two groups was that service-class couples had been living together for considerably longer than had the middle-class couples. This is consistent with the national data.[57] The service class was also far more racially and ethnically diverse, while the middle-class couples were more likely to have grown up with parents who were married throughout their childhood. Of course, the two groups differed in other subtle ways. Style of dress, modes of speaking, and life goals, as well as when respondents expected to achieve them, varied by social class. While these may influence what they discussed or how we interacted with them, we worked hard to ensure that they were all able to express their views about their relationships, that we captured the meaning of what they were telling us, and that their stories are told here in their own words.

TABLE I DEMOGRAPHIC CHARACTERISTICS OF COHABITING COUPLES

Variables	Measures	Service Class (means/N/$)	Middle Class (means/N/$)
Age	Mean age: Men	26.4 years	28.3 years
	Mean age: Women	24.4 years	25.2 years
Relative Age	Men > 4 years older	4	11
	Women > 4 years older	2	1
	Both within 4 years	24	19
Educational Attainment	Both high school (HS) or less	1	–
	1 ≤ HS, 1 some college	6	–
	Both some college/associate's degree	19	–
	1 HS, 1 BA (bachelor's degree)	1	–
	One some college, one BA	3	4
	Both BA	–	14
	One BA, one MA (master's degree)	–	10
	Both MA+	–	3
Race	Both non-Hispanic white	16	24
	Both Hispanic	1	1
	Both non-Hispanic black	4	2
	Mixed-race couple	9	4
Couple-Level Earnings[a]	Mean couple earnings	$38,971	$67,672
	$18,000–$24,999	8	–
	$25,000–$34,999	7	5
	$35,000–$49,999	8	6
	$50,000–$74,999	6	10
	$75,000–$99,999	1	5
	$100,000 or more	–	5
Relative Earnings	Man earns more	13	14
	Woman earns more	6	3
	Each partner earns 40–60% of the income	11	14
Marital Status	Both never married (NM)	24	26
	One NM, one previously married	6	5
Parental Status	Both no children	16	27
	Both share children[b]	5	2
	Man has children (not woman)	6	2
	Woman has children (not man)	2	0
	Each has a child from a previous relationship	1	0
Duration of Cohabitation	3–6 months	8	12
	7–11 months	2	1
	12–23 months	5	12
	24–35 months	7	4
	3 years or more	8	2
N		30	31

[a] Couple-level income is determined by summing each partner's reported individual income. One man in the service class and one man and one woman in the middle class refused to report their income. Their partners' reports were used to determine their couple-level income. In another instance, neither partner reported a middle-class man's income; instead, it was set to the mean of men's income for his social class.

[b] In two service-class couples the partners share a child and the male partner also has a child from a previous relationship.

A READER'S GUIDE TO OUR BOOK

In the following chapters we showcase the thoughts and feelings of our couples about what it means to live together in 21st century America. This book uses their stories to reveal how contemporary relationships progress and how social class and gender shape the ways that men and women negotiate change or maintain stability in relationships that lack clear rules or guidelines. We focus on the relationship processes that form the underlying layers of romantic relationships, expectations, and behaviors. Our book documents how individual men and women cope with creating families in the midst of transitioning into adulthood during a time of economic flux. We show the ways in which traditional aspects of relationships can change and how in some ways gender norms remain entrenched. More important, we examine how social class shapes virtually every aspect of relationship progression, from dating to moving in together to discussing the future. Our respondents' experiences shed light on the factors contributing to the diverging destinies of young adults from more and less advantaged backgrounds and how that is reflected in the families they form.

In the next two chapters we explore the stages leading up to and into shared living. Discussions of such experiences are largely absent in the academic literature on relationships, especially cohabitation. In Chapter 2 we explore how couples' relationships began, with a focus on the role that gender norms played in shaping who initiated the romance and determined when it would advance into shared living. Chapter 3 examines the speed of couples' entrance into cohabitation after the start of their relationships. We utilize our respondents' stories about what shaped their decision to move in together and highlight how these reasons differ by social class. These variations, we argue, reverberate through subsequent stages of couples' relationships.

Then we explore the nitty gritty of daily life among our cohabiting couples. Chapter 4 delves into how couples manage the division of housework, while Chapter 5 explores their desire to plan or defer childbearing, detailing the contraceptive behaviors of couples, their idealized time frame for having children, and their responses to pregnancy scares or actual conceptions. We consider these the underlying scaffolding helping to support or undermine the relationship. Couples who are best able to achieve a balance of domestic work that is mutually satisfying to both partners have a greater likelihood of remaining together, while couples that are on the same page regarding whether or when to bear children, as well as how to avoid conception until the timing is right, should also be better able to address the other challenges that life throws at them. These chapters provide some of the first and most in-depth studies of the factors shaping the daily lives of cohabiting young adults.

Finally we explore factors shaping relationship stability and progression. Chapter 6 examines couples' attitudes toward marriage relative to dating or cohabitation. Chapter 7 explores our couples' relationship futures—if and how they actually discuss marriage and negotiate whether or not to become engaged. In Chapter 8, we draw out the implications of these results for the future of the family and suggest some policies for narrowing the bifurcating outcomes of young adults from more and less advantaged backgrounds.

In what ways have the family formation processes of young American adults changed over the past few decades, and are there ways in which they have largely remained the same? Chapter 2 examines who made the key moves as these young adults met and became couples, along the way exploring if those who enter cohabiting unions engage in behaviors that could set them apart from married couples, perhaps flipping the normative gender script to enable women to be more assertive or minimizing the costs of the sexual double standard. What happens once couples begin dating, and how do relationships that in the past might have transitioned directly into marriage instead lead to cohabitation? Let's find out.

2

In the Beginning

Becoming a Couple

The process of partnering has changed radically over the past few decades. Internet dating apps have proliferated, providing seemingly limitless opportunities along with possibilities for liberation, danger, and uncertainty. While the concept of a matchmaker is not new (cue the music to *Fiddler on the Roof*), helping individuals find their true love has become increasingly commercialized in today's busy world.[1] Niche sites now promise to help individuals find soul mates based on demographic characteristics, religious beliefs, or even hobbies.[2] But have contemporary courtship processes—based on 21st century notions of open sexuality and personal fulfillment—changed the way young people behave in seeking out relationships?

Our research reveals the complexity behind modern day courtships. Women are increasingly pursuing advanced education, working in the paid labor force, and when they partner, living in dual-earner couples. Many young adults profess a desire for egalitarian partnerships, where work and home responsibilities are shared. In such a world, gender distinctions in how relationships begin—who initiates dating, for example, or proposes that couples live together—should disappear. But when it comes to the dating and mating scene, change has been slow. The stories our respondents told about how they met revealed that men generally retained the upper hand in initiating romantic relationships.

While new ways of courtship are evident, change in the processes used by young adults to advance relationships is not yet fully accepted. This is true even though the relatively new courtship phase of cohabitation gives both women and men the opportunity to push the boundaries in various ways. Women who attempted to initiate romantic relationships were often met with male resistance—and experienced considerable anxiety themselves. On the other hand, waiting to be asked out is far from comfortable, and men also feel burdened by having to be the date initiator, especially when signals are hard to read. Men with few resources, furthermore, may worry that they lack the means to be a good date because of expectations that they pay for some kind of social activity.

That said, we found that when it came to relationship initiation, gender trumped social class. College-educated women may have imbibed notions of equality to a greater extent than less educated women, but all women remained unified in the gender bind that left them waiting for the man to ask them out. In this chapter, we explore who initiated "the ask" that launched our couples' romantic relationships. Then we see whether the gender balance changed when it came to progressing into shared living. Our bird's eye view into how men and women become couples reveals how gender norms are established, reified, and challenged. But mainly, it highlights how traditional the early stages of romance remain.

A BRIEF HISTORY OF COURTSHIP: FROM FRONT PORCH TO SHACKING UP

Changes in the nature of courtship have transformed the progression of romantic relationships in the United States. In the 18th and 19th centuries, courtship rituals took place almost entirely within the purview of one's family and friends. Young men and women had ample opportunities to interact with one another at religious meetings and community gatherings or, for more privileged families, in a young woman's home. Upon finding a prospective partner, the young woman and her parents would decide whether or not to allow a young man to court her further. This often took the form of showing increasing trust in the burgeoning relationship by allowing the man to stay at the woman's home long after her parents had retired for the evening or, in some instances, even overnight in her bed.[3] Although men were still expected to woo the objects of their affection, young women (and their mothers) often acted as gatekeepers and had a great deal of power over men's behavior.[4]

In her book on courtship in 20th century America, *From Front Porch to Back Seat* Beth Bailey details how power shifted in the 1920s with the rise of automobile ownership and the paid date.[5] Suddenly, young people's actions moved beyond the eyes and ears of watchful community and family members to the soda shop, the movie theater, or lover's lane. Young men were expected to ask out a girl, drive her to a formal date, and pay the tab. In exchange, social custom specified that the woman repay him with a kiss—or more—at the end of the evening. As dating moved from the private to the public sphere and became commercialized, power dynamics within these youthful romances shifted as well. Men, especially those with more disposable income to cover the costs of dates, assumed power over relationship initiation and progression. Women's power, on the other hand, was increasingly relegated to more passive roles, such as accepting a date or a proposal. Furthermore, women were expected to control what was thought of as young men's "natural" sexuality by reciprocating a bit for the date, but stopping things before they went too far.[6]

Another turn in courtship norms occurred in the 1960s and accelerated during the 1970s, as the birth control pill enabled the sexual revolution and ushered in the era of "free love." Between 1970 and 1990, the median age at first marriage climbed for both women and men, jumping from 20.8 to 23.9 for women, and 23.2 to 26.1 for men.[7] Given the delayed age at marriage, many young adults spent more time dating, and the proportion that ended up living with a partner without marriage inexorably increased. The growing proportion of single young adults, as well as new expectations regarding sexuality within nonmarital relationships, challenged conventional notions about how relationships "should" progress. Given high rates of divorce and greater public attention to new relationship forms, some began to question whether marriage was a workable institution or was best left behind to founder on the dust heap of history.[8]

Fast-forward to the early years of the 21st century, when the median age at first marriage reached the late twenties for both sexes. Although many young adults believe that they will marry, they are less certain about how or when they will be ready for that commitment.[9] Furthermore, there is far less clarity regarding how romantic relationships *should* progress. The very term "date" conveys a musty, archaic image of a man with a firm jaw line in a blue business suit asking a woman in a bouffant hairdo out to dinner and a movie. And the decline of such rigid rules has long been touted in venues where young adults are densely congregated, such as on college campuses, where news stories around Valentine's Day regularly proclaim that dating is dead.

The rules regarding relationship initiation are also unclear. At a time when women are more likely than men to graduate from college and women increasingly contribute an equal amount, if not more, to the couple's income than the male, can a woman pursue the man of her dreams? Or does a lack of male initiation indicate that a man is, in the words of a popular movie, "just not that into you"? Must women adhere to the roles set out by Disney fantasies like Cinderella or Snow White and wait to be courted, or sacrifice themselves for love like the Little Mermaid, or are today's crop of princesses more proactive? A popular book of the 1990s asserted that women should return to well-established practices of letting men take the lead. This book, *The Rules: Time-Tested Secrets for Capturing the Heart of Mr. Right,* has been updated for the internet age (with sequels such as *The Rules for Marriage* and *The Rules for Online Dating,* published in 2002, or the most recent release, *Not Your Mother's Rules: The New Secrets for Dating,* released in 2013), but the message remains the same.[10] Men should be the ones to initiate relationships, and women must learn how to manage men to achieve their desired ends.

These traditional messages (or, in the words of advice books, rules) are well integrated into the American collective cultural psyche. Even though dating has changed in various ways over time, men are still expected to initiate relationships. Many couples find that they are unable to overcome powerful internal norms about traditional gender roles. In a study that asked women to simulate date initiation, for example, researchers found that nearly a third of the women in their study (31%) did not actually ask for the date; instead, they showed responsiveness to get the men to ask them out. These women were unable to overcome the dominant discourse of male as initiator, female as accepter.[11] Even among college students, who are generally socially liberal, the male partner is expected to initiate and plan a date. Such expectations have changed little over the recent past, persisting for at least the last 35 years.[12]

The rise of cohabitation might signal the emergence of new scripts for relationship formation and advancement among contemporary young adults. Those who enter into cohabiting unions differ in important ways from individuals who marry before living together. The men and women who live together tend to express different attitudes toward gender roles than their counterparts who marry without cohabiting; cohabiting women are more career-oriented and the men are less likely to adhere to traditional notions of providing for the family.[13] Cohabitors are also less religious than those who elect not to live together outside of marriage. Cohabitation itself provides young adults with the opportunity to create new norms and new ways of interacting within romantic relationships. Because it is incompletely institutionalized, there are fewer long-standing rules about how to be a cohabitor. Is it possible, then, that the kinds of people who enter into cohabiting relationships (or the nature of the relationship itself) have altered the ways in which relationships are initiated or forwarded?

As was true historically, social class may differentiate the process of dating (and the content of those dates). The service class has long expressed more traditional attitudes regarding appropriate gender roles. In Lillian Rubin's classic 1976 study of the working class, the antecedent of what we term the "service class," those she interviewed rarely planned for the future, whether for work or their romantic lives; rather, things just happened. Both the men and women said they married because it was expected or because they got pregnant. But over four decades have passed since Rubin documented the family experiences of America's working class. Studies of more advantaged young adults' relationships are also rare, limited largely to the realm of fiction or film or focused more on the dearth of children than the absence of partners.[14] As a result, information on couples' experiences in the early days or months of their unions remains thin, at best. What does exist suggests that institutionalized gender norms are hard to overcome.[15]

BECOMING A COUPLE

In our study, date initiation remained largely a male bastion of either privilege or responsibility. The majority of the couples in our sample credited the man with instigating their romances. This occurred in a variety of ways: conversations that took place while couples were hanging out, as well as more conventional approaches where the man asked the woman on a date to signify romantic interest. Women initiated the relationship only about one-fifth of the time. A handful of couples disagreed regarding who was responsible for forwarding the romantic relationship or felt that it had been a mutual decision. How individual partners described this initial step highlights how gendered the early stages of romantic relationships tend to be, though many individuals and a few couples contested or attempted to rearrange normative gendered patterns of relationship advancement.

Among the couples we interviewed, male-dominated relationship initiation remained the standard, regardless of social class. Among the service-class, men were responsible for initiating 63% of relationships

(n = 19), whereas 58% of the middle-class couples indicated that the man had been the instigator (n = 18). Men were assigned this initiator role in a variety of ways. Among some couples, flirtations transitioned into something more via a conversation about where the relationship was heading or with the man expressing definite sexual interest, with kisses, flowers, and flattery. Andre, a 25-year-old mortgage underwriter, explained that he and Stacy had spent about two months getting to know each other as they participated in a large role-playing group where they had met. One night, while driving her to a restaurant where a bunch of the other participants were going to be, he indicated, "I told her pretty much that I was interested in her and she was pretty happy, because she'd been interested in me. Then we *really* started talking." Stacy was gratified that Andre had finally broached the subject; she responded to him, "Yeah, I got a crush on you, too."

Even though men were generally quite forward in their attempts, they did not always feel confident playing the role of initiator. Several noted that, in the words of one respondent, "liquid courage" helped facilitate their pursuits. Chad, for example, who met Jackie when she was running the karaoke machine at a bar, found mustering the nerve to ask her out quite challenging as she was, in his words, "intimidatingly gorgeous." He explained: "I was probably a tiny bit tipsy and I think I had taken a Percocet earlier, so I was feeling somewhat confident. And I just went up, and just straight up hit on her and totally made an ass of myself but, it seems apparently not in a negative way (*laughs*), and we just got talking and like right before I left I just, I asked her out and we went on a date." Other men expressed discomfort with making the first move, even when faced with clear interest. Jake, who worked in computer support, spent several months hanging out with Stephanie but was hesitant about how to transition from a friendship to a romance. As he recalled, "I am not necessarily the kind of person that is the first kiss aggressor all the time, but I definitely did this time."

Still others resorted to indirect approaches to establish that they were officially in a relationship. Jorge, a 22-year-old mortgage processor, explained how he assessed Valencia's interest by inquiring, "If people ask, what should I say? Do I tell them you're my girlfriend or say we're just talking?" In fact, nearly equal numbers of men from service- and middle-class couples experienced anxiety about asking their current partner out. Nonetheless, the men in both our samples—notwithstanding the nervousness they felt—were about three times more likely than the women to be credited with initiating the relationship.

Women initiated the romance (or attempted to) only about a fifth of the time. This generally took the form of asking the man to do something, from going to a wedding as their date or coming for a visit (among long-distance couples who met online), to raising the question of whether a "friends with benefits" sexual relationship had changed to something more. Frequently, these women used less-than-direct approaches. Aliyah, a 20-year-old administrative assistant, explained her tactic for clarifying her relationship status with Terrell. "I asked him one day, 'Well, what do you consider me as?' And he was like, 'Well, you're my girlfriend.' I was like, 'Well, you never asked me, so how do you know?' He said, 'Because I just told you that you're my girlfriend.'" Others took a more direct approach. Rachel, a 24-year-old graduate student in the sciences, met her partner while swing dancing and later called Nicholas and asked if he would be her date for her department's Christmas party.

Sometimes men needed to be persuaded to become involved. A few of the women who initiated their relationship demonstrated great doggedness. Keisha, a 30-year-old bookkeeper who met her partner, Stan, while visiting Atlantic City with a friend, laughingly told the story of how they met. The two were playing pool together, and she tried to draw his notice, saying "I was shaking my chest, like trying to distract his attention." This gambit didn't work. So, Keisha and her girlfriend invited Stan and his friend to go dancing, and in the early morning hours, when Keisha was boarding a bus to return home, she gave him a big kiss. Later, she called him up to explain herself. "I said, 'You know, that's not me. I'm more a lady than that.' So you know, I called him on the telephone and I really deeply apologized to him." They ended up talking, and she soon went to see him. While initially she attempted to pique his interest, in the end she took the bull by the horns and called him herself.

A handful of middle-class women also demonstrated great determination in pursuing partners, even in the face of initial disinterest. Jeff, a computer networker, had tried to avoid Sabrina's early advances when she approached him around town several times. "I saw her out and so I acted like I was on my cell phone and didn't see her because I didn't want to engage at that point in time . . ." he explained. "The next day I happened to run into her. She's like 'Oh hey, I wanted to talk to you but you were on your phone.' I'm like, 'Oh, yeah.' I wasn't playing games, I just wasn't ready to engage, and so she asked me out to go somewhere and I was like 'No.'" Eventually he mentioned a movie he wanted to see and accepted Sabrina's request to go together. Janelle, who owned a yoga studio, was even more straightforward. After Jonathan acted, in Janelle's words, "chilly" the first two times they hung out with mutual friends, she decided to rely on what she was sure Jonathan would not refuse. Jonathan describes that first encounter as, "constant sex, for like a week." Asked if she had planned it, Janelle said, "Yeah. I had somebody pick me up so I would have to get a ride home because I'm manipulative. So I left my car at home so that I would (*makes air quotes*) need a ride home." This type of assertive pursuit was more common among the middle-class women.

More frequently, women showed they were receptive to being asked out and waited for the man to make that move. Conventional gender scripts assign men to do the asking while women wait to be asked, as most women in this sample did. They did not necessarily appreciate waiting. Quite a few women mentioned their frustration with partners slow to pick up on their interest, which they thought they telegraphed with great clarity. Natasha, a college-educated small business owner, remembered that after spending weeks actively flirting with her current fiancé at the gym, her membership was about to expire and he still had not asked her out. "So that last week I'm like, 'Hey, are you going to miss me? This is my last week.' Because we still hadn't exchanged numbers or anything. [I was] trying to get [him to do] something." Middle-class women in particular commented on the ways they let men know that they were receptive to being asked out, though they were often unable to answer why it was so important that the man do the asking. Several of the college-educated women in our sample, for example, approached their partners first (at a bar or party, for example) and flirted, demonstrating their receptivity.

Others commented that at times, more than flirting was required. Jack, a 24-year-old financial planner, said of his partner Audrey, "She actually approached me," recalling that as she was dropping him off at his parents' house after a party, "she goes 'Well, you think you're ever going to call me?'" He later called her up and they went on their first date. Explaining the process, Jack stated, "I mean, she probably initiated us even talking, but I'm probably fairly confident that I initiated the first date." These indirect approaches reveal how women—particularly the college educated—were not just passively waiting for men to do the asking, even when they were not directly overturning normative gender prescriptions that men be the one to invite them out.

Women are, nonetheless, somewhat loathe to nominate themselves as the relationship initiator. Amy, who first approached her current fiancé, Kevin, at a high-end Irish pub, commented, "I always said I never wanted to pick up a guy at a bar, but I kind of did." Explaining how she had first seen Kevin, she said, "[My girlfriends] were just out drinking at the Dubliner and he was there by himself, and he was sitting at the bar. I was like 'I'm going to go talk to that guy' because I'm not shy and I was like, 'he looks nice. I need to find a nice guy.'" Nonetheless, both Amy and Kevin say he initiated what he called "our first *real* date," as he phoned her the next day and took her out to dinner.

The women we interviewed, especially the middle-class women, clearly expressed some ambivalence about being seen as too assertive or, in the words of one woman, "desperate." Women's discomfort with flipping the conventional social script highlights normative acceptance of how relationships "should" proceed, as well as their concern with transgressing these social boundaries. But their comments and actions reveal the difficulties contemporary women face in navigating expected gender norms. Women do not have total confidence that men will hold up their end of the gendered bargain. But they remain unsure how assertive to be, yet are unwilling to just passively wait for a man's notice. After talking to Kevin at the bar, Amy said "We exchanged numbers, and he was like, 'I'll call you.' I was like, 'Yeah, Right!'" She was pleasantly surprised when he actually did, stating "He did, he called me the next day."

Some women also expressed uncertainty about what distinguished a romantic gesture from one that was purely platonic. Emma described how puzzled she was at the start of her relationship with Aaron. Although he asked for her phone number and called her up to go out, when they did go out he never paid for her. As she explained, "We'd talk on the phone and go out to dinner and I would go to pay my half and he would pay his half, so I thought, 'What is this? It doesn't seem like a date!' So we did that a few times, and I said, 'Well if you want to date me you have to pay.'" Asked what about Aaron paying transformed it into a date, Emma replied, "Because in that way he's arranged the evening and he's taken care of it, and there's some sort of romantic undertones to that, I guess."

Women who adhered too closely to gendered norms, however, risked making the man feel like she was not interested, as Travis revealed. He and Kathryn met in Cancun and spent several days together. But when Kathryn got back to her home town, she took the advice of friends who relied on *The Rules* manifesto; they encouraged her not to call him for at least three days. This left Travis feeling like Kathryn had blown him off and was not interested. While the women in our sample clearly did not all follow *The Rules,* and those who did may not have followed all of them at the same time, they often abided by gendered proscriptions or worried about how it might be perceived when they did not.

In fact, the dance of courtship sometimes made it too complicated to determine which partner initiated their relationships. Six middle-class and five service-class couples either disagreed over which partner initiated their relationships, assumed the initiation was mutual, or were not able to determine the exact sequence of how things happened. The gradual build-ups of these relationships may be one reason that couples did not always agree on how things became official. Service-class couples were less likely to begin with a traditional date, instead hanging out together at work or playing video games. Eugene and Susan, for example, met when they were working together at the same store. Susan said of Eugene and their coworkers, "We'd all go to each other's house and play video games." Brian and Shelly also began talking to one another while at the restaurant where both worked. Shelly explained, "Well we were just kind of buddies for a little while . . . and then one day he just came over and we just talked, we just decided that we liked each other and we started hanging out and then he would stay [over.]"

Other couples had a difficult time establishing when they began dating because the transition was so gradual. Sandra, a 21-year-old service-class manager at a restaurant, explained, "I don't know if we ever actually went out, I mean we'd go to [a video store] a lot, I don't know. I think that it was just kind of like, we weren't together and then we were together." Some service-class women expressed resentment regarding relationships that evolved without a clear demarcation like a first date. Diana said in response to the question about how her relationship with Anthony evolved, "I kind of throw that in his face sometimes. I'll be like, 'We never go on dates anymore!' But I don't know if we ever really did." The greater reliance of service-class couples on hanging out may be the result of their somewhat younger age or more constrained economic circumstances.

Among the middle class, dates were more common, but several couples revealed that they discovered their interest in each other while at least one partner was dating someone else. In these cases, determining who initiated the relationship or even when it began was difficult. Emma, mentioned above, realized that one reason for the mixed messages she was receiving from Aaron was that he was still involved with another woman. Tara indicated that she spent a fair amount of time talking with Drew about relationship problems she was having with a friend of his, before realizing how much more fun she had with Drew. Evan described why it took a while before he and Juliana actually started dating, explaining, "She was dating somebody else, and I was pursuing her . . . we'd see each other out, and we'd talk, and then she broke up with him, and I started dating somebody. So we were just talking at that point. . . . And then I kind of came to my senses and dumped the girl that I was with at that point and Juliana and I started dating that following weekend."

While some couples could not tell how their relationship started, or viewed the decision to become a couple as mutual, a few couples disagreed on who initiated the relationship. Evan and Juliana, for example, both nominated themselves as the relationship initiator, while Aaron believes that when he paid for their dinner he was the instigator, even as Emma explained that she had to tell him what she expected after several dinners where they had split the bill. And finally, two of the middle-class couples reported knowing each other for a while at college and could not recall when they became a couple. As Bree, an accountant, explained, "It was kind of like friends seeing each other, like I couldn't even tell you when it turned into dating."

The Dance of Pursuit?

Egalitarian relationships also contradict classical norms regarding the dance of pursuit. Books like *The Rules* suggest that women play hard to get, or at least do not indicate that they are totally accessible and willing to accept a date at the eleventh hour. A handful of the women in our sample indicated that they either enjoyed being pursued or were not initially interested in being in a relationship. They therefore had to be persuaded that their partners were worth their time. Such behavioral patterns were more common among the middle class than among the service class. Several middle-class women, for example, were not yet ready to be serious or were unwilling to become exclusive with one person.

Justin, a landscaper, said about his current girlfriend that "there was a part of her that didn't want to get involved with anybody." Rebekah, a graduate student and bartender, explained that she paced her relationship with Andrew, who was also a customer at the bar where she worked, saying, "I mean he was obviously in pursuit, but in a very understated way, and I kind of enjoyed that game." But some partners needed more persuading than others. Martin explained that he essentially had to drag Jessica through the various stages of their relationship, recalling how she had said to him, "I'm glad we got to this point, but if you hadn't basically pushed the issue we would have never gotten to this point."

There were also a handful of service-class women whose male partners had to do some convincing to persuade them to be in exclusive
relationships. As with the middle-class women, these women also were
reluctant to close off other options. Explaining how they became exclusive, Artie said, "I know initially she didn't, she wasn't even sure if she
wanted a boyfriend and I guess it just kind of happened." When Artie
asked her if she wanted to become exclusive, Brandi explained, "I just
kind of pushed it aside, because I really wasn't ready." Another service-
class woman was reluctant to get involved with her current partner as
he had dated many of her high school friends; it took her talking with
these former girlfriends before she felt ready to get involved with Shane.
While some women also pursued men, women's pursuits were generally
short lived.[16] Studies of relationship progression seem to miss this dance,
where one partner is initially more interested in pursuing the relationship while the other paces the union to their liking.

WHO DECIDES WHEN TO LIVE TOGETHER

Examining which partner initiated discussions of moving in together
allows us to explore whether this new step is a venue where these roles
are challenged and transformed. Cohabitation is "uninstitutionalized,"
meaning there is little in the way of shared understanding regarding who
can raise the topic of living together or what happens when one partner
is more ready for such a move than the other. Social norms are largely
missing. This would seem to open the door to the challenging of normative gender roles. In fact, the women in our sample were much more
active in initiating the move to shared living than they were in beginning
the dating relationship.

Asked how the topic of living together was broached, the most common pattern described by those we interviewed—more than 40% of
both the service- and middle-class couples—was for the female partners
to suggest moving in together. Nearly as many service- class men were
attributed with initially raising the possibility of living together. Middle-
class men were the least likely to raise the subject of living together. The
college-educated couples in our sample, however, were more likely than
the service class to say the decision to move in together was a mutual
one. The remaining couples disagreed on or were unable to determine
which partner first suggested moving in together.

The absence of one clear pattern indicates that cohabitation is not yet
institutionalized. Because sexual relationships were already established

and couples were often spending many nights together, discussions of entering into a shared living arrangement often arose naturally. Caleb, for example, recalled Sophie telling him, "[My roommate's] moving out and you know, we sleep in the other's bed every night anyway and it would just make a lot more sense for a lot of reasons to move in together." Similarly, Stan, a 31-year-old hospital orderly, explained that it just made sense to live with Keisha; he had been having financial difficulties and his living situation was unstable. He described how she raised the idea "because she already had an apartment, she was established, she came up with the suggestion of me moving and coming to stay with her."

Anxiety and Hesitation

Of course, given their general adherence to traditional gender roles when it came to date initiation, women, especially those among the service class, were not always comfortable suggesting the couple move in together. As a result, some raised the possibility indirectly. Jake found his partner's method of suggesting the possibility of sharing one apartment, rather than commuting between two, endearing. As Jake recalled, "She did one of those, like, 'I'm going to ask you a question and I don't want you to freak out about it, because it's like one of those things where I am being too forward.'" Sherry's partner, Tyrone, also recalled her way of suggesting they live together with amusement. "She was like, 'We move in together, we could split the rent, we could be roommates,' and she stressed the point of roommates," after which he laughed. While these women appeared hesitant about overturning normative gender expectations (being "too forward"), Jake and Tyrone enjoyed being asked and were receptive.

Among the middle class, women did a fair bit of hedging in how they initiated the move-in. Travis said his partner, Katherine, "kept referring to how she didn't want to live out of a handbag, out of her travel bag," which spurred them to decide to live together. Similarly, Brad and Carrie credit her with initiating the move-in, but as Brad explained, she did so in a roundabout way. He explained, "She didn't say like 'Let's move in' she said something like, 'Do you realize how much money we're wasting?' I said, 'Yeah' and then we started talking about it." Among middle-class couples where the female partner was ultimately credited with initiating living together, the topic of cohabiting was like an elephant in the room, and both partners often reported that the other hinted at it, or that both did so. Audrey, a 22-year-old graduate student who had dated her partner all through college, for example, explained that they had been "skating around the issue." She said, "We were both always kind of hinting." Finally, she said, "I was the one to actually first verbalize it," indicating that she told her partner, "If I am living with you, I'll start looking for two bedrooms . . . but I need an answer. Do you want to live with me?" Similarly, when asked who initiated moving in, Paul, a lobbyist, said, "I think we kind of took playful stabs at it for a while" before Kate came out and asked if they should live together. Whether this hesitance to discuss living together resulted from discomfort with overturning gender roles or uncertainty about how to progress into shared living, this dance was more prevalent among the college educated, perhaps because they dated for longer periods of time, on average, before taking this step than did the service-class couples.

Yet while the majority of the men whose female partners initially raised the subject thought living together was a good idea, there were valid reasons for women's anxiety. Quite a few men were unwilling to accept these offers right away, effectively putting the brakes on any decision. Jonathan, the 28-year-old middle-class computer systems administrator, asked how he responded to the initial discussion with Janelle, said, "I told her that I wanted to wait a little while." Eric, who worked part-time as a security officer while attending school, said he initially laughed when Dawn raised the possibility. The women's responses indicated that they were quite aware of these delays. Sophie revealed, "I needed a roommate and Caleb was a little bit hesitant at first because he didn't want to move in for the wrong reasons. His way of thinking is more level headed." In Caleb's words, however, "I just didn't know if I wanted to step into that type of whole world where you live with your girlfriend and you share space and share everything, like being married, basically." Kirsten, a 24-year-old research assistant, attributed her partner's hesitation about what he called her "standing offer" to similar concerns, explaining, "He was kind of reluctant at first and I can understand why. It's a commitment thing. It's kind of scary."

The service-class men who sought time to decide on their living arrangements differed somewhat from their middle-class counterparts. Stan was, in the words of his partner, "rather leery" about moving in because he was reluctant to move away from his child, and Jorge was concerned because he was from a very religious family that would not approve of his cohabiting with Valencia. The final service-class man who sought to slow down the process expressed uncertainty about the relationship, saying he told his partner, "We're not ready to move in together." Any delay, however, was relatively short-lived. All three of the service-class men who hesitated did move in with their partner within six months of the relationship's start, as did two of the middle-class men. Even when women do initiate relationship progression, we conclude, their male partners frequently continue to have the final deciding power by controlling the timing of moving in together.

When Men Suggest Living Together

Men were somewhat less likely to raise the idea of cohabiting than were women. Several of the service-class men who did ask their partners about living together were looking for an apartment and, in lieu of seeking out new roommates, suggested that they cohabit. Of note is that in nearly half of the service-class couples where the man initiated the topic, the relationship would have likely ended had the couple not moved in together, either because it was initially long distance or because one partner was moving away. Maria, who met her partner online, explained that Bill asked her to move in together "because he didn't want the long-distance relationship. So I think it was him anyways bringing it up and saying, 'Why don't you just move in, we'll have this and work it out as best as we can.'"

Of the eight middle-class men who raised the possibility of cohabiting, the partners of two expressed reservations about cohabiting. But the men took quite different tacks in persuading their female partners that the decision was the right one. After raising the possibility of living together, Kevin also assured Amy about his intentions. "I told her, I said, 'I don't want to push you into anything. I don't want you to do anything you're not comfortable with. I want you to do it if you want to do it.'" He then intimated that a proposal was imminent. But gentle persuasion was not the tactic used by Martin; though his girlfriend, Jessica, wanted to take things a little slower, in his words, "I just laid it out. 'This is the deal. If I'm coming there [to your town], I'm not going to live down the street, and you need to decide for yourself if you can handle that." Few of the women in these couples expressed reservations that moving in might signify a higher level of commitment than they were ready for, in contrast to the response of several middle-class women during the dating stage of the relationship.

A handful of couples asserted that decisions to move in together were made mutually, as well as gradually, though this was more common among the middle than the service class. Tara, a 28-year-old computer programmer, said, "I don't think we ever made a conscious decision." The remaining couples, both working and middle class, did not agree regarding who initially broached the possibility of living together. Although it is difficult to discern any clear patterns in the responses of these couples, many of these disagreements appear to be the result of misunderstandings or the initial reluctance that one partner felt about cohabiting. These misunderstandings suggest how struggles over power and resources operate to advantage men. In one example, Natasha told her partner, Soliman, that she did not want to cohabit, only to give up after several months of his staying at her apartment every night; she finally determined to ask him to at least help pay the rent, as her financial situation was precarious. Juliana, who wanted to move into her boyfriend's apartment, was taken aback by his reaction to her discussing the possibility. He told her, "Well, you can't just decide, you have to be invited." Disagreements among the service-class couples less often took the form of such power exertions, instead resulting more frequently from basic communication glitches.

Your Place or Mine?

And where did our couples begin their shared lives together? Among the middle class, couples most frequently moved into the woman's abode, then the man's, and a few moved into a new apartment (n = 12, 11, and 8, respectively). The hierarchy among the service class differed, with couples most often moving into the man's apartment, followed by a new apartment, and last the woman's place of residence (n = 11, 10, and 9, respectively).

Among the middle class, the transition into "her" space may have resulted because the women were the ones to suggest cohabiting or their resources allowed them to afford nicer places. But for service-class women, economic exigencies often precipitated the move into shared living, most often not in their current households. In fact, nearly half of the service-class couples were not living alone (or with just their partners and children) after they moved in together, instead sharing their homes with either a parent(s), a sibling, friends, or roommates. In contrast, only five of the middle-class couples initially lived with others, and those who did so often owned their home and relied on others to help make the mortgage payments.

WHAT WE LEARNED: HAVE WE COME A LONG WAY (BABY)?

Although young people often express a desire for more egalitarian relationships, our results suggest that cohabitation does not represent a dramatic break with the past, at least in terms of relationship initiation. Men retained responsibility for instigating the majority of the relationships among the couples we interviewed. Women continued to demonstrate their receptiveness to being asked out or posed their attempts to gauge a potential partner's interest as "jokes." The prevailing way that couples began their romantic relationship was via a male expression of interest or requests for a date. That is not to say that male hegemony was unchallenged. Some women did initiate the relationship, or attempted to. A handful of couples mutually decided that they would go out together, yet another indication that gender norms are changing. Yet change is slow. Several generations after the sexual revolution, at a time when women now account for half of the paid labor force, they remain in subordinate positions with regards to jump-starting romantic relationships.

The gender status quo is far weaker when it comes to raising the possibility of moving in together, a step which is not yet institutionalized and has few guidelines. Although no one pattern predominates, women are somewhat more likely than men to push the relationship to the next stage (living together) once the romance is established. Their approach was not always direct. But their ability and desire to forward the relationship into shared living highlights one way in which women are pushing the envelope and seeking to take advantage of new relationship forms. Once a relationship was underway, women did not passively wait for the next step. Many took a firmer hand in the advancement of their intimate unions. In fact, women are somewhat more likely to push the relationship to the next stage (living together) once the romance is established than are men.

Men are not always compliant when women flip the conventional script. For starters, they sometimes wrest control of date initiation from the women. They also put the brakes on progression to shared living when they believe it's too soon. After initial resistance, however, men often reconsidered and entered into shared living—if not always on the time frame their partner desired. Men's responses to women's attempts to forward their relationships highlight the importance of couple-level analysis for studies of relationship power. Even as some men welcomed their female partner's assertiveness, considering it appealing, the reverse was often true. Some men did not accept women's attempts to play a more assertive role in the progression of intimate relationships, expressing concerns with being "trapped" that echo the sentiments of Rubin's working class men of the 1970s.

To sum up, our results indicate that women are more likely to raise the topic of living together, although often in indirect ways, than they are to initiate the first date. Notwithstanding their upending of conventional gender norms, however, men—middle-class men in particular—sometimes wrest control of the situation from their female partners, either by deferring on the decision making, shutting down a discussion of a partner moving in (by telling them they have to be "invited" first), or in a few instances, acting in opposition to their partner's wishes or time frame. Service-class men, in contrast, are nearly as likely as their female counterparts to suggest the couple live together, in part because they have less in the way of a financial cushion to allow them to live alone. The larger story, however, is one of gender, not social class. The less institutionalized nature of cohabitation appears to give women more freedom to take charge in furthering their relationships into shared living. Strongly established gender scripts, even within these new unions, mean that changing the process is not easy.

Initiating talk of living together, of course, is often a result of numerous factors, such as the need for a place to live or a desire to take the next step in relationship progression. These factors also shape when, in the course of a relationship, one or both partners begin to contemplate shared living. In the next chapter we explore the tempo of relationship progression, or how couples paced the timing of entering into shared living from the relationship's beginning. We also consider the varied reasons our respondents gave for entering into their shared living arrangements. While this chapter reveals that gender played the predominant role in how relationships progressed in the early stages, our next chapter suggests that social class better accounts for how rapidly couples moved in together.

3

Shacking Up, Living in Sin, Saving on Rent?

The Process of Moving In Together

"We have fun and we enjoy each other's company, so why shouldn't we just move in together?" asked Lauren, a 23-year-old grant writer. She and Justin had reconnected after college, after bumping into each other at a bar. Along with many other cohabitors, Lauren and Justin stated that a desire to spend more time together was among the main reasons they determined to live together, though saving money and the convenience didn't hurt. But Lauren didn't think they'd been dating long enough to jump into marriage. "I mean, Justin and I have talked about getting married," she said, "but we're just really not ready for it. We're on the same page there," she asserted. "We haven't even been together for a year." Like many of the other cohabitors we interviewed, Lauren viewed living with Justin sans marriage as the right thing to do. At some point, she thought, they might marry—but not now.

Others, however, were less sanguine about cohabiting. Asked about the factors influencing her decision to move in with her boyfriend, Sherry, a 21-year-old African American working on her bachelor's degree and waitressing to make ends meet, mentioned sheepishly, "And my main motivation, this is so bad, was money." She was not alone in viewing cohabitation as less than optimal. Those expressing such sentiments were more often young, less educated, and struggling to make ends meet. Susan, a 20-year-old woman attending college off and on and working at a call center in the interim, explained why she moved in with Eugene only four months after they became involved, saying, "It's not what I really wanted to do but I just, we couldn't afford to live by ourselves and separately so we just ended up moving in together." Asked what she might have done if she had the resources to forego cohabiting, Susan indicated she would have deferred shared living until after they were married, given her religious beliefs; nonetheless, her financial situation and lack of parental assistance for independent living precipitated her move into cohabitation. Such stories tend to be overlooked in the media coverage of young people's movement into shared living. Instead, cohabitation is often represented as a bid (usually by the female partner) to progress the relationship toward marriage or as a carefree decision entered into as did Lauren and Justin (described above), because it is convenient and playing house is fun.

There are, of course, those for whom moving in together represents a deepening commitment or, possibly, a step toward marriage. Asked why he decided to live with his girlfriend, Kevin, a 27-year-old manager for a small manufacturing company, said "You know, it was a pain in the ass not living together. So we just decided, let's move in together, see how things progress and go for a few months and then we'll get engaged and kind of go from there." Kevin and Amy had been dating for about a year before they moved into their own apartment together. Amy expressed a reluctance to move in with Kevin unless she knew that he would, in her words, "take that next step." Within three months of moving in together they were engaged, and when we interviewed them, they were planning their wedding. For Kevin and Amy, moving in together was a precursor to engagement and marriage. But that is less and less often how cohabiting unions resolve. In particular, this specific sequence is increasingly a middle-class phenomenon. It represents the culmination of a very different process than that demonstrated by Sherry or Susan, or even Lauren and Justin.

As our respondents indicated, people move in with a romantic partner for a variety of reasons. Despite how common living together is, however, relatively little is known about how or why couples end up sharing an abode. This chapter addresses that gap. We detail when in the course of relationships couples begin to live together full-time, what motivated our respondents to take that step, and how they felt about the way this process unfolded. The process of moving in together is shaped by reasons for moving in: economic need, housing emergencies, as well as relationship progression. Many of our respondents moved in together very quickly—often within just a few months. But as we show, service-class respondents moved in together far more rapidly, on average, than did their middle-class counterparts. Class engenders particular dynamics that shape how and why these relationships unfold as they do, in ways that result in more successful and stable relationships for the more educated and greater challenges for the less economically privileged.

WHAT DO WE KNOW ABOUT THE PROCESS OF MOVING IN TOGETHER?

Cohabitation has become the majority experience among contemporary young adults. Yet there are few accepted standards surrounding the decision to enter into shared living.[1] It is unclear, for example, when in the course of a romantic relationship is the optimal time to move in together. Diving in too quickly can raise eyebrows, causing some to think "What's the rush?" Taking too long, however, may suggest that partners are ambivalent about the relationship or each other. Some reasons for moving in together may contribute to relationship quality more than others. Finally, notwithstanding greater acceptance of alternative living arrangements, moving in with a romantic partner often causes others—family members, friends, and even distant acquaintances—to ask when couples are going to get married.

Numerous psychologists, family sociologists, and self-help gurus have sought to understand the optimal approach to building trusting, committed, and quality relationships. While movies like *He's Just Not That Into You* utilize popular psychology to explain romantic dilemmas, a large body of academic research has focused on the concept of commitment: the positive attributes such as high levels of emotional or sexual satisfaction that make an individual desire to remain in a relationship, as well as the sometimes negative aspects, such as barriers to leaving a relationship and the mechanisms binding partners together.[2] Some psychologists have argued that cohabitation is different from marriage, and that living together represents an ambiguous state of commitment.[3] Uncertainty regarding what "living together" means may make it difficult for individuals to determine the nature of their relationship. Cohabitation lacks clear markers to the outside world that couples are committed to each other for the long term. There is no ring, no announcements in local papers that couples have moved in together; the banns are not read in church, as in days gone by. Sometimes couples are not even aware (or in agreement) that they are living together![4]

One major challenge to understanding how cohabitation fits into relationship progression is that few studies explicitly examine how long couples are romantically involved before they move in together, even though it takes time for commitment to develop and deepen.[5] They also fail to ascertain why respondents move in with a partner, whether such reasons are similar for both partners, or if plans for the future were discussed prior to entering into shared living. These are serious omissions. Each of these factors on their own, or in conjunction, may shape relationship quality and stability.[6]

The importance of time is a foundational element in the study of relationship processes; numerous studies have found that slowly developing relationships, at least among marrieds, are often of higher quality than those that developed rapidly.[7] Such may be the case for cohabiting relationships, as well. The reasons why individuals move in with their partners may also signal something about the nature of the relationship. In this chapter, we present our respondents' stories of how their relationships progressed, focusing on tempo, reasons for moving in together, and how our respondents feel about the pace of their relationship progression. Our findings indicate that social class plays a very important role in how rapidly relationships progress as well as reasons for moving in together, something which popular portrayals of cohabitation generally ignore. Furthermore, the pace at which individuals enter into shared living reverberate across relationships in ways that often strongly impact the futures of these unions.

RELATIONSHIP TEMPOS: HOW RAPIDLY DO COUPLES MOVE IN TOGETHER?

During their interviews respondents described how their romances progressed, when in the course of their relationships they determined to move into one space, and their reasons for doing so. These responses allowed us to estimate the length of time from when couples became romantically involved to when they began cohabiting. Although partners did not always agree on how long they were romantically involved before moving in together, responses generally differed only by a few months. On the basis of our prior research, we divided our time frames in several intervals, examining the duration from when respondents started to date or hang out to when they reported moving in to a shared home together.[8] We estimate the couples' timing to shared living, averaging couple responses.

Our results reveal two important findings. First, transitions into shared living occurred relatively rapidly. But we also find notable social class differences, which is our second major result; the service-class respondents progressed into cohabitation considerably more quickly

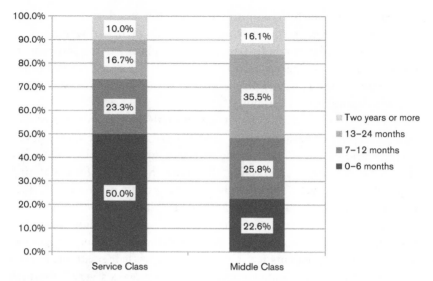

FIGURE 3. Couple Reports of Duration from Start of Relationship to Cohabitation, by Social Class

than their college-educated counterparts. This can be seen in Figure 3. Half of the service-class couples—fifteen of them—moved in together within six months of the start of their relationships, compared with only seven of the college-educated couples.

About one in four (eight middle-class and seven service-class couples) took between seven to twelve months before entering their cohabiting unions. In total, nearly three-quarters of the less educated couples had begun living together within their first year of involvement. Less than half of the college-educated couples had moved in with their partner within the first year of involvement. The general findings of quantitative studies based on nationally representative data largely substantiate ours, revealing that the majority of cohabiting unions were formed quite rapidly.[9] Simply understanding when couples make union transitions, however, does not tell us why they decided to do so. For this, we turn to their insider accounts to better understand the reasons couples decided to share a home.

WHY MOVE IN TOGETHER? THE TOP SEVEN REASONS

Our interview respondents often mentioned reasons motivating their entrance into shared living as they discussed how their relationships

TABLE 2   REASONS FOR MOVING IN WITH ROMANTIC PARTNER, BY SOCIAL CLASS
AND SEX

	Combined Sample		Service Class		Middle Class	
Reasons	N	%	N	%	N	%
Convenience	60	20.5	23	16.7	37	23.9
Housing	54	18.4	27	19.6	27	17.4
Economic rationality	46	15.7	16	11.6	30	19.4
To be together	37	12.6	27	19.6	10	6.5
Next step	39	13.3	10	7.2	29	18.7
Family	27	9.2	18	13.0	9	5.8
Financial necessity	23	7.8	15	10.9	8	5.2
Security	4	1.4	0	0.0	4	2.6
Other	3	1.0	2	1.4	1	0.6
Number of reasons	293		138		155	
Number of respondents	122		60		62	

unfolded. We also specifically asked them an open-ended question about why they had moved in with their partners. While respondents often mentioned several reasons, often in tandem, generally they focused on one or two explanations.[10] Because partners' reasons for moving in together often differed, we examine responses individually, giving precedence to the top three reasons individuals mentioned. Overall, we focused on the 293 reasons our interviewees provided. How these answers are distributed, overall and by social class, are presented in Table 2.[11] Most of the reasons respondents gave fell into seven broad categories: convenience, housing needs, economic rationality, choosing to spend more time together because of mutual enjoyment, as a "next step" in the relationship to demonstrate deepening commitment, in response to a family situation, or as a result of financial necessity. A handful of respondents also cited other factors—such as concerns about safety that arose from living alone—but never as a first reason.

"Practical" Reasons: Convenience, Economic Rationality, Financial Necessity

Despite Harlequin (and Hollywood) storylines where couples are inexorably drawn to shared living because they cannot stand to sleep apart, reasons that might be considered "practical"—convenience, economic rationality, and financial necessity—made up nearly half of the justifications respondents gave for moving in together. *Convenience* accounted for over one-fifth of all the justifications mentioned, though it was referred to far more often by the middle class.[12] The notion that living together was easier than living apart and therefore that sharing a household would simplify life was raised in several similar ways. Describing why he and Amy moved in with each other after dating for about a year, Kevin, a 27-year-old middle-class plant manager, said: "It got to the point where we were just, like it was just wearing us out, her driving all the way home to get her bag or get showered, then come to my place. It was just more of a strain on our relationship to not live together than it was to live together, because we were always driving back and forth and, you know, leaving curling irons at one house. It was just a pain in the butt." Andre, a 25-year-old high school-educated mortgage broker, explained, "We're spending all the time together anyways, and basically all we were doing was living together with a commute. So why not just live together and then not have to worry about taking stuff back and forth, having clean clothes at the other person's place, deciding whose place to stay at?"

Even when partners lived close to each other, the constant back and forth seemed a bother. Emma, who literally lived next door to Aaron before giving up her apartment, explained:

> I do love him very much, but it was a lot of convenience, most of it, which is pretty sad to say. But we'd be making dinner and he'd say, "Oh, we need poppy seeds," and I'd be like, "I'll just run next door and get them." But like, I'm tired of running next door all the time! So it just made sense, you know, with the amount of time that we were spending together, it just seemed right and natural and really good.

In addition to the commute, those who said it was more convenient to cohabit often referenced how their possessions were constantly migrating between places. Soliman, Natasha's partner, explained, "I found more of my clothes started seeping into her apartment." But travel distance or wardrobe challenges were not sufficient to result in shared living; one other aspect was central, as Josh, a 22-year-old part-time community college student and data entry clerk, made clear. Asked why he and Patty decided to share a home, he reported, "Well, just because by that point we were probably spending almost every night together."

In fact, many convenience cohabitors spent almost every night together from very early on in their relationships. Amy, a 28-year-old respiratory therapist, mentioned, "We spent a lot of time together initially, and we were like together all the time, and we'd stay at each other's places." Lauren, whose vignette begins this chapter, reported that the frequency with which she and Justin spent time together certified that they would be able to live together, explaining, "We realized after spending every single day together for about four months that it would just work." But she reiterated that the decision was not made rashly, clarifying, "Well, we thought about it for a full month before we officially made the decision, but it just felt right." In the end, many of our respondents felt that living together was the simpler, most expedient option.

Other respondents put a particular economic emphasis on their decisions to share a home. We term the belief that living together just made good economic sense *economic rationality,* to distinguish it from *convenience* and *financial necessity.*[13] A total of 46 respondents said that, although they could afford to live alone, it just made more sense fiscally to live together as opposed to apart. Moving in with Chad after dating for about four months was not planned in great detail, according to 24-year-old Jackie, who was pursuing an associates' degree while working as an art counselor for youth. According to her, "It was easier economically, I mean if I would have got my own place and he would have gotten his own place, you know, that's spending a lot more money but probably only like sleeping at one house, so that was kind of a reason." Other respondents who moved in quickly explained economic rationality was a primary reason for cohabiting.

Middle-class respondents were nearly twice as likely as their service-class counterparts to explain that they moved in because it was the economically rational thing to do, even if it was not financially necessary.[14] Carrie, a 24-year-old high school teacher, explained her decision by stating, "Obviously, just money-wise it made so much more sense, because we're spending two rents, two cables, two this, two that, and we're obviously never using any of them at the same time, so it just made more sense." Others viewed maintaining the façade of separate residences as wasteful. Karen, a 25-year-old research coordinator at a center for children with disabilities, said, "I was basically living with him anyway and throwing money away." For these respondents, there was little point to maintaining separate apartments with the ensuing costs if they were spending their time in only one location. Justin, a 24-year-old college-educated landscaper, explained, "Well, it has a lot to do with practicality," clarifying, "So if we're going to be together all the time, why pay the rent over there and why get separate groceries? We might as well just

get [an apartment] together and be together. We like being together anyways, so why not make it more financially feasible as well?" Those who
saw cohabitation as economically rational thought everyone reasoned as
they did. "I'm sure that's why most people do it," asserted Greg, a
35-year-old owner of a construction company.

Of course, there were some cohabitors who expressed reservations
about attributing their decisions to move in with their partners to financial convenience, worried that such an emphasis on rational calculation
signified something unsavory. Drew, who had moved into his partner's
house, expressed frustration that others might view their decision to
cohabit as based on financial reasons, perhaps because he worried that
reflected poorly on his provider abilities. He argued, "So it's not like now
we're going 'OK, now we got to move in because if we don't we're going
to both go bankrupt.' That was never the issue." Matthew, a 30-year-old
architect, attempted to provide a fuller justification of his decision to
move in with his partner, Kristina:

> I mean, you know, the romantic answer is that because we know that even-
> tually we're going to be married, and that I didn't see any point in not spend-
> ing time with each other simply because some tradition says that we shouldn't
> be living together, which I didn't necessarily believe and luckily she didn't
> either. But I would say the other part of it is the fiscal reason. You know, she
> wasn't going to make a lot of money starting right out of college, and she
> didn't have a lot of money. She probably couldn't afford to live the lifestyle
> that I was used to living at that point. So it just made sense to pool our
> resources.

Matthew was not alone in his desire to portray a full array of reasons
for cohabiting. Brad, the 29-year-old graduate student whose partner,
Carrie, had suggested cohabiting because they were wasting so much
money, said about the role financial convenience played in their decision, "It wasn't, like, *the* reason, but it was a good supporting reason,
another reason to do what we thought was the normal thing to do."

Fewer respondents mentioned that *financial necessity* was a major
factor in their decision to move in with their partners, with only 24 of
those we interviewed discussing economic challenges as an impetus. Yet
research on cohabitation has seldom considered this option, or explored
the factors—whether the steep costs of adequate housing, excessive
monetary demands necessary to obtain available housing, or economic
uncertainty—which contribute to economically driven reasons for living together. Varied reasons, including job losses, reductions in work
hours, a desire to quit one's job, and not earning enough to cover rent

or pull together a deposit for an apartment (which often amounted to two or three months' rent) made it difficult to cover living costs, and necessitated moving in with a partner. Having a partner help with expenses, even temporarily, was essential for many of these respondents. Simon, a 25-year-old carpenter who had an accident that severed part of his finger, recalled that when he and Laura moved in together, "Finances were very, very hard. I was laid off. I was actually in between jobs." Eugene, a 22-year-old call center employee, also revealed how a lack of employment conditioned his rapid move in with Susan. "I needed help with the money and she was willing to help me," he explained, "because there was a time, after I quit Videogame Superstore, that I didn't have a job for about a month." His partner, Susan, represented the financial need as mutual, saying, "I actually didn't have the money to pay the rent where I was currently living, so I was in a financial bind," even though she had a job at that time.

Several of these respondents mentioned the difficulties of finding roommates to share the rent, whether because they didn't know anyone in town or because their pool of eligible roommates was limited. Julie, who moved to another state to live with her boyfriend, Ray, after about three months, knew no one in her new location and had not even thought about how doubling or tripling up with others might enable her to afford an apartment. "I wasn't able to sustain a sort of life outside of anyone else's home," she explained:

> I didn't make enough money. It just wasn't even an option. I had always thought if you lived on your own it's because either you came from money, or you had a real job, and so it didn't even cross my mind that I could, you know, work a couple of jobs and live on my own. It was just never even an option.

Others expressed frustration with affording apartments that required considerable money up front for a security deposit. Sherry, a 21-year-old African American waitress attending college part time, wanted to move to her own place but felt stymied finding something. "Like all my girlfriends are just, they have gone on, they move out, they live by themselves or they have a roommate and they're set. I look around for one-bedrooms, I could not afford it. I didn't have any savings; I didn't save up a dime. And those down-payments and things like that, they cost, while paying 400 dollars a month for my place. You know? So I'm like, 'Shit.'"

Financial need was not limited to service-class cohabitors, though it was a far more common justification among them.[15] Financial problems of the middle-class respondents, furthermore, were shorter lived. Taylor said it took him a while after finishing his college degree to find a job and that he had moved in with Bree "mainly because I financially could not support myself, and that's pretty much what it came down to." But he did find work within a few months, and as time went by he obtained several promotions and changed jobs. At the time of his interview, he was earning slightly less than the median household income for Ohio in 2006, though he still earned less than his partner.[16] Another man who moved to Columbus because the woman he was involved with lived and worked there reported how moving in with his partner was a non-negotiable condition of his relocation. Martin described their initial discussion of where he would live:

> So she kind of said, "Well, maybe you could look for an apartment here." I said, "I'm broke, I can't afford an apartment and even if I found one I could afford, I'm going to spend all my time with you anyways, because I'll know no one in Columbus but you." And again, I looked at it objectively, like if I'm going to be moving there I have to save money, and the cheapest way is "I'll move into your place, we'll split the rent." So I just laid that out. "This is the deal. If I'm coming there, I'm not going to live down the street, and you need to decide for yourself if you can handle that."

He went on to talk about how difficult it was to find a professional position that suited his qualifications and the lengths he went to—including managing a pizza parlor—in order to be able to contribute to the rent. Nonetheless, he soon found a job as an editor at an educational publisher and at the time of his interview felt economically established enough to have proposed to his partner, Jessica. Natasha, who worked as a freelance translator, also mentioned that at the time she had asked her partner, Soliman, to move in, her business had begun to founder, given the proliferation of computer translation programs. Because her partner had been staying over her apartment every night anyway, she decided that enough was enough. "Like I said, I kind of pressured him into it, like, 'Look, if you're going to live here, live here. Let's make it official, maybe you could help me with the rent a bit.' Because like I said, I was kind of struggling at that point." She went on to say, "I just couldn't afford to pay it all on my own."

That financial resources feature so prominently in cohabitors' discussions of why they move in together is not unexpected. The old adage encouraging marriage—that two can live as cheaply as one—is also applicable to cohabitation. But too seldom is the topic of financial need featured in discussions of why young adults cohabit. This is surprising, given how much attention has been paid since the advent of the Great Recession in 2008 to young adults who move back in with parents because of the lack of jobs or the costs of independent living. Many of our respondents felt that this option—moving in with parents—was not available to them or was a situation that they desperately wanted to avoid.

In fact, several of our young, less educated respondents felt that they were *pushed* into cohabiting with their partners, as they could not see any other options. Patty, who moved in with her partner, Josh, when she was 18, explained the financial bind she and her young friends who needed housing found themselves in:

> I think probably what spurred us living together is when my sister kicked me out. I was like, "What am I going to do? I don't have enough money to live by myself." All my friends were my age, you know, and they were still in high school, and if they had graduated earlier, you know, they got their GED and were in no position to have an apartment with somebody, 'cause they didn't have a job. So I don't know if that kind of forced us to live together or what.

Susan, who moved in with Eugene within four months of the start of their romantic relationship, was also a reluctant cohabitor, but explained, "We understand that this was not our first option, to move in with each other, but we knew that it was financially what we needed to do." Her partner, Eugene, verified that economic need resulted in their moving in together, despite their religious qualms. "If something were to happen and my girlfriend was to leave," he said, "I would not have enough to pay minimum payments on all of my debts that I have, plus pay for rent and all the utilities since everything's in my name, and afford gas and food. I would not make enough. I barely break even as it is right now, with both of us working." Eugene was working several jobs for a combined 60 hours a week, while Susan reported working about 50 hours a week at an array of jobs she held. Debts from attending college, emergency car repairs, and the learning process of becoming financially independent make the transition to adulthood particularly challenging for youth whose parents are not middle class. But while financial need pushed several reluctant cohabitors into shared living, the decision to do so weighed heavily on their conscience. Tyrone, whose partner, Sherry, could not afford to cover the initial deposit for a new apartment, also felt that cohabitation was not optimal given their religious convictions, explaining, "I mean, we ain't livin' right," while Sherry worried that their relationship would not be, in her words, "blessed by God," and was frequently in tears over their arrangement.

Housing Need

Nearly a fifth of all our respondents reported that housing needs spurred their decisions to live together. Cohabitors described a variety of residence-related factors, including the necessity of finding a new place to live or someone with whom to share housing costs. Discussions about housing, however, differed from mentions of financial need or economic rationality in that they were specifically focused on shelter. Even though housing needs were mentioned just as often by service-class as middle-class respondents, more service-class couples were in long-distance relationships that required one partner to relocate if the relationship was to persist or intensify; this was the case for six service-class couples but only one of the middle-class couples.

Cohabitors whose need for housing precipitated their moves mentioned the sudden and often unexpected departure of a roommate or growing discomfort with a roommate situation, as well as leases ending. Stephanie, a call center employee, said, "I mean, my roommate was moving out, and he [Jake] was already staying with me, and it just seemed like the thing to do." Chad, a 24-year-old who worked at several unskilled service jobs, said of his decision to move in with Jackie, "We both needed to find another place." Jackie's version matched Chad's, though she put more of the impetus on him. "He had to move out of his place and I was looking for my own place," she said, "so I think we were kind of doing some looking on our own, and you know, he kept dropping hints about needing a roommate but he can't find anybody that he'd want to live with. And so I think finally he had some friends that were moving out of their place and they wanted somebody to sublease and he just couldn't afford it by himself, and I'm looking for a place and we could just live together." In fact, the sublease option made it more attractive to her, as she recalled, "Plus the lease, since we sublet it, was only six months, so I mean, you know, if things didn't work out we could easily kind of do something else."

The middle-class respondents more often had greater control over their housing situations. Evan, a 27-year-old account executive who owned his home, recalled, "I had a roommate who had worn out his welcome greatly and I was going to get rid of him regardless. So it was good timing on that." The middle-class respondents who referenced housing needs as a reason for moving in with their partners were far more likely to mention the expiration of a lease, often in the future. Audrey had graduated from college and was going to be pursuing her master's degree in the fall; she explained the challenge of having leases end at different times. "I was getting to the end of my lease. All of my friends had essentially graduated. I hadn't really met anyone in my program yet that I would be interested in moving in with. . . . And Jack's lease was up in the end of September, so we were kind of skating around the issue." Nathan, a 24-year-old purchasing manager, said about his partner, Andrea, "She had brought up living together because we both were kind of in a position where we didn't know where we were going to live once our leases were up." In fact, among the middle class, those who mentioned leases tended to have dated for well over two years before moving in together. Evan, mentioned above, epitomized this group in explaining how the need for housing featured in their decision to cohabit. He said, "Her lease was ending, I was ready to kick him [the roommate] out. We had already been dating for over a year. Put all those things together, it led to her living with me."

To Be Together versus as the Next Step

Over one-quarter of the reasons mentioned for moving in with a partner relate specifically to the intensification of the romantic relationship. Respondents' discussions seemed to fall into two distinct categories: those who mentioned that moving in with a partner was a means of spending more time together because they enjoyed each other's company, versus as a "step," or sign of increased commitment. About half of those in this category mentioned a desire to spend more time together, while the other half viewed moving in as the next relationship stage. Ming, who had been involved with her partner, Randy, for several years, simply explained, "We liked to be together." Nicholas, a 29-year-old architect, replied, "because we really like each other, actually for time, partially for convenience, partially because we like to optimize the amount of time we could spend together." Others thought that shared living would work given how well they got along. Monica, a 26-year-old college graduate who worked as an animal handler, said in response to why she decided to live with James, "I thought it'd be fun. I mean, why not? No reason not to, I mean there's no specific reason why, we just wanted to." Carly, an 18-year-old library clerk, explained, "It was, like, the time we spent together was so good, like we would always have so much fun. That's about it."

Service-class respondents mentioned a desire to be together as a reason for cohabiting nearly twice as often as middle-class cohabitors. But while wanting to spend time together may result in deepening intimacy and trust, this reason did *not* signify that the relationship was becoming more serious or that they were assessing compatibility for marriage. The explanation given by Ray, a 31-year-old bookkeeper who sporadically took a few credits toward an associate's degree, highlights this. Asked why he decided to live with his partner, 30-year-old Julie, he responded that it was "just something that ended up happening. We were both attracted to one another and both wanted to be together and so I really don't know, other than that."

In contrast, respondents who mentioned moving in as the *next step* in their unions discussed living together as a way to signify a higher level of commitment, to assess compatibility prior to marriage, or because they knew that a wedding was in the cards. Their justifications therefore differ significantly from those stating that they just wanted to spend more time together. Tracy, who moved cross-country to be with her partner and was one of our most occupationally successful high school graduates, managing a branch of a national coffee shop, described moving in as a step to demonstrate and deepen commitment. Even though she and her partner got engaged before moving in together, she said, "So it was naturally the progression to take, was to live together, because I wasn't ready to get married, and I don't think he was either." Others discussed living together as a means to "test" the strength of the relationship. Jack, a 24-year-old financial planner, phrased it this way: "I guess it's just being better prepared to maybe take the next step into marriage." These responses highlight how cohabitation has become naturalized as part of the courtship sequence, epitomized in the response of Martin, the 31-year-old editor, who said about his initial discussions of moving in with Jessica, "I was like thinking, if our relationship's going to continue, we've been dating for a year, I've met your family, we're having sex, I mean we might as well. The next step for most people now is not to jump to engagement. It's to live together."

Still others commented that they already knew that they would marry their partners and therefore moving in together was just part of the natural progression. Kevin, a 27-year-old manager at an industrial plant, said, "At that point I knew that I wanted to marry her, and she knew that she wanted to marry me. So we knew that we were going to become engaged and we wanted to spend the rest of our lives together." Evan, a 27-year-old sales representative, replied, "It was kind of a timing, slash, I know this was the girl I was going to marry thing" in response to the question about why he decided to live with his partner.

These respondents differed from those who indicated that living together was a means to "test" out the relationship; they often state that they would not have lived with their partners were marriage *not* in the cards. Matthew, the architect who gave both a practical and romantic answer to why he had decided to live with his partner affirmed, "If I had any doubt, then I wouldn't have. I do see some value in living with the person before you officially say, 'OK, this is forever.' But if I already knew that I had a doubt, I certainly would've never gone through with it, I would've kept it at arm's length." These respondents indicated that they were confident their relationships would lead to marriage, and that conditioned their willingness to cohabit. Of note is that most of these respondents were not engaged at the time they moved in with their partners, and most are men.

Family Reasons

The final reason mentioned in sufficient numbers by our respondents for cohabiting related to family issues—such as the desire to move out of a parent's (or sibling's) home, an attempt to avoid moving back in with family, or due to a pregnancy. Nearly 10% of the sample mentioned such reasons for moving in with their partners. Regardless of their social class, those who mentioned family reasons were often in their late teens or early twenties when they moved in together. But nearly twice as many service-class respondents as middle-class ones mentioned family reasons as a motivator for cohabiting, and for many of them, moving in with a partner was the first time they had lived apart from parents.

Conflict with parents and a desire to feel more like an adult were mentioned repeatedly by these respondents. Even though many did not feel that residing with parents was stigmatized, they did express strong desires for greater freedom than coresidence with parents allowed. This was most clearly stated by those who had never lived outside of their parents' homes. Shane, who at 22 worked as a part-time stocker at a popular clothing store, recalled, "I had been wanting to get out of my parents' house and she wanted to be getting out of her parents' house." He continued on to say, "We'd talk about not wanting to live with our parents, and then we'd just talk about living together instead, because it'd be easier for rent." At the time of their interviews, however, Shane had moved back in with his parents, bringing his partner, Sandra, with him.[17] Eighteen-year-old Patty moved in with her sister after fighting with her parents but soon left that situation to live with her partner.

Josh. Wanting more autonomy spurred her to move out of her parents' home and into her sister's, as she explained:

> When I moved in to my sister's, I think the big reason I was so ready to move out of my parents' house was just because I was upset that I couldn't spend time with him [Josh]. He would like to do things later at night and I had to be in by midnight, even though I was 18. My parents were like, "You know, we don't like you being out late," and I would just get really upset. I think when I moved into my sister's, immediately we started hanging out at each other's house all the time and sleeping at each other's house.

But the conflict moved with her, and her sister soon kicked her out of the house for repeatedly coming home late. This spurred her move-in with Josh, she recalled. "I'd say probably we were both in a tight spot. I didn't want to go back to my parents, and he didn't want to go back to his parents either, and it was both like we had nobody else to fall back on."

Moving in with a significant other was also perceived as the best way to avoid family conflict. Ray remembered that Julie's family situation was not so great when they first started dating, and he hypothesized that a desire to get away from the tensions may have motivated her decision. "I think at that time she wasn't getting along with her parents. Her parents were separated or I should say they were divorced, so I don't think she was getting along with her mom real well at the time. That's why she was staying with her dad, and I think, at first I thought maybe she was [moving in with me] just to get away from her family." A desire to relieve family strains was also expressed by Dawn, who had never lived independent of her family prior to moving in with Eric:

> I wanted to get away from my parents. I mean I love my parents, I love to hang out with them but you just want to have that separation, feeling like you are kind of moving on with your life and doing what you want to do. Don't get me wrong, I love my parents. I love spending time with them. I visit them almost every weekend. But I wanted to get out on my own. Plus, you know, I wasn't getting along with my dad too well. We get along great now, we get along fine. He still lectures me a lot about things I'm not doing right but, you know, I just kind of wanted to get away from it.

Those who had already lived independent of parents reported feeling more stigma about returning to the parental home or explained that their partners did not view it as a desirable option. Adam, who was in his late twenties when he began seeing Sheryl, recalled, "I was really eager to get out of the house. It was hard living with my parents again, you know, so we moved in together pretty early, in my opinion, but I was really eager to get out of my parents' house, so it seemed like the next right thing to do." Jeremy, who divorced and went back to graduate school, explained his decision, saying "When I was in [graduate] school I was in a dorm, I got out of school at the very beginning of May, and I was just kind of like, 'I have nowhere to live,' and I didn't want to live at home with Mom and Dad. It's an option, I just didn't want to."

Another four respondents, all from our service-class sample, detailed how pregnancy served as the motivator for moving in together. All four were in their teens when their conceptions occurred.[18] Terrell described how this event propelled him into living with Aliyah, though neither had a full-time job at the time, and she was trying to complete her bachelor's degree. "I wasn't trying to move in," he asserted, "but after we found out she was pregnant it wasn't no ands, ifs, or buts about it." The progression into shared living tended to occur more gradually for those who moved from their parents' homes or whose shared living was precipitated by pregnancy.

Partners often did not provide the same reasons for why they decided to move in together. Women were more likely than men to mention convenience as a reason to move in with a partner. Men were more likely to mention housing. But men—especially middle-class men—were considerably more likely than women to mention that they moved in as a step toward greater commitment or marriage. This is notable, given research documenting that men often control when a proposal takes place, and many had not yet discussed their intentions with their partner. Our findings therefore suggest that what cohabitation means at the time individuals move in with their partner, as well as the factors living up to shared living, differ in important ways by social class and sex.

IS FASTER BETTER? FEELINGS ABOUT RELATIONSHIP TEMPO

Many of the service-class respondents felt their relationships progressed quickly, which is perhaps not surprising given that over half had moved in within six months of their relationship's start. Nearly two-thirds of the less educated respondents (or 38 of 60) described their relationship tempos as very fast or declared that things had progressed rapidly. Carly, at 18 one of our youngest respondents, had moved in with her 28-year-old partner, Vic, within three months. She recalled, "We moved really quickly and just everything progressed really fast, you know? I was living there right away, we were having sex right away. And I think that it might've been a little bit different, but I don't know how."

Among the middle-class respondents, many also felt that their relationships had progressed, in the words of Greg, "overwhelmingly quickly." But quite a few of those middle-class respondents who described their progressions as rapid—particularly the women—qualified their responses. Karen, a 24-year-old research assistant in a university lab, described how serious her relationship felt within six weeks of meeting, but while she said they had rapidly progressed in intimacy, she went on to say, "Well, we didn't move in officially for almost a year and a half." Karen wasn't the only woman to clarify that while the romance had moved along at a brisk pace, they had not moved in together immediately. Kristina also replied that her relationship had progressed "very quickly," but the 24-year-old architect went on to say, "Like it was not really fast, I mean, I feel like the appropriate amount of time went by for us to date before we moved in." Nonetheless, she stated breathlessly, "I feel like our relationship has been such a whirlwind, that it's gone by so fast. Even now I'm like, 'Oh My God!' We've been dating two years. It does NOT feel like two years." Such responses indicate that at least for the middle class, there may be an implicit amount of time, or a "testing period" between the romance's start and when it is deemed acceptable for couples to move in together. That period appears to be a little over a year.

One factor that expedited relationships, or made respondents feel their romances had evolved rapidly, was that many of these couples had already been spending most nights together. Stephanie explained, "It was pretty easy for things to go really fast once we got together. And moving in together after only a few months was a big step, but at the same time, he was already living with me." Justine, a 27-year-old graduate student in psychology, asked how her relationship had evolved, stated, "Really fast, because we just really hit it off right away. I mean, even though we technically didn't move in until about a year, it felt like we were living together almost right away, like within a few weeks." Brad, a graduate student in his late twenties, also felt his relationship had progressed very quickly, responding to a question about how many nights a week they spent together by stating, "At the beginning? I would say pretty much, for the most part, seven out of seven." Asked if he would change the tempo, he said, "No, because it was just pretty natural, so it worked out well."

Many of those in the middle class who described their relationship progressions as rapid also suggested that the high level of comfort indicated that their relationships were good for the long haul. Kevin, a 27-year-old branch manager at a small manufacturing plant, described how good a fit he and his fiancée, Amy, were, explaining, "From very early on in our relationship, we clicked and we hung out a lot." He continued on to say, "We were just, had a ton in common and you know, I understood her humor, she understood mine, so it was just, it was an instant click." Evan, a 27-year-old sales manager, explained his feeling about their progression by saying, "I saw we were both extremely happy with each other. I think I knew probably within six months that I was going to propose to her at some point. I think she knew before that, at least that's what she tells me." Few among the less educated cohabitors used such language to describe their relationship tempos. Such differences in perceptions may come into play as individuals contemplate the future, as we discuss in Chapter 6.

Not all cohabitors were happy about how rapidly they had moved in with their partners. But dissatisfaction with too rapid a pace was only expressed by the less educated respondents. A total of eight service-class respondents expressed qualms regarding their relationship tempos, with many wishing, in retrospect, that they had moved more slowly, and a few commenting that they wish they had not begun their relationships at all. Most of these respondents (six) had moved in with their partners within the first six months, often because of the financial necessity of one or both partners. Asked why they would have slowed things down in hindsight, these respondents mentioned that living together went against their religious convictions, that it had caused problems with their children or other family members, or that it had detracted them from focusing on their own self-development. They also attributed high levels of conflict to their rapid transitions.

In fact, several of the service-class respondents seemed to wish that they could "redo" some aspects of how their relationship unfolded, even if they were satisfied with their partners. Susan, who moved in with Eugene when both were experiencing job instability, regretted her rapid entrance into shared living because cohabiting went against her religious beliefs and also upset her family. Nonetheless, she expressed a sense of fatalism regarding what else she could have done and how it had progressed. Asked how she would describe her relationship tempo, she replied, "I think it progressed really fast, and I kind of wish it didn't progress so fast, but at the same time it really didn't matter." Asked why she thought it had progressed quickly, Susan said, "Because to me, normally when couples start dating, I don't think they should move in like two or three months right after they meet each other. Usually you want to get to know each other a little bit more, you know? That part just seemed like it was just really, really fast." When asked if she would have moved in if she had the money to stay in her own place, Susan replied, "We wouldn't have moved in with each other." Probed further about when she might have moved in with Eugene, Susan answered, "Probably not until we got married because both of our religions, really you're supposed to marry and then move in with each other and we were trying but it didn't work out that way. So you know, our families aren't happy with the situation because it makes it a little hard, and it's a little stressful. They're a little irritated with that and they're not happy with the fact that we're living together, but they understand at the same time that financially that's what we had to do."

Other respondents who felt their relationships had progressed too quickly thought that they had set aside their own interests or that their partners did not put as much into their relationships as they did. Stacy said, "I think if I have to do this again I'm definitely going to go slower. It's intoxicating to go that quickly. It's like, 'Oh, I'm having the best time of my life!' But in all rationality it's not the best situation, because you get so lost in somebody else that all your real life stuff starts to go like . . . " At that point, Stacy made noises and hand motions of a building crumbling to indicate how other aspects of her life had imploded. Patty also felt that the way the situation had unfolded had not been optimal for her:

> If I could redo it at my own pace, I would probably have things go slower. I think if I could redo things, I don't think I would want to live with him, like at this point in time. I think we both are not as sure of ourselves, and you know, I don't think we both equally put into our relationship living together. And I think it would probably be better for me personally if I had experienced living on my own, or with a friend first, instead of my first experience with a roommate is with my boyfriend, which is difficult.

The majority of those expressing reservations about how rapidly they had moved in together, or who would have deferred doing so if they had only had more resources, were women. These sentiments reveal that it is not marriage alone that can deflect women from self-development; living with a romantic partner may also require time and attention that detracts from their ability to invest in their own human capital.

A few of those who had progressed rapidly also expressed in hindsight that if they had the opportunity to do it again, they would not. All but one of the respondents who expressed how difficult the transition had been were from the service class. Vanessa, who invited her partner, Robert, to live with her within the first week, explained, "I never really expected it to happen as quick as it did, and by the time it happened, I mean we got into lots of arguments and there's some times that I would regret that I had him around, you know? I wish I had thought about it a little bit more before I just moved somebody in, but it happened quickly, I mean like real quick." Asked if she would do it differently, she retorted, "I wouldn't move them in the first week of dating. That's for sure." Ron, a 31-year-old disk jockey at a gentleman's club, replied to the question about whether he would do it again, saying, "Do it over? I wouldn't do it. I wouldn't date her." His partner, Crystal, a dancer at the club where Ron worked, also replied, "On one hand I almost want to say I would have never done it at all, but I think I would have slowed it down, because like you don't get to learn that much about a person when you move that fast, so that once you're already in love, you're like, 'I don't like the person.'" Only one college-educated respondent expressed dissatisfaction with her tempo into shared living. Expedited entrance into shared living may be associated with poorer relationship quality, which may account for why many cohabitating unions dissolve quickly.

College-educated cohabitors were far more likely than their service-class counterparts to say their relationships had advanced at a good or steady pace. Over a quarter of the middle-class respondents described their relationships as gradually building over time. Thirty-year-old Jessica explained how taking time to get to know each other provided a solid foundation for her relationship with Martin, though she was initially hesitant about his moving in with her. Asked to describe the tempo of her relationship progression, she stated, "I think it was just about right. You know, because we had the friendship beforehand and I knew so much about him as a friend, you know, and then we have the year of long-distance dating. And I guess now that I look back on it, like that year was very important as far as like trust and building your trust with each other, being honest with each other." Less educated respondents also mentioned that taking more time to get to know one's partner also benefitted their relationships, though given differences in progression tempos there were just fewer of them—only five—in this category. Some commented that though it was difficult not rushing into things, they thought it was better for their relationships. Simon, a 25-year-old carpenter, explained how challenging it was to hold off for seven months before moving in with his partner. Laura:

> I thought we did good for that point and not just diving right in, because it's, you know, you feel all these things and stuff for a month and then you move in with the person and find out 'She's crazy!' and she's stalking you at work,

you know what I mean? But we did, I thought we did good. We did it right, you know? I thought that was a proper time period, and I mean, it was agony. We waited that long, it was really hard, it really was.

Respondents who assessed their progressions as more tempered also tended to compare their current relationships with previous ones. Two of the service-class women, both of whom had previously been married, reported that their current relationships had progressed at a more gradual pace, or, in the words of 29-year-old Sheryl, "naturally."

There are also those who described their relationships as progressing fairly slowly, though their numbers are small.[19] Several of these respondents explained that things moved at a slower pace in part because they had relationship troubles or had on-again/off-again relationships with their partners. Max, who was 29 at the time of his interview, explained why it took him and Tameka over four years before they moved in together. "It took a while because I wasn't trying to do the right thing. I was still out running around, going to clubs and meeting people and doing different things." Concerns with closing off one's options were also expressed by college-educated respondents. Andrea, who began dating her partner, Nathan, when she was 21, explained, "I was a little apprehensive at first. I was trying not to fall too fast and too hard, so I think that it was a relatively simple, easy pace." Asked why she would describe her pace as slow, Andrea replied, "Considering we've been together four years and we're just now getting engaged, a lot of my friends are moving a lot faster than that. I don't think we moved very fast." These respondents tended to be young, in their late teens or early twenties, when they initially met their partners.

But not all of those who described their relationship progression as slow had done so because of an unwillingness to limit their options. Twenty-two-year-old Brian, who worked as both an auto mechanic and a waiter at the time he was interviewed, thought a gradual progression was good for their relationship, explaining: "We had that year of friendship to learn each other, know each other, you know? And then, waiting to have sex is definitely always a good thing because, you know, you don't want to weight a relationship on sex, especially if you're looking for a serious one, I mean depending on what you're looking for. I would say I would do it again the same way." Travis, a 29-year-old CPA at the time of his interview, also suggested that tempo was in the eye of the respondent and referenced that what was a comfortable pace for him had not been so for his partner, Katherine. Asked to describe how his relationship had progressed, he stated, "Probably kind of slow. I know *she* would say it's slow. *I* don't think it's rushing into anything. I mean, I think it's an appropriate pace."

WHAT WE LEARNED ABOUT THE REASONS FOR AND TEMPO TO COHABITATION

The early stages of a romantic relationship are filled with new discoveries, anticipation of what is to come, and assessments of whether the relationship will last. For many contemporary young adults, romantic relationships quickly transition into shared living arrangements, often for reasons beyond the couples' desires to assess the next step in their unions. Financial need or the greater practicality of sharing a home, the end of a lease or departure of a roommate, or the desire to get away from family members seemed to precipitate the entrance into shared living at least as much—if not more—than careful assessments of where relationships were headed.

But event-driven transitions into shared living—those associated with job fluctuation or other financial necessities, as well as housing needs—are more likely to occur among the less educated than among those who have completed their college degrees. They also tend to occur earlier in the course of the relationship among service-class cohabitors than middle-class cohabitors. Couples that are romantically involved for over a year before moving in together are substantially more likely to be considering their relationship futures than are couples who begin shared living within three or four months as a result of a need for a place to live or because they lost their jobs or had their hours cut at work. For starters, instability in employment and attaining economic and career stability are strongly associated with marital delay. Numerous qualitative studies report that young adults feel that they must be able to demonstrate they are established in their jobs or moving up in their careers, have completed their schooling, and are financially secure before getting engaged or married. Those who end up living with a partner because they do *not* have these very important markers would therefore be unlikely to contemplate marriage in the near term. But it is not just their better economic positions that explain why college-educated cohabitors are more likely than their less educated counterparts to transition into marital unions. Those who progress more slowly into shared living often attribute their decisions to move in with their partners to relationship-driven reasons. They have had more time to assess the strength of their unions and determine if they are worth advancing.

Their rapid entrance into shared living was often a source of concern among many of those who felt that they had few other alternatives. A lack of a financial cushion was the motivator for more than a few; the difficulty of making ends meet on a collection of minimum or near-minimum wage jobs, the absence of enough money to pay for a security deposit and first month's rent for an apartment, sudden costs imposed by cars that needed to be repaired in order to get to work, and the pressure of repaying debt from both credit cards and school weighed far more heavily on our service-class respondents than they did for their better educated peers and were frequently mentioned in discussions about how their decisions to live with their partners had been made. But while the tempo to shared living generally differed by social class, our results suggest that for many, it was not different norms regarding tempo that shaped faster transitions into shared living; rather, class differences in practical realities—what proportion of one's earnings went toward paying rent, the need for assistance with keeping a roof over one's head, or job instability—was often the driver. That so many of the less educated made decisions to move in with their partners relatively rapidly and often while feeling less than ready might hamper further relationship development.

Of course, rapid moves into shared living may open up new doors and close others. While several of our respondents mentioned that a pregnancy precipitated their decision to cohabit, other respondents—all from the service-class sample—mentioned that a conception early on in their relationship delayed considerations of marriage. Other respondents, however, transitioned into engagement; some set firm wedding dates, though our service-class respondents were often content to refer to themselves as engaged but with no clear time line to marriage. Still others discovered that living together, in part due to frequent arguments, was not all that it was cracked up to be. In the next few chapters, we discuss what couples experienced once they moved in together. In Chapter 4, we examine the ways that dividing the housework lead to domestic bliss for some and relationship woes for others. We discuss the fertility desires and behaviors of both sets of couples in Chapter 5 and follow it up with an analysis of the evolution of couples' relationships after moving in together, both in terms of how they felt about marriage and the steps they took toward it. The timing to cohabitation continues to reverberate in these subsequent outcomes, spreading ripples through their relationships that, while growing less evident to the eye over time, persist in influencing the trajectory of these unions.

4

"I Like Hugs, I Like Kisses, but What I Really Love Is Help with the Dishes"

The Dance of Domesticity

"Honestly, at the beginning I thought I would only allow a 50–50 situation. I did exactly 50% of the housework, as did he. I cooked 50% of the meals and if I cooked a meal he always did the dishes. I thought it was going to be this very modern woman-man type relationship," said Julie, a 30-year-old nanny and full-time student who had been living with her partner, Ray, for about seven years at the time of her interview. Asked if the division of labor now was what she thought it would be, Julie replied, "No, but I wouldn't call it unfair," then clarified. "It's different now, but not unfair. It's me doing all of the housework because he's working twice as much as I am. He works full time, is a part-time student. I am a full-time student and part time [worker]. He brings in the majority of the money; he makes more money than I do per hour, so it's like 100% tackling different roles. I am the homemaker, take care of the apartment, do all of the grocery shopping, any kind of social things I set up, and he is work and school. I don't mind the arrangement at all. It's kind of just something we fell into, kind of settled into." Ray was also quite content with their division of home and work responsibilities. Other women said that they always expected to shoulder the majority of domestic labor, frequently attributing that to their high standards. As Karen, a 25-year-old research coordinator explained, "I don't trust anyone else to clean it the way I want it cleaned."

Not all of our respondents—particularly the women—were so satisfied with how they balanced domestic labor. Quite a few struggled with a slide into conventional arrangements that seem more typical of 1950s married couples than free-spirited cohabitors, or were mystified at how to change their situations. Describing how different the actual division of domestic labor was from what she assumed it would be, 18-year-old Patty, who worked at a coffee shop, remarked, "It's not really the same as what you would expect, you know, everybody to be equal and help each other. It doesn't work out that way most of the time." This did not sit well with Patty. She went on to explain, "I know Josh can clean and I know he can cook, but for some reason, it's like I have to, that's my responsibility. But I think it should be pretty even." Accounting for why she thinks the division of domestic labor devolves largely to women, Patty stated, "I find that most men are just too lazy or neglect to note that they *do* know how to do these things, so they just leave it to other people."

Still other couples had achieved what they described as a relatively equal division of labor. These respondents, who were disproportionately college educated, were generally happy with their arrangements, even if they had not arrived at them overnight. Few of these couples consciously attributed their approach to a feminist philosophy. Instead, most viewed their more equal divisions of domestic work as fair, natural, or a reflection of their domestic inclinations, rather than resulting from a desire to challenge conventional-gendered behaviors. Tabitha explained why she and her partner, Edward, divided chores, including the care of their newborn son, stating, "We both work, so we share everything." Alisha said, "I cook, because I love to cook, and he will do the dishes. I never had to say, you know, 'I cook, you clean,' he just automatically did it." Others commented that they were not interested in keeping a score card about who did what, like Jeff, who said, "I'm not like on like the tick system like 'one for me, one for you.'" Yet many of the men in these couples who ended up sharing housework relatively equally never expected such an arrangement. What characterizes those couples who are able and willing to divide housework more equitably?

There is not one uniform pattern regarding how cohabiting couples arrange their household labor, which our results suggest. Men did the bulk of the domestic labor in a few of the couples we interviewed, and others managed to arrive at a relatively equal division of labor. Yet the most prevalent situation was for couples to rely on the woman to shoulder the majority of the housework. Men sometimes expressed embarrassment at not doing more, even if their partners attributed them with sharing relatively equitably, implicitly acknowledging the inequity. Kevin, a 28-year-old manager at a local manufacturing firm whose partner, Amy, said that they roughly shared the domestic labor explained somewhat sheepishly, "You know, I thought I would do it [housework] voluntarily and I don't do it. I'm not as quick to volunteer to do the dishes and take out the trash, that sort of thing. I'm lazy, I'm not going to lie about it." But men far more frequently asserted that they did less domestic labor because their partners were "better" at it or had higher standards. Other men felt it was just too onerous for them. Robert, a 26-year-old part-time roofer, explained, "every little bit I do I feel like it's a lot, you know?" Men were far more likely than their female counterparts to state that they had not even thought about how the household work would get done; a few even asserted that domestic labor was just not a man's responsibility.

New living arrangements may challenge established family patterns, but our findings reveal that they do not completely transform gendered expectations regarding who performs housework and who benefits from the fruits of that labor. In part due to their better ability to negotiate what they wanted in their relationships, our middle-class couples were more content with how they divided up the domestic work than were service-class couples. Dissatisfaction with how the work in the home was managed was most pronounced among service-class women; not only does their share of the work feel inequitable, but attempts to advocate for a more equal division of labor failed or required more effort than seemed worthwhile and were ultimately abandoned. This chapter explores the nitty-gritty of how couples collaborate or fail to coordinate their household activities. Our in-depth assessment into the negotiation of the daily activities of cohabiting couples showed how couples constructed (or destructed!) gendered behaviors, reified or challenged the exercise of power, and expressed respect or intimacy. Attempts to arrive at satisfactory divisions of housework reveal yet another avenue of continued gender inequality between more and less advantaged couples, a theme we return to in subsequent chapters.

WHAT DO WE KNOW ABOUT EXPECTATIONS FOR HOUSEWORK?

The division of labor shapes the daily rhythms of couples' lives and is among the most common sources of tension between partners.[1] Few young men today have issues with women working outside the home; many think dual-worker families are necessary, given the challenges of maintaining a decent standard of living.[2] Furthermore, the majority of women nowadays expect to work full time and increasingly remain there throughout their working lives.[3] As work in the paid labor force has become increasingly the norm for women, women's expectations that their male partners will pitch in on the domestic front have grown. In fact, contemporary young adults increasingly express a preference for egalitarian partnerships.[4] Nonetheless, the work place has not changed enough to accommodate two working partners; instead, it remains a "greedy" institution, and good jobs often seem to be in short supply.[5] But a key factor impeding the widespread embrace of sharing domestic labor is that the work is often tedious, repetitive, and unappreciated. Few people look forward to cleaning bathrooms or making sure that the toilet bowl is "sparkling fresh and clean!"[6] Such work has long been perceived as the domain of either "the weaker sex" or those in disadvantaged positions.[7] Finally, sharing the domestic load often requires that the male partner relinquish at least some of the prerogatives that used to come with his sex—the ability to opt out of household labor.[8]

Recent research on how young adults expect to manage their work lives and family lives highlights the dramatic impasse between idealized expectations and what young people feel may really unfold in their lives, and how men and women anticipate they will manage the tensions. In her expansive study of young adults who came of age in the late 20th and early 21st century, aptly titled *The Unfinished Revolution*, Kathleen Gerson (2009) reveals that while young men and women generally aspire to egalitarian relationships, most believe that they are not attainable given the inflexibility of the American work world. They therefore devise "fall-back" strategies that serve to perpetuate the divide between breadwinning and caretaking. The men Gerson interviewed, for example, reported that their "Plan B" involved prioritizing their own jobs over those of their partners. Though still expecting that both would work for pay, these men anticipated that their wives or partners would remain primarily responsible for domestic responsibilities. Gerson labeled this approach "neo-traditional": men were accepting of women's new roles in the workplace but did not challenge men's conventional roles at home. The women Gerson interviewed, in contrast, felt that if they could not find egalitarian partnerships—if their only option was a man who expected them to do it all—they would prefer to be alone and adopt children or have them without marriage. The dissonance in what men and women anticipate happening with work and care relationships emerges in studies of both high flying professionals and less economically advantaged couples.[9]

In her research, Gerson did not distinguish between individuals who were cohabiting, married, or had recently separated. But a sizable body of research documents important ways in which the behaviors of cohabitors and marrieds differ. Married women do considerably more domestic labor than do married men, even though the proportion of housework married men do has increased significantly over the past few decades.[10] If couples can live together without the formal contract of marriage, however, perhaps they may also jettison some of the old rules and roles of marriage—such as conventional gendered behaviors. Cohabiting couples engage in more equal division of domestic labor, in part because they are less likely to be parents; cohabitors are also somewhat younger than marrieds, and cohabiting women are more likely than married women to be in the paid labor force.[11] But gender trumps union status; cohabiting women continue to spend significantly more time in domestic labor than do cohabiting men.[12] Furthermore, when men move into cohabiting unions they decrease the hours they spend in domestic labor, whereas women's housework hours increase upon moving in with a partner.[13] Whether such behaviors persist among this generation of cohabitors, entering their informal unions when living together is more normative and expectations for egalitarianism even greater, is an open question.

Even when couples arrive at egalitarian arrangements, doing so is not without consequences. Studies of couples who have managed to create relatively equal unions, where work outside the home and inside are shared, find that such unions can be difficult to sustain. Couples may face various roadblocks—from family members, the workplace, or even their own community.[14] Such relationships also required a great deal of maintenance. Earlier studies showed that couples practicing equality reported more feelings of resentment and depression, less satisfying sex lives, and greater risks of divorce than did those with more conventional arrangements.[15] Recent research suggests that outcomes associated with more equal relationships may differ, as they have become more common.[16] But has there been a dramatic shift to egalitarianism? Partners also do not always agree on expectations for housework. When gender norms are unclear, or where partners hold differing opinions about what is fair or equitable, couples may experience a good deal of conflict.[17]

Of course, not all couples experience this flux in the same way. Social class, as well as gender, differentiates how young Americans participate in both the paid labor force and their contributions to the household labor. The service class, particularly the men, have traditionally expressed more gender-traditional attitudes than middle-class individuals regarding the division of paid and domestic labor.[18] This may be due in part to the "liberalizing" effect of higher education.[19] Historically, men's elevated status within the workplace also led to extra privileges at home, including greater decision-making power and the ability to "opt out" of onerous household tasks.[20] However, less advantaged men have experienced far more threats to their prerogatives as their labor market position has eroded and many find their female partners with more education than they have.[21] Additionally, because the wage gap is smaller among men and women with lower levels of educational attainment, there may therefore be more resistance on the part of men to giving up their few (and ever diminishing) masculine advantages and "helping out" more around the house. While higher-income women may reduce time strain and domestic disputes by outsourcing traditional feminine roles (such as eating out more or hiring cleaning help), this option is much less available to their less affluent counterparts.[22]

Nearly all of these studies of household labor examined married couples. Whether social class differentiates the ways cohabitors negotiate the division of paid work and housework, then, remains to be seen. Clearly, attitudes about appropriate gendered behaviors are always changing. In fact, Gerson (2009) found that among contemporary young adults, lower-income and less educated respondents were only slightly less likely to expect equal relationships than their more educated and upper-middle-class peers. It is possible, then, that the less institutionalized nature of cohabitation may afford today's cohabitors an opportunity to share paid and household responsibilities more equally, regardless of social class.

COHABITORS INVOLVEMENT IN THE PAID LABOR FORCE

Members of our study who were employed full time (35 or more hours per week) like Randy, an airplane mechanic, or Monica, a zookeeper, clearly had less availability to engage in domestic work than cohabitors who worked part time or attended school in lieu of full-time work. Looking at the employment status of our respondents suggests one reason why cohabiting men perform less housework: they are more likely to be working full time (see Table 3, Panel A). Nearly two-thirds of our sample worked full time. But there was considerable variability by social class and sex. The middle class—both the men and women—was generally working full time, while many service-class respondents worked part time while pursuing more schooling.[23] Men from both

TABLE 3   INDIVIDUAL EXPECTATIONS FOR AND DIFFERENCES IN THE DIVISION
OF LABOR (BY PERCENTAGE)

	All Individuals		Service-Class Individuals		Middle-Class Individuals	
	Men	Women	Men	Women	Men	Women
Number	61	61	30	30	31	31
Panel A: Employment						
Full time worker	78.7	55.7	63.3	40.0	93.6	71.0
Part-time worker, not a student	4.9	11.5	6.7	10.0	3.2	12.9
Part-time worker and a student	11.5	27.9	20.0	43.3	3.2	12.9
Not working for pay	4.9	4.9	10.0	6.7	0.0	3.2
Panel B: Initial Expectations for the Division of Housework						
Expected they'd share it equally	32.8	45.9	26.7	43.4	38.7	48.4
Expected she'd do majority	29.5	41.0	26.7	33.3	32.3	48.4
Expected he'd do majority	8.2	6.6	10.0	10.0	6.5	3.2
No initial expectations	29.5	6.6	36.7	13.3	22.6	0.0
Panel C: Actual Division of Housework						
She does majority	55.7	57.4	66.7	66.7	48.4	51.6
Shared equally	32.8	32.8	16.7	13.3	45.2	48.4
He does majority	11.5	9.8	16.7	20.0	6.5	0.0

groups were more likely to be working full time than their female counterparts. We turn now to our respondents' stories to determine whether
these class and gender differences were reflected in housework expectations and behaviors.

COHABITORS' EXPECTATIONS ABOUT HOUSEWORK

The employment and educational pursuits of our respondents varied
over the course of their relationships, something that our static measure
of employment at the time of interview does not capture. We therefore
asked our respondents about their expectations for domestic labor upon
first moving in with their partners, and then followed up to determine
what aspects of housework had changed since moving in together. Our
findings surprised us (see Table 3, Panel B). Given frequently cited attitudes about young adults' expectations for equality, we had anticipated

that many more of our respondents would want to share housework. But we found that the majority of both men and women in our sample did not express such desires. Although the largest proportion of women had expected that housework would be divided equally, that view was expressed by less than half of all women (45.9%, or 28 of the 61). Nearly as many women thought that they would do the majority of the housework (25 of 61). Men, in contrast, were roughly equally divided into three groups. Less than a third of the men assumed domestic labor would be split relatively equally (20 of the 61 men), 30% thought that their partner would do the majority of the housework, and another 30% had not even thought about how domestic work would be divided—demonstrating a form of male privilege in itself, implying as it does that housework was the responsibility of someone else.[24]

Large differences in expectations by social class also emerge, though these are far more evident among the men. College-educated men were more likely than service-class men to expect to share housework equally (38.7% vs. 26.7%). The service-class men, in contrast, were most likely to say that they had no initial expectations for how the work would get done, with equal proportions of service-class men expecting that the housework would be shared or that their female partner would do it all. As for the women, those with college degrees were as likely to expect that they would be doing the majority of the housework as to anticipate equality, while fewer service-class women thought that they would do the lion's share of the housework.

A closer look at how couples negotiated important aspects of their relationships reveals why men's and women's expectations differ so radically, even among those who are living together. Only twelve of our respondents expressly discussed housework expectations before moving in together. Of those who had, the six middle-class individuals were much more specific and directive. Kristina, an architect, said that she knew that she would be the one to do most of the housework but clarified how she conveyed to Matthew that he needed to help. "I also laid down rules," she said. "I'm like, 'Look, if we're going to move in together, you're going to do the dishes. You're cutting the grass.'" Paul, a 26-year-old political lobbyist, recalled how they had detailed their intended domestic arrangements. "We said that we were going to make a list, right, and we would have like this dry erase board," he chuckled. Service-class respondents' conversations about expectations for housework tended to be rather vague, more along the lines of how Vickie explained her discussion with Howard: "Any mess you make, you clean up," before elaborating, "nobody was assigned to do dishes or anything like that." In fact, these discussions were often not detailed enough to be workable, if Shane's revelations of what happened are any indication. "We planned for most of the chores ahead of time," he recalled, "and those chores that we didn't plan for would just get ignored, 'cause no one was supposed to do them. And that caused more problems. But it was never really anything too big. It was usually just like keeping the bathroom clean, when like soap scum or just dirt and stuff like that get on the counter and table."

A few respondents who did not explicitly discuss ahead of time how they would divide domestic responsibilities sometimes made assumptions on the basis of what they had observed before moving in together. Sherry, a 21-year-old waitress, explained, "When we were just dating, he always had his house clean." She added, "I'm so used to living with roommates, you know? So you're used to having this part, 'You clean the kitchen, I'm going to clean this.' . . . So I'm thinking that we're both going to do it." Unfortunately, that did not happen. Sherry, like quite a few women, ruefully remarked that they thought the men had been making special efforts to keep things clean to impress them while they were just dating.

Past experiences and global attitudes shaped expectations for the division of labor for men. Men who expected things to be equally split, especially those from the service-class sample, often had some link to the military, either having served themselves or having grown up with a father in the armed forces. Randy, for example, stated that he expected to do the bulk of the housework because his partner, Ming, would never be able to live up to the standard for cleanliness he had developed in the Army. Stan also anticipated sharing the domestic labor, stating, "I can't have anybody doing everything for me. I'm so independent. The military did that, you know, me being so independent, I can't just sit around." Middle-class men who expected to share chores equally attributed their expectations to personal proclivities, namely that they were good about keeping their spaces clean and tidy. Jack, a 24-year-old financial planner, commented, "I'm pretty domesticated and open minded, I don't mind sharing responsibilities." James, another young middle-class male, also described expecting that they would arrange domestic chores equally, saying, "We sort of just were going to split everything down the middle, and like everything would get done." Middle-class men may have had greater expectations of sharing domestic work with partners than the working-class men because they had more often lived with roommates in the past, in college or after graduation.

Two groups stand out, given research that couples increasingly desire egalitarian roles: women and men who anticipated that women would do the majority of the domestic labor. Their comments reveal several important themes in how individuals rationalize behavior in intimate unions that perpetuates inequality. A closer look at the many women in our sample who believed that they would end up doing the majority of housework in their new shared living arrangements provides some evidence as to why women still do most of the housework. Women often attributed their expectations to their very high standards of cleanliness or to their partners' tolerance for mess. This was particularly the case among college-educated women, some of whom, like Natasha or Tabitha, described themselves as "neat freaks." Bree, whose exacting work as a financial auditor required strong organization skills, accounted for her expectations by saying that her views on cleanliness differed from that of her partner's, explaining, "his threshold for dirt was a lot higher than mine was." Personal observation of how boyfriends kept their apartment before they moved in together also shaped their views, as Amy explained:

> Well, I would say, like I was in this boy's apartment. It was DIRTY. Like I was in there every day and I knew what he would do and not do. I knew he would do his own laundry and that's totally how I wanted it, so that's fine. I knew he would not ever clean a bathroom and I knew I would be doing like most of the cleaning kind of things.

A few of the service-class women expressed similar justifications. Jackie, who commented on her need for a clean, well-organized living space, explained that she expected to do the lion's share of the cleaning in her new place with Chad, saying, "I knew before we moved in together he didn't do chores."

A handful of respondents also attributed their expectations to their own gender socialization, based on their experiences in their families of origin or in earlier relationships. Emily, a 28-year-old pastry chef explained, "Yeah, it's kind of always what I've expected. My mom always did more housework than my father. I always did more housework than my ex-husband. Actually, I did all of the housework." Alisha also attributed her expectations to her experience with a previous live-in boyfriend, as did Keisha. But service-class women were far less able to account for why they expected to do the bulk of the domestic labor, most often just viewing it as a given. Diana, who was only 17 when she began living with her partner, had just given birth, and was also completing her high school degree, explained, "During the week I normally did everything because I didn't really expect him to." Carly, who moved in with Vic when she was 18, indicated that she had assumed her role as primary cleaner without any discussion, saying, "When we first started dating I would do like all the chores and help him out and stuff, when he was in school." Valencia, who said that the idea of her partner, Jorge, doing the laundry "makes me worried," went on to say, "I mean, I've always just did the laundry," and seemed not to find it unusual that she now did Jorge's laundry, as well as all the cooking and cleaning. These two perspectives—attributing their assumption of the majority of the domestic labor because of their personal need for cleanliness and order or because that was "how they were raised" may enable these women to navigate the dissonance between their desires for equality on other fronts and how it played out in the realm of domestic labor.

What about the nearly 30% of men who expected that their female partners would do the majority of the housework? The reason proffered most frequently by these men related to personal proclivities, both theirs and their partners. Several men indicated that they were either too messy or indolent to do the housework. Sam, an 18-year-old part-time student and call center employee, said, "I mean, I don't really do [housework]. That's the thing, I'll admit, I'm lazy. When I get home from work, I don't really want to do much," going on to state that that was the reason his partner, Rhoda, ended up doing the bulk of the cleaning. Brad, also attending school but for a graduate degree, expressed similar sentiments (while using gold-plated words). "I'm kind of lackadaisical," he explained. "I don't want dust bunnies all over the floor, but I don't really care if the toilet bowl gets scrubbed every two months or every week." Other men indicated that their partners were adamant about doing the cleaning. Jorge justified his lack of domestic participation by saying "Well, she's the one that likes to do all of the cooking and she likes to do all that stuff." Simon, who described his role as "helping," explained about his partner, Laura, "For the most part, she took that upon herself." Jonathan attributed his reason for presuming his partner, Janelle, would do most of domestic work to her views on order and cleanliness. "Janelle is, like, completely obsessive-compulsive and neurotic about the cleaning," he explained. He also suggested that he had effectively been trained to not participate, saying, "I do so few things around the house because she just doesn't, like if I were to clean the bathroom or the bedroom she'd just clean it over again. She's just that way."

A few men justified their expectations that their partners would perform most of the domestic work by attributing their poor domestic skills to a lack of training, practice, or interest. They suggested that women were naturally better at domestic labor. Robert, who worked part time as a roofer, explained that while he was growing up, "We had a maid come, so I really didn't have to clean much. And when I was younger, my Mom would just do all the dishes and clean everything. So I've never really had to clean, you know, I've never had to do all that stuff, so it's hard for me now, you know?" Anthony, who lived with his 19-year-old partner, Diana, and their two-year-old daughter, explained why he expected that Diana would do most of the housework. "Just stereotype, you know? I mean, because honestly, like when she was growing up her mom would have her do that stuff all the time, and I never cooked or anything." He added that he felt a sense of accomplishment in just making a peanut butter sandwich for their daughter. Two of the middle-class men who were foreign born also clarified that they were not practiced at domestic labor. Soliman explained, "I had never washed dishes in my life before, I never washed dishes. We had a maid, you know?" Peter pointed to his home country to highlight how separate spheres worked to benefit men:

> Back in Kenya men kind of just chill out and the women do most of the stuff in the house and most of the cooking. Actually, pretty much everything. Men just get into the house, you pick up your newspaper and watch your TV. You wait for the food to be on the table and all of that.

Discussing what he observed men doing, he stated, "I kind of grew up not seeing my Dad do anything. So that's how you kind of see yourself or picture yourself as a married person." Of note is that even when women stated that they had not done much in the way of housework while growing up or did not feel like they were cleaning experts, they did not assume that their lack of skills on this front freed them from domestic work.

Finally, a handful of men, mostly from the less educated group, expected that their partners would do the majority of the domestic labor because they, in their own words, provided the finances. In essence, they suggested that their partners exchanged domestic labor for the men's financial provision. Jorge explained that because he was working and his partner, Valencia, was not at the moment, she could not complain about doing the majority of the housework. Simon, whose partner, Laura, had supported him while he recuperated from a work accident for which he did not receive compensation, explained, "She understands that, you know, I work 10, 11 hours every single day, 5 or 6 days a week. She sees that and she knows when I get home I want to sit down, drink a beer and just relax, you know?" Travis, the one middle-class man in this group, explained that he assumed that his partner would do the bulk of the cleaning "because I pay for the dinners and pay for a few other things, and she's living well above her means." Clearly, vestiges of the benefits that accrue to men who are providers remain, even if the amount these men provided was not that great. Their earnings enabled them to believe that domestic labor was not their bailiwick.

THE ACTUAL DIVISION OF HOUSEWORK: BETTER THAN EXPECTED OR LEAVING A LOT TO BE DESIRED?

Do expectations map closely onto what actually transpires regarding cooking, cleaning, and other forms of reproductive labor? Looking at how our respondents describe who actually does what in the household reveals that the majority of the couples in our sample follow rather conventional practices, where the woman does the bulk of the domestic labor (see Table 3, Panel C). This is much more often the case among our service-class couples. But the proportion of couples who share the housework relatively equally is sizable, accounting for nearly a third of the total sample. Equality in domestic labor is far more common among the middle-class couples, however, who are almost as likely to state that domestic work is shared as to report a conventional arrangement. Finally, a small group—about 10% of all couples—reported that the male partner did most of the domestic labor, though this is largely concentrated among the service class. Our less educated respondents, then, appear to be more distributed along the poles with regards to how domestic labor gets done, weighted toward conventional behaviors but with a sizable minority practicing a counter-conventional (male-dominated) housework division. The college-educated, in contrast, are nearly equally divided between egalitarianism and conventional practices. Of note is that childcare responsibilities did not automatically shift the burden of responsibility more heavily to the women. Even though research shows that the arrival of children tends to make the division of household labor more conventional, that was not the case for the parents in our sample, where the birth of children were just as likely to make couples' divisions of household labor more equal as less equal.[25] We explore how couples describe their balance, before discussing how their practices contributed to or detracted from relationship satisfaction.

Conventional Divisions, Traditional Couples

Over half of the couples in our sample followed an arrangement where the female partner performed more than 60% of the domestic work. We classify this group as *conventional*. Although the majority of these women also worked, men were often attributed with being the primary economic provider, consistent with role complementary, while the women performed the lion's share of the domestic work.[26] The service class more often engaged in conventional divisions of household labor than did middle-class cohabitors; 20 of the men and 20 women in this group attributed women with performing the largest share of their domestic labor. Diana and Anthony were partners who followed this particular arrangement. Anthony, who worked part-time unloading crates at a local dock, explained in response to a question about what kinds of chores he did around the house, "I try and keep up. I try. I do laundry and all that stuff." He and Diana both noted that each took turns cleaning the house and taking out the garbage, but when asked what percentage of the tasks each partner did, Anthony replied, "It's probably like a 70/30 [with her doing 70%] or something like that."

Middle-class couples who practiced conventional arrangements also described men as "chipping in" with housework. Aaron, who managed an office supply store, explained that he and his partner, Emma, did not have a real system for determining who did what around the house. "It's not like we made up a chore list or something," he stated, "where it's divided up of who is supposed to do what on what day or something like that, but I think it's really an informal hope that it gets done, and hope that neither one of us gets stuck with too much of the stuff." Both he and Emma, however, admitted that she is the one who "gets stuck with too much of the stuff." Emma explained that Aaron just failed to see the need for housekeeping like she did. Though men like Aaron and Anthony do occasionally perform some of the labor essential to keeping the house functioning, they do so less frequently than their partners.

Quite a few of the couples in this conventional group describe how they practice a traditional, "indoor/outdoor" division of labor, where the man performs all of the "outdoor" or "physically demanding" jobs while the woman assumes responsibility for all of the "indoor" chores. Evan, who was a sales manager for a well-known motorcycle distributor, described their division of labor as "the traditional male/female roles where she cooks and cleans and I, like, [do] yard work and washing cars." He also identified the chores that were off limits. "I don't do bathrooms. Bathrooms are icky to me," he declared, continuing on to state, "I don't do floors. If I have to scrub, I don't do it." Drew, who worked in IT security, expressed a similar disinclination to performing indoor chores, stating, "I like to do the man work." Service-class men also commented on their responsibility for the outdoor chores or other tasks they viewed as particularly masculine, such as taking out the garbage. Simon, a 25-year-old carpenter, explained why he viewed trash removal as the man's job: "Garbage of course I think is a man's job, 'cause lots of times it's heavier. You've got to walk out in the cold and being a gentleman you know, you take that on." In fact, men took particular pride in garbage duty. Max, a 29-year-old middle school administrative assistant and a part-time basketball coach, explained his and Tameka's division of labor by stating, "She does more of, like, the cooking and more of the dishes. I do the trash. I'll take trash out all over the house any time. It doesn't matter if it's trash in the bedroom, bathroom, kitchen, whatever. I'm doing trash, and sometimes that may be two times a day. It may be, you know, once every two or three days. It just balances." Among the service class, however, this indoor/outdoor arrangement disproportionately disadvantaged women, because almost all of these couples lived in apartments, with little in the way of outdoor chores. Middle-class cohabiting couples with these conventional arrangements, in contrast, all lived in houses, owned by one or both of the partners; because many of their houses were fixer-uppers, there was considerable maintenance work to be done. It is important to note that whether men are responsible for trash or installing shelving units, their chores are often less routine than those that their partners complete.

The majority of women in these conventional couples reported being satisfied with their traditional arrangements, regardless of social class. Quite a few of these women viewed their roles as equitable (if not equal), in part because their male partners often provided a larger share of the household income. Asked to describe how they divided their household labor, Janelle, who owned a yoga studio, explained, "I do it all. I do it all, but he provides the finances." Likewise, Natasha, who had recently opened up her own fitness center, said about her partner, Greg, "He brings home the money. The least I can do is clean up!" Service-class Stephanie, who was working at a call center after a recent spell of unemployment, explained that her partner, Jake, will do some of the chores if she reminded him to do them, but felt that she did about 80% of the housework. Still, she expressed satisfaction with their arrangement, noting, "But he also buys me groceries. Like, when we go grocery shopping he buys the groceries, 'cause he makes a lot more money than I do. So that kind of makes up for it."

Male partners were also quick to point out their role as financial provider when their partners did the bulk of the household chores—even if, as with the service-class men, their relative contributions were not that much more than their partners'.[27] Sam, an 18-year-old part-time student at community college who also worked in a call center, explained why he thought his partner, Rhoda, should do more of the housework, such as putting away the dishes and the groceries. "I figure, I paid for it, you all can at least put it away and stuff. I ain't about to do that, either, I paid for it and carried it into the house." Simon, whose partner, Laura, performed the majority of the housework, explained:

> I think that's her way, you know? Because she does feel really sensitive and it kind of makes her feel bad that she can't contribute more money, and she knows how hard I work for my money and you know, how much I actually put out compared to what she does. But she, she contributes so much in other ways and I remind her all the time how valuable she is, you know? So she does her fair share and she makes up for a lot of things, for stuff at home that I don't [do].

Men in particular often relish the prerogatives of the provider role. Ray, who worked full time as a bookkeeper while taking courses part time to complete his bachelor's degree, had experienced an improved employment situation over the years. Commenting on how his improved provider ability altered the couple's expectations of who would do what in the house, he said, "I can just come home and . . . I can just sit and relax, and so I mean there's a lot of things that she does for me that I really appreciate." Asked what he did for his partner, Julie, he responded: "Well, not as much as she does for me (*laughs*), not physically, but you know, I'm supporting her. I make a lot of money and so financially I support her." The presumption that their assumption of the provider role enabled these men to opt out of housework highlights how persistent gendered expectations for men remain. This may be particularly true for less educated men whose jobs are often in male-dominated industries that serve to reinforce their fairly gender-traditional attitudes.[28]

The college-educated couples who engaged in conventional divisions of domestic labor were more likely to express satisfaction with their arrangements than their service-class counterparts. This difference was particularly marked among the women. There appear to be two main reasons for these distinctions. First, there was a smaller gap between initial expectations and actual divisions among the college educated. The proportion of middle-class women who expected they would do the bulk of the housework and the percent that actually did the majority of it are approximately equal—48.4% compared to 51.6%. Among service-class women, in contrast, only a third had expected to engage in traditional roles, but two-thirds (66.7%) of both the women and men reported that the women did the majority of the household labor. In other words, the expectations and behaviors of middle-class women were far more closely aligned than among the service-class women.

Women who had desired equality in domestic labor often expressed frustration with their current housework burdens and wished their partners would do more. Kate, a 29-year-old manager of a state-run internship program, described the lack of equal sharing of domestic work as "a real bone of contention for me," then said, "and I'm not even a neat freak!" Some of the men also commented that their attitude toward housework disadvantaged their partner, like Derek, describing the early years of living with Kathleen. "She was very concerned with housework but didn't like to do it. I was less concerned with housework and didn't like to do it. So that caused a lot of friction. My attitude [ten years ago] was sort of that the first person who really felt like something needed to be done should do it. And that left her with cleaning the house all the time, so that didn't work out so well." Service-class women also expressed dissatisfaction with how housework was allocated. Brandi, who at 24 was working to complete her associate's degree, said of Artie, "He just doesn't, like, take care. You know, I want to take care of my stuff and you take care of your stuff, and he does not. I mean, it's not that he won't pick up dishes and stuff like that, but he'll just do it on his time, and they can sit there a week and I will go in and do it. And laundry is the same way." But while both middle- and service-class women expressed discontent when their expectations were not met, many more of the service-class than middle-class women had their hopes for equality dashed.

A second reason that helps account for middle-class conventional couples greater satisfaction with the division of domestic labor results from middle-class women's more successful strategies to get "help" from their partners. In addition to the women utilizing more positive and effective approaches to garner assistance, middle-class men also seemed more amenable to assisting their partners with some of the domestic chores when asked. While noting that she did almost all of the laundry and cleaning the house, Emma noted about Aaron that "He actually does a lot of the grocery buying and he actually does a lot of the cooking." Karen described the work that her partner, Jeremy, did in glowing terms, stating, "Jeremy's been so great with helping. There's so much that has to be done to my house, so many repairs, and he's doing a lot of that. Like the dry-walling, and we just cleaned out my garage. He's got some big work to do!"

A few service-class women also describe how their partners were learning to do more, but many of the service-class women who asked for "help" around the house found that their requests were ignored. Brittany, who said she did about 75% of the housework but who had expected it to be equally shared, said of her partner, Spencer, "Well, I wish that he would do more because neither one of us have a lot of time to dedicate to cleaning." But her attempt to get Spencer to realize how much more of the housework she was doing—posting a chore chart—failed. Diana explained that she sometimes asked Anthony to do more, but to little avail. Describing her reaction, she said: "I'd more or less get like pissed off and be like, 'Anthony, why couldn't you do this before I got home?' You know, after I like threw a big fit about it. Then he would [say], 'OK, well I'll do it.' I'm like, 'No! It's pointless now, I already started.' You know, that kind of thing."

The service-class men also affirmed that when their partners desired them to do more of the domestic labor, it often resulted in even more work for the women, who had to motivate and oversee the work. Artie confessed that his partner, Brandi, "has to really give me a good kick in the butt to sometimes get some stuff done." But not all the women felt that the continued effort and struggle to get partners to share more of the housework was worthwhile. Several women indicated that they had given up asking their partners to do their fair (or a fairer) share, a demonstration of men's manifest power.[29] Vanessa explained her abortive attempts to get Robert to do more around the house. Asked about their division of labor, she said:

> He doesn't do any labor and I do it all (laughs). I mean he doesn't wash dishes or if he washes, I have found that just asking him to wash dishes or doing any type of housework is like pulling teeth. He doesn't like to do that. So I mean, now the division of labor is I clean. Sometimes he'll clean if he sees that I'm just really mad or frustrated at him, but I basically do all of it to avoid arguments now.

In fact, several service-class women who were disappointed at being responsible for the majority of domestic labor voiced doubt about their relationships' futures.

Egalitarian Divisions

Despite the assumption that equal sharing of domestic work should be very common among cohabitors, such a division was not the majority experience among the couples we interviewed. Nearly a third of our sample reported that at the time of their survey, they were sharing the housework relatively equally. By this, they meant that each partner performed between 40% to 60% of the domestic labor. We therefore classify these couples as *egalitarian*. Averages for our sample, however, are extremely misleading. Whereas nearly half of the men and women in our middle-class sample report a relatively equal sharing of domestic work (fourteen of the men and fifteen of the women), only a handful of service-class men and women described their divisions of labor as egalitarian—five of the men and four of the women. Why are service-class couples so much less likely to practice equal sharing than they had initially expected, and why are the middle class—mainly the men—so much more likely to engage in egalitarian behavior?

Men who engaged in an egalitarian division of housework repeatedly stated that they had no problem with doing domestic chores. Jared's reply was typical. Asked how they divided up the household chores, he replied, "I'm just one of those people that if I see it needs done, I'll do it." Martin laughingly stated that he "loves doing chores." Unlike many of the women in the conventional group, he did not express dissatisfaction with how his partner, Jessica, did the housework. Instead he said, "Now of course, she'll vacuum, she'll clean the bathroom, and I'm not offended. I'm like 'Great, I didn't have to do that,' but I had no preconceived ideas like 'the woman does this or that.'" Another factor that differentiated these couples from their conventional counterparts is that both partners generally did chores without being told to.

Men's descriptions of themselves as "domestic" or "neat" played a sizable role in how household chores were divided. Middle-class men were particularly likely to describe their desires for order and cleanliness. Jeff, a 32-year-old computer consultant, attributed their domestic arrangement to their zodiac signs, before going on to detail his modus operandi:

> I knew going into it she was messy. I accepted that, and I'm a neat freak, so she's a Cancer, I'm a Virgo, so Cancerians are messy. I'm fine with that, so I just clean up. I don't say anything. So like actually yesterday I scrubbed out the kitchen, put away all the dishes, ran the dishwasher, scrubbed the floor, did the bathroom, cleaned up all the clothes and folded them, hung them up and, you know, I didn't look for a badge. I didn't even mention it. When she came in the apartment she's like "Oh, you cleaned!" I'm like, "Yeah, it's done."

While some men described having higher standards for cleanliness than their partners, most of the couples in the egalitarian group explained that they were actually quite similar in their orientations toward chores. Jared described himself as "a clean freak" but then went on to state, "so it worked out, because she pretty much is, too." Dean, a 36-year-old lawyer who had been involved with his partner, Lindsey, for 18 years, said, "It's not like one of us is a slob and one of us is really neat or the other way. We end up having the same instincts that lead to us doing about equal work."

Not all the couples who report sharing domestic work relatively equally are self-described "neat freaks." Five of the egalitarian couples say that they are all right with a certain amount of disorder. These couples suggest that they have learned to go with the flow and their homes would not pass the white glove test at all times. Mark, a 31-year-old stay-at-home dad who hoped to complete his degree after his children started school, stated, "If the house is messy, you know, fine. When it bothers one of us it will get picked up." Others talked about how work schedules sometimes meant less time to devote to housework or how busy times of the school year resulted in things being left for later. Lisette, a 26-year-old graduate student in economics, explained, "Obviously from time to time it's messy, but it's just from time to time." An ability to take the long view helps these couples feel positive about their labor divisions.

Several respondents in the egalitarian group also viewed their cohabiting arrangement as similar to previous roommate experiences, where shared domestic work was expected. In fact, the contrast between a roommate situation and cohabitation often shed a positive light on the partnership. Sophie, for example, had a high commendation for her experience with Caleb, stating, "He's really clean and takes care of his space, and he's a good roommate." Jack, a 24-year-old financial planner, clarified what he took from previous living arrangements that worked for his current relationship, stating, "I kind of am still in the roommate mind, where we share a lot of the cleaning responsibilities and stuff." Such respondents had observed in previous living situations what the ingredients were for a good roommate and a bad one, and had erred on the side of performing the labor necessary to be placed in the "good" category.

Were the couples who shared domestic labor relatively equally seeking to overturn normative-gendered behaviors, view themselves as gender trendsetters, or describe themselves as feminists? The answer to these questions is a resounding no. Only three of the men in this group of equally sharing couples attributed their behavior, at least partially, to a feminist philosophy. All were college educated, demonstrating how higher education can liberalize gendered expectations. Justin, 24, explained his attitude regarding equal sharing:

> We try our hardest for everything to be equal, because we're also trying to set a good example for people out there. I'm trying to set an example for men that, "Hey, your wife can be equal to you." And she's trying to send an example to women, saying, "Hey, your husband can be equal to you. He doesn't need to be better or do more than you, or less than you." You know? We're definitely trying to lead by example.

But the two other middle-class men who might be classified as feminists focused their justifications on the need for fairness and equality. Jeff, a 32-year-old computer consultant, said he put himself in his partner's footsteps in thinking about how things should be:

> I think people should be able to complement each other in terms of work, and I think if there are inequalities in the domestic chores then that leads to resentment and it can present itself in, like, total other forms. So I'm really conscientious of the fact that, like, if she was doing everything and I'm just sitting around watching TV or something, then that would suck. I wouldn't, if I was her I wouldn't feel good, and so I wouldn't want to feel like that.

Dean pointed to his and Lindsey's desires to be, in his words, "very principled that it was going to be very equal." But the majority of the men in the egalitarian group that share the domestic labor relatively equally with their partners just describe their labor as what they should be doing. They do not view their actions as part of a great feminist revival, but instead as merely something they prefer to do, whether due to their own personal proclivities, because it is better to share, or a desire to make their partners happy.

Negotiating Equality

Egalitarian couples were not always as equal in their behaviors as they were at the time of their interviews. Several mentioned that achieving a more equitable balance was not something that happened overnight. Natasha, whose partner grew up in a very traditional family, described Soliman's conversion to an equally sharing partner in very positive terms. "He's like been so good about it," she explained, "he helps so much now." Like some of her conventional counterparts, she still falls into describing her partner as a "helper" rather than someone who shares the load with her equally. However, unlike most of the conventional women, who were often dissatisfied with their labor divisions but felt powerless to change them (or had given up their attempts), egalitarian women's efforts had been more productive. Their male partners were also more amenable to change than appeared to be the case among many of the service-class couples. Natasha reveals that the process to reach equality with Soliman had not been a path that was necessarily easy. "Like, we had to go through so many ridiculous stupid, stupid arguments to get to that point, and I know it's such a cliché, like 'woman thing,' but you know, to keep the place clean," she revealed. Asked if they had initially talked about how the chores would get done, Natasha explained, "We eventually had that conversation, exactly. So it's like, it's at a point where it's okay now." She concluded her review about the chores that he and she now do by proclaiming, "He's completely met me half way." How couples manage to arrive at a mutually agreeable division highlights both egalitarian women's abilities to persuade their partners to change and male partners' receptivity to the women's wishes.

Overall, egalitarian couples expressed a good deal of satisfaction with their relationships. This was particularly the case when the female partner had initially expected to do the bulk of the household labor. Alisha, who had initially been concerned about how the chores would be divided, stated, "It's actually been better than I thought it would." Rebekah, who had a previous, negative roommate experience, enthused about how happy she was with her relationship, stating, "Living together is, I mean obviously we're only four months into it, but so far it's been really great!" While the middle-class women were more likely to benefit from having partners who shared housework with them relatively equally, service-class women also expressed relief that they were not left to do the majority of the domestic labor and satisfaction with their partners for what they did do. Keisha explained that she had not pictured having a partner who would share the domestic work with her; she described how shocked she was at what Stan actually did. "I mean, he'll keep the house clean. He'll vacuum, he'll wash dishes. I mean, he'll clean the whole house! When I come home, the house is clean and I don't worry about nothing. If I need clothes washed, he'll wash the clothes. As I say, I got a prize possession, I got a gift. I got a gift." Her partner, Stan, clearly feels that appreciation. Asked how satisfied he was with his relationship, he promptly replied "Ten."

Satisfaction with an egalitarian division was not universal. Ron, for example, expressed some dissatisfaction with doing what he viewed as more than his fair share (60% to Crystal's 40%.) Nonetheless, his ideal division was still egalitarian. Asked how he would like it to change, he said, "I think it would more of a, it would be 60–40 her way. Like she'd be doing more than I do." While few couples kept tabs the way that Ron did, a few other men also mentioned that they thought it could be more equal—though in their cases that meant that they thought they themselves could do a bit more. Attempts to attain equality are, in the eyes of our couples, often a bit more challenging than they had initially thought. Nonetheless, most of those who engaged in egalitarian divisions expressed satisfaction with how they were currently managing their domestic chores, and this often seemed to extend to other aspects of their lives.

Counter-conventional Arrangements

Couples that turn convention on its head, where both partners say that the man does the majority of the housework, are rare. In only five couples—all service class—do partners agree that the man does the bulk of domestic chores. Two men from our middle-class sample claim that they do more than 60% of the housework, though their partners believe it is equally split, and one service-class woman attributes her partner with doing far more than she does, though he himself states that the division is 50–50. How prevalent such nonconventional arrangements are among contemporary couples is difficult to ascertain, though recent studies support our finding that it is relatively infrequent.[30] This pattern is somewhat outside of the box, and a closer exploration of why couples arrange their housework in this fashion is warranted to determine what factors contribute to this arrangement.

Men in the *counter-conventional* group often described themselves as neat freaks or attributed their cleaning habits to how they were raised. Three of the five men either mentioned their predispositions to order or were described as tidy by their partners. Asked how she anticipated the housework would get done, Marta explained, "Harry was always a neat freak. So I knew my house would be clean." Randy also described his orientation toward housework as long standing, saying, "I actually do most of it, 'cause I did growing up too. I'm just in that in that mode, for some reason." As previously mentioned, Randy and Harry both had military exposure, as Randy had served while Harry's father was a veteran. Adam, on the other hand, said that he had been expected by his mother to play a role in domestic chores, explaining, "When I grew up I always had to, every week I cleaned the bathroom and I dusted the furniture and every night I did the dishes." Such ingrained patterns carried over into their relationships.

But not all men who were doing most of the housework attributed their labor to their penchant for neatness. Both Andre and Terrell described their roles as the mainstay for domestic chores as relatively recent, while Adam and Randy had also picked up more of the work in response to their partners' work or school loads. In all of these cases, their partners' exceedingly busy schedules accounted for this. Randy's partner, Ming, and Terrell's partner, Aliyah, were hoping to finish their degrees within the next year, and so both were taking a very heavy credit load. Stacy was also working long hours and attempting to finish up her certificate in court reporting. But while the female partners pointed to their school obligations to justify their scaling back their domestic labor, both Stacy and Aliyah also commented that they had grown tired of doing all the housework. Their heavy work and school loads were strategies of avoidance, as they were then unavailable to perform much of the housework. Explaining how the division of housework had changed, Stacy stated, "So for a while I was doing all the chores and it was pretty shitty, 'cause I got very little help. But Andre was very busy and our [male] roommate was very busy, and this and that. But now *I'm* the one with the [busy] schedule, so for the past month, two months, Andre does all the laundry, Andre does the dishes, cleans out the cat boxes, he does the grocery shopping, like we totally role switched." While Stacy did not foresee going back to how it had been before, Andre was hopeful that it would. Unlike Stacy and Andre, both Aliyah and Terrell acknowledged that Terrell had exploited Aliyah early on in their shared living experience by expecting her to do everything. Accounting for how they had gone from her doing the majority of housework to him doing it, he said, "She said I took advantage of her, like I would come home and just throw my clothes anywhere, because I knew she would pick them up. So after a while it took a toll on her. And with school and my daughter, she just started declining womanly duties."

While several of these men explained that their domestic roles resulted from a partner's very busy schedules, other men just had more time on their hands. Adam, Harry, and Terrell held jobs only intermittently, which resulted in their female partners picking up more paid work hours where possible. Adam had left his previous job, which Sheryl said paid relatively well. She was upset that he had quit this job, as their financial situation was quite precarious:

It has been like the tightest three months, four months, you know? And then these student loans being all screwy, our rent's late. It's all fine now. But we just borrowed money. I mean, I've picked up more hours at work. If he just would have stayed at the first job it would have been fine. I have a little anger towards that that I've discussed and worked through, for the most part. I had to pick up a lot of extra hours. And he borrowed money from people. And my parents paid my school fees because my loans weren't in. Lots of family help.

Adam did not necessarily appreciate being the one primarily responsible for the domestic work, though he did acknowledge that there were mitigating circumstances. "I'd like it to be 50/50," he said, "but then like, you know, one's doing more than the other and then I think somebody else should pick up the slack. Like there was a quarter where she was working 30 hours a week and going to school full time, and I was just doing, you know, school, so I tried to do more. I tried not to complain about doing the dishes all the time because, you know, I mean she's doing more than me, so I tried to pick up the slack on that end." The way counter-conventional men and women responded to the overturning of conventional roles differs from the reactions of the more conventional men and women to how domestic work and paid work were divided. Whereas conventional women often viewed domestic work as a means of "making up" for their lesser financial contributions, several men in counter-conventional couples were more grudging, viewing their housekeeping roles as temporary rather than a way to substitute for lower earnings. Furthermore, counter-conventional women did not laud their men for doing the bulk of the housework, nor did counter-conventional men make flattering comments about their female partners' earnings abilities. The economy of gratitude operated differently for conventional and counter-conventional women. Even when women do "bring home the bacon," their contributions have a different meaning than when men provide the couples' finances. Furthermore, the performance of domestic work is less valued than income-producing work, regardless of who performs it.

WHAT WE LEARNED ABOUT COHABITORS AND DOMESTIC LABOR

The couples we interviewed displayed a wide variety of behaviors when it came to performing the domestic labor necessary to keep their households functioning. For some, this meant taking on specialized roles; other couples forged more equal divisions or completely overturned established gender conventions. Individuals' satisfaction with how they as a couple arranged their accomplishment of domestic labor varied as widely as the gender roles they enacted within their unions. Even though cohabitors often expressed preferences for egalitarian unions, our couples found that attaining arrangements that satisfied both partners' expectations for how domestic work would get done was often difficult. Furthermore, those that accomplished their goals were nearly always middle class.

On the whole, men from both groups were content with their current divisions; few expressed dissatisfaction with the ways they and their partners organized their paid labor or housework, and few men were attempting to affect change, at least in the short run. Women in general offered up more complaints than did their partners, though middle-class women were far happier with their arrangements than were their service-class counterparts. Of course, being able to achieve the kind of arrangement (such as a fairly egalitarian one) that one desires is cause enough to celebrate. But these middle-class cohabiting couples offer additional hints for achieving greater satisfaction in the chore wars.

Three factors seemed to permeate the relationships of the (mostly middle class) couples who had created satisfactory divisions of labor. First, these couples were much more intentional in their attempts to keep things equitable. Middle-class couples, for example, often put very specific strategies in place (such as a chore chart) to help ensure their housework arrangements stayed fair, rather than relying on each person to just "pitch in" or "do their part." Second, the give and take of the middle class was qualitatively different from that of their service-class peers. It often involved both partners working together. Middle-class women tended to be much more direct in asking for what they wanted, primarily in the arena of housework, such as demanding an equal arrangement. Even the most conventional of these middle-class women were very clear in requesting that their partners complete a certain chore. However, if those requests fall upon deaf ears, they are futile. The third, and perhaps most important factor contributing to the greater satisfaction of middle-class couples, and particularly middle-class women, was that middle-class men were far more apt to compromise than were service-class men. When asked to be a "helper" or to do an equal share of the housework, they nearly always complied, though some ruled out doing particular chores (i.e., dusting or mopping). A few of the men performed housework out of a broader philosophical sense of gender equality, but most did so out of a sense of fairness and a desire to promote their relationships' well-being. Service-class men, in contrast, often minimized inequality or ignored their partners' pleas for greater help around the house, leading a number of the service-class women to just stop asking for it, lest it lead to yet another argument.

We do not mean to imply that everything is sunshine and roses for the sample of college-educated cohabitors. Very few of these couples attained an egalitarian division without some effort. Many of the college-educated women who pushed for (and received) partner's participation in the domestic labor still found themselves doing closer to 60% of the housework than 40%, with the added responsibility of making sure things remained that way. But both the women and the men in these couples were quite a bit happier with their household divisions of labor than their service-class counterparts. So why is achieving equality among our service-class couples such a struggle?

To begin with, a number of structural factors make it more challenging for these service-class couples to attain the egalitarian unions that cohabitors purportedly want. Although we interviewed these couples prior to the start of the Great Recession, and jobs were plentiful in Columbus (both according to official statistics and our respondents), the decline in jobs that paid men a family wage is long standing. Always more gender-traditional than their middle-class peers, less educated men may be clinging ever more tightly to one of the last vestiges of the breadwinner role—not having to do housework—even as they have seen their provider abilities decline.[31] And service-class cohabiting couples, including those we interviewed, more often live with children. Most of the service-class couples we interviewed could not afford to live on one income, so when children were present, both continued to work. What appears to be happening among many of the service-class couples in this sample, though, is that they represent families in flux, or what scholars have termed "transitional families." Whether or not they have children, the women in these couples are often triply disadvantaged, relative to middle-class women. They frequently hold low-status irregular jobs and earn a large proportion of the household income, yet still perform the bulk of the housework.

Notions of equality have permeated young adults' views of how housework in intimate relationships should be apportioned, but to a much greater extent for women than for men. This is not a novel assertion, though our findings extend this conclusion to unmarried, cohabiting couples.[32] While intimate relationships continue to evolve more rapidly for contemporary women than they do for men, we also provide evidence that middle-class men have changed their behaviors to a greater extent than have service-class men. Our middle-class couples, for example, more often challenged established gendered practices by achieving greater parity in how housework was divided. College-educated men, in particular, appear to be undoing gender via their actions, thereby contesting essentialist notions of men's and women's "natural" roles. And middle-class women also speed along this process, by discussing their expectations, encouraging their partners to rise to their expectations, and expressing appreciation for the balance achieved.

Yet even as cohabitation has provided an opportunity for middle-class couples to create more equal relationships (at least prior to having children), it may further disadvantage service-class women. Their division of housework is often unequal during cohabitation, and there is little evidence that it will improve even (or especially) if they get married, given service-class men's adherence to their prerogatives and their reluctance to change.[33] What this means is that service-class women are once again at a disadvantage, beginning from when they move in. The moderately educated women in our sample were, unfortunately, less able to achieve what for many of them was their desired goal of greater egalitarianism within their intimate relationships. Furthermore, rather than attributing their struggles over housework to how gender is currently institutionalized in American society, these women tended to individualize their problems, viewing them as "personal." Still, there is clear evidence that class has emerged as an important axis whereby men and women can challenge the construction of gender, or reify how it has long operated, even in new situations that might lend themselves to gender-transformative behaviors.

We turn now to yet another venue where couples can work together to attain desired ends or leave one partner to bear the burden of unequal responsibility—contraception.

Family Planning or Failing to Plan?

Communication, Contraception, and Conception

Every pregnancy scare that I have is like a bullet
through my chest.

—Stacy, 21-year-old student and call center worker

During the first decade of the 21st century, the proportion of all U.S. births to unmarried women reached its highest level ever—over 40%. Demographers attribute much of the increase in nonmarital births to the growth in cohabitation, which raises couples' risks of conceiving.[1] Many of these pregnancies are unintended. The risks of getting pregnant loomed large in the minds of many of our respondents. While some looked forward to that possibility, most were not seeking to conceive at the time we interviewed them. Tara, a 28-year-old computer programmer who had been cohabiting with Drew for eight of the nine months they had been romantically involved, explained, "We've talked about having kids down the road." As for her time frame for parenting, Tara stated, "I'd like to get the school loans paid off and the other stuff paid off. Maybe be together a few years, just continue enjoying each other's company before that dynamic changes and you bring somebody else, a child, into it." Her partner, Drew, who worked in internet securities, felt similarly, though his priorities were slightly different. "I want to get married first and then I want to get some life going first and then maybe some money and then go, Okay, now let's start trying," he said, adding that two years after marriage seemed like an ideal time to think about getting pregnant. Despite being together for less than a year, this couple had discussed their fertility goals and time frame, and reported taking steps to ensure that a pregnancy did not occur to disrupt their carefully laid plans.

Other couples, however, were not on the same page, either regarding their fertility goals or means of preventing conception. A number of couples concurred that the present moment was not the right time to bring a child into the world but admitted being less than one hundred percent careful to take precautions to prevent that from happening. Chad, 24, explained that "there have been, like, little forgetful moments." These moments often resulted in a good deal of anxiety for our couples. Recalling their last pregnancy scare, Chad's partner, Jackie, also 24, described her panic. "Maybe six months ago I thought I was pregnant. I didn't feel well, I missed a period. I'm like, 'Oh my God! This is the worst thing ever! What am I going to do?' And so I made him go out and buy one of those little tests. I felt so bad. . . . I mean, I was freaked out, but I think he was just, like, terrified." When the test turned out negative, Chad said, "We jumped around the room, overjoyed!"

Not all of our couples were so happy at the results of their pregnancy tests; 15 of these 61 couples discovered that they were expecting, quite unexpectedly. None of these respondents intended or planned these conceptions, even though some experienced more than one pregnancy. Vic, a 28-year-old library clerk whose 18-year-old partner, Carly, was due in a few months, said, "I was thinking that we would have a kid in about three years, maybe four at the most." Carly concurred that they had discussed having children in the future. "We decided we wanted one," she said, "but we didn't want one until we were out of school. And then it happened." Why, when birth control is readily available, do so many cohabiting couples experience unintended pregnancies? Do men and women take equal responsibility for preventing pregnancies that are not (yet) desired? And how does this vary by social class?

In this chapter, we explore whether and when couples wished to have children (or more children), how couples discussed and utilized birth control, the worries they felt when faced with possible pregnancies, and the decisions made by those couples who reported experiencing a conception in their current relationship. The middle-class couples we interviewed demonstrated more effective planning and communication skills than did their less educated counterparts regarding their reproductive choices. But even service-class respondents who most strongly worked to prevent pregnancy often faced greater challenges to do so than their more advantaged counterparts, largely due to structural factors (like unstable jobs with inadequate health insurance coverage), but also resulting from interpersonal difficulties. At the same time, middle-class couples exhibited a greater ability to work together as a team, and a larger number took personal responsibility to prevent pregnancy than was evident among service-class couples. As a result, their more consistent usage of birth control, reliance on the most effective methods, and greater willingness to utilize two methods of protection set their contraceptive behavior apart from their service-class counterparts. Couples' reproductive strategies are yet another arena where social class differentiates the family trajectories of respondents from more and less privileged backgrounds. Even when the intentions of our service- and middle-class couples were largely the same, their behaviors and the resulting outcomes differed.

WHAT DO WE KNOW ABOUT THE CONTRACEPTIVE BEHAVIORS OF COHABITING COUPLES?

In the closing decades of the 20th century, the proportion of births to unmarried women who were living with the father of their child jumped. Whereas conceptions outside of marriage in the past often led to what were termed shotgun marriages, by the late 1970s less than a third of women who conceived outside of marriage got married prior to the birth of the child, and that share continued to decline in the waning years of the 20th century.[2] At the same time, a growing percentage of cohabiting women were giving birth. By the end of the first decade of the 21st century, 56% of nonmarital births were to women who were cohabiting with a romantic partner. Among women under the age of 35, fewer than half were married upon giving birth to their first child.[3]

Many of these births, however, were unplanned. Younger cohabiting women, particularly those in their twenties, have higher contraceptive failure rates than do married and single women, regardless of the type of contraception used.[4] In the early years of the 21st century, three decades after the Supreme Court ruling that legalized birth control for women in the United States irrespective of marital status, nearly three-quarters of cohabiting women's pregnancies were unintended, and more than half of them ended in abortion.[5] Those most likely to terminate their pregnancies include younger cohabitors, cohabiting women with less than a college degree, and women in lower-quality relationships.[6] Yet many, particularly those with moderate levels of education, carry their pregnancies to term.

Little is known about the relational processes that may help explain social class variation in contraceptive usage and efficacy. That is not to say that a good deal is not known about what drives some groups of women to become mothers. Numerous researchers have sought to understand the childbearing decisions of unmarried women. Notwithstanding the key tenet of modern fertility control, which holds that women can determine when (or if) they bear children, there is considerable variation in how fertility control plays out. Less advantaged women often view the concept of planning a pregnancy as "unnatural." In fact, pregnant, low-income women frequently assert that despite not being ready to become mothers, bearing the child is the adult, responsible action.[7] Women from more economically advantaged families, in contrast, particularly those focused on obtaining professional degrees and getting established in a career, are more likely to view nonmarital parenting as irresponsible. Those who have become parents outside of marriage are not well represented among their social milieu.[8]

The male perspective on the factors contributing to unintended pregnancies is also largely absent. Despite the costs that unintended pregnancy imposes on men, including financial obligations, the research on men tends to focus on men as "players," and what studies exist focus predominantly on the least advantaged men, rather than those who are neither the worst nor the best off.[9] When men's reproductive responsibilities are assessed, they are often minimized, though some research suggests that this is due to the social framing of contraception as primarily the responsibility of women.[10]

Recent scholarship on the contraceptive utilization of sexually involved young adults has focused on efficacy, or the self-confidence required to complete the steps necessary to achieve their goals (such as fertility avoidance or delay).[11] Contraceptive efficacy often requires considerable effort and forethought. One must make and keep appointments to obtain a prescription for birth control, for example, as well as regularly fill prescriptions or purchase over-the-counter contraceptives. In other words, to be efficacious with regards to delaying or avoiding a pregnancy requires that individuals be organized, persistent enough to follow through with a particular preventative regime, and consistent.[12] A range of factors—such as relationship quality and partner supportiveness—are important in shaping individual and couple-level efficacy. Unmarried women are less likely to conceive in higher quality, supportive relationships, and couple dynamics are also important in determining whether conceptions are carried to term, as well as whether relationships persist after a child is born.[13]

But social class and educational attainment appear to play a particularly large role in contraceptive efficacy. Those who are college educated are more likely to utilize contraception, and also experience lower levels of contraceptive failure.[14] Beyond structural considerations, few studies have unpacked reasons for lower levels of contraceptive efficacy among more and less advantaged women.[15] Many factors facilitate individual women's orientations to contraception or shape couples' engagement in pregnancy prevention; individual and couple-level factors can also reduce vigilance in pregnancy prevention. A better understanding of how contraceptive dynamics play out, how individuals and couples describe the contraceptive norms that shape their behaviors, as well as ways in which manifestations of self-efficacy differ by social class, is needed to shed light on the growing disparities in the fertility experiences of young service- and middle-class cohabitors.

WHICH COHABITORS WANT CHILDREN?

Whether or not couples believe they will have children (or more children) varies widely by social class, in part because service-class respondents were far more likely than their middle-class counterparts to already be parents. Only two middle-class couples in our sample had borne biological children; another two middle-class men had nonresident children from prior relationships. In contrast, nearly half of the service-class sample—14 couples—lived with children, were expecting them, or had nonresident children. Several of these parents had been married before. The majority of the service-class cohabiting parents in our sample, however, were unmarried at the birth of their child(ren). The service class may have already attained their desired fertility goals. Nonetheless, their responses highlight the importance of conception and contraception as ongoing features of their lives.

Parenting Goals

Almost all our service- and middle-class respondents affirmed that they were not currently attempting to get pregnant. Two couples were expecting at the time they were interviewed. In another two couples, one of the partners had taken steps to ensure that they could not become a parent again, with one man obtaining a vasectomy and one woman reporting a tubal ligation; nonetheless, the male partner of the woman who was permanently sterilized desired to become a father one day. All told, there were 26 couples in our less educated sample at risk of becoming pregnant, compared with 31 college-educated couples. While many, especially those who are not already parents, say that they would like to have children, they almost universally affirm that this is a future goal. Julie, a 30-year-old nanny and part-time student, explained, "I feel like I'm such a late bloomer that there's still things that I want to do and not have to worry about kids and the fact that I'm, I can't imagine having kids and going to school. I don't know that I'd be able to split my attention like that." Most respondents echoed her sentiments, but couples were not always in agreement about their fertility desires.

Couples Who Agree about Their Fertility Desires

Three service-class couples and four middle-class ones concurred that they never wanted to have any (or any more) children. One service-class couple already shared a child together and the man had a son from a previous marriage; he had gotten a vasectomy to ensure that he could not father more children. Both the two other service-class couples did not have children and were young, with one partner in each couple holding strong views about overpopulation. Although they were not themselves wanting to bear or father children, all members of these two couples were open to adopting. Mitch explained, "I have this theory that there's too many people in the world and you know, there's overpopulation, there's too many people having, like, 12 children and people having children that they can't support and there's plenty of children out there that need love and support, so I'd rather try to take one of those."

Even though only four middle-class couples shared a disinclination to become parents, none attributed their decision to concerns with overpopulation or stated that they would consider adopting. Rather, they focused on other aspects of their lives. Justin, a middle-class salesman, explained, "We love each other way too much to have kids thrown in the mix," commenting on the strain children had imposed on their friends' relationships. His partner, Lauren, stated that while she enjoyed children, she was too motivated by other goals, saying:

> We're both very career-minded people, so I want to focus on my career, and I don't want to have children, and he feels that way too. We both love kids, like other people's children, to a certain extent. I've always worked with kids, and I've been a counselor at camp, and I love kids. I just don't want my own.

Lindsey, a professor, asserted "I have never wanted kids." She and her partner have been together for almost two decades, and she thought it unlikely that either would suddenly change their minds. Her partner,

Dean, agreed, "I'm not very interested in having children. I mean, my family is Lindsey." The literature suggests that such couples would be active in preventing pregnancy.

By far the largest segment of couples in our sample, accounting for over half of the couples interviewed (n = 34), desired to become parents at some future point. In general, this goal was a couple-level one, though there were a few respondents who did not believe their current partners would make good parents or were uncertain about their futures together. Respondents openly talked about their wishes to be parents at some point. Harry, currently unemployed, talked in great detail about how he and Marta had seriously discussed having their own child together. Whereas he had not in the past been that keen for children, living with Marta and her two children from a previous marriage had completely revised his notion of what parenting was like. As he explained, "I just love kids. I didn't used to but I do now." He then detailed how he notices babies all over the place, explaining, "We just want one so bad. I just love children." Middle-class men like Martin also waxed enthusiastic about children. Explaining why, he said, "All our friends had babies, so you're hanging out with cute babies and, you know, like it [baby fever] starts to happen." His partner, Jessica, laughingly seconded Martin's effusions regarding the children in their future, saying, "I think he would have kids right now if I let him. You know, like, he's all excited." While not all our respondents conveyed so much eagerness, in large numbers they believed that children were in their future and looked forward to it.

Couple Disagreement Regarding Parenting Desires

Nearly 30% of our cohabiting couples—eleven of the service class and seven of the middle-class couples—were not on the same page regarding their fertility desires. Arriving at agreement is more complicated among the service-class couples, as a sizable number already have children, often with a previous partner. But while one partner might feel that they do not want another child, the other may have an inclination to see what parenting is all about. Spencer and Brittany are a good example of this dilemma. Spencer, a 29-year-old sound engineer, got married very young, in response to a pregnancy. Explaining his views on parenting, he stated, "I've got a 9 ½ year old, you know, I don't want to start in diapers again because, whew, it's rough!" He went on to say that he is contemplating having a vasectomy, because "then I know that I won't have any." Brittany, his 23-year-old partner, was unsure about whether she wanted children. Though she initially stated that she did not, she added, "I mean, sometimes I do, but it's nothing, my clock hasn't even ticked yet." When asked whether she ever planned to have children, she responded, "I don't know. I thought about maybe having one just to have the experience," suggesting that she had not totally ruled out motherhood. Other couples disagree even if they are both parents. Adam, an unemployed service-class father of one is certain that he does not want any more children, stating, "Babies take a lot of time, and I don't know if I want to do that. I don't really like kids." His partner, Sheryl, who also had one child from an earlier marriage, was less certain she was done having children. "About another child," she explained, "I don't know, sometimes I really want one. And then sometimes there's just a lot of things that I want to do, like that I could do with this career that I wouldn't be able to do." Because more of the service-class men already had children from prior relationships, it is perhaps not surprising that consensus regarding fertility desires is lower among the service-class couples than it is among the middle-class couples.

Prerequisites for Parenting

Most of the individuals we interviewed, regardless of social class, were not seeking to become parents or have more children at the present time. They listed a variety of reasons for deferring childbearing. The reason that surfaced most frequently, among both the service- and middle-class respondents, was the need to achieve financial stability first. More than half of the respondents in both groups mentioned this as an important prerequisite for parenting. What financial stability actually meant, however, differed by social class. Among service-class respondents, having a job that paid enough to build an emergency savings fund and the ability to afford more than just the basics was considered essential. Susan explained that she was not yet ready to have children, stating, "Before I have kids I want to know that I can financially support them, because I don't want to end up in the same spot as my mom, and feed them rice and tuna fish." She added that she would rather forego having children than to raise them in poverty. Finishing their schooling was also important to a large number of service-class young adults, in part because it was associated in their mind with greater earnings. Ray, a 31-year-old bookkeeper, explained that before having children, "I know that I want to finish school. I want to be making enough money to where I can support a wife and kids." Crystal, a 21-year-old exotic dancer, explained, "I'd like to have kids, but I want to get out of college first, I think, and then go with it." In fact, service-class women were particularly concerned with finishing their degrees, whether they were aiming for an associate's or a bachelor's, before having children.

Most of the respondents in our middle-class sample had already attained several important markers of adulthood—having completed college and found rewarding jobs. Financial stability therefore meant something more than providing their children an adequate diet. David, a 30-year-old retirement planner, elaborated what financial stability meant to him. "I guess that means to have a certain balance in your bank account, a certain cash flow every month, knowing that you don't have to rent, you can buy a house, that's what financially stable means to me." In light of parenting, he explained that it meant "knowing that you can afford more for the kids, their activities and this and that." Middle-class respondents often mentioned that they wanted to settle into their jobs or climb the corporate ladder prior to embarking on parenthood, or that they wanted their partners to do that. Bree, a 25-year-old accountant, earned more than her partner but wanted to stay home with her children for the first few years of their lives. She explained, "Financially right now everything is really good. I know that he wants to move up in his job, so it would probably be good to wait a couple of years, until he's really comfortable where he is." Karen, a 24-year-old graduate student, wanted to defer children to a point in the future where she would be "more established at that point with my career, where I want to be and what I want to be doing and hopefully settled in, you know, where he will have worked for long enough too that we can be in a steady place." For these respondents, becoming established took time, and therefore childbearing would have to be delayed.

Many college graduates pursue additional schooling, a practice that was common in our sample, particularly among the women. Those who were in graduate school or whose partners were, were aware of the costs that early parenting could impose on their career prospects. James, who was moving across country with his fiancée, Monica, to attend law school in the fall, thought well beyond the three-year term that his schooling process imposed. Explaining the factors shaping his parenting time frame, he said:

> I think I need to finish school, and I think she needs to finish school, and I think she needs to decide what path she wants to go and what she's happy with, because if we ended up having kids now and she hasn't gotten into grad school and hasn't completed or even gotten, like, on the path she wants

to be on, I think she'd be hurt by that, by having kids. I think she'd feel like it was kind of holding her back, and I don't want that.

Soliman expressed similar concerns that having children could derail his partner's future plans and potentially cause resentment, saying about Natasha, "I want her also to come to a point in a career where she feels comfortable enough to have kids."

One important prerequisite mentioned by many of the respondents in each group might be surprising, given the dramatic increase in parenting among cohabitors. A substantial number of respondents, both male and female, wanted to be married prior to become parents. Marriage was often mentioned in conjunction with financial security. Sherry, a waitress attending college part time mentioned that having children was "a lifetime dream of mine" but clarified that it had to happen "in the *right* context, in the right lifestyle, environment, that will make me happy." Asked what that was, she stated, "Married. Financially secure, financially stable with support [from] family." Kristina, an architect, echoed Sherry's views that marriage prior to children was the proper sequence. Asked what she would like to happen before becoming a mother, she said, "Of course I want to be married. I really want that to happen first."

Even though many of the important prerequisites for childbearing were similar across social class, there were some conditions that were mentioned exclusively by the middle class. The need to be ready for the "parenting lifestyle," defined as being less selfish, partying less frequently, and developing more patience, were mentioned by both service- and middle-class respondents. Only the middle class, however, articulated a desire to spend time together exclusively as a married couple prior to having children. Andrea, a 25-year-old social worker, articulated how important it was to "have our freedom first together, I guess that newlywed freedom." Katherine specified, "I want to be married to him for a couple of years and just be married before we bring kids into it." These very expressions denote middle-class perceptions of parenting as something to be planned, avoided until the time was right, and managed to ensure optimal couple-level readiness.

To achieve these goals—financial readiness, marriage, time together, the completion of graduate degrees—means that many cohabitors who plan on becoming parents intend to delay conceiving for considerable lengths of time. But such planning is far more often the practice of the middle class than the service class. Middle-class cohabitors in particular discussed optimal ages for bearing children. For the women, this is often in their late twenties or early thirties, with a somewhat greater range among the men. Rebekah, a graduate student and bartender, explained that she wanted to have children in her late twenties or early thirties because, as she noted, "hopefully by that time the majority of my schooling will be behind me." While both service-class and middle-class men express concerns about being "old" fathers, the middle-class men have a somewhat later time frame than their less educated counterparts. Mason, who was 26 at the time he was interviewed, said of fatherhood, "It's not something that I feel a huge hurry, but I know I want to have my first kid by the time I'm 35." These individuals are more often "planners" who envision a particular future, and have good reason to believe that such a pathway is attainable.[16] It is this planning, in part, that motivates their contraceptive behaviors.

CONTRACEPTIVE DISCUSSIONS

Most couples in our sample discussed contraception, at least minimally. Such conversations often covered widely divergent topics and also varied by social class. Cohabitors mentioned concerns with both avoiding sexually transmitted infections and pregnancy. The ways couples discussed (or did not discuss) birth control utilization in the early stages of their relationship provide hints as to why middle-class cohabitors were less likely to become pregnant than their service-class counterparts.

In an ideal, rational world, couples would discuss the issue of contraception prior to becoming sexually intimate. But the world is rarely a rational place, especially when it comes to sexual desire. Our middle-class respondents were far more likely to say they discussed birth control in advance of actually engaging in sexual intercourse, with at least one partner in nearly half of these couples stating that such a conversation had been held; only one of the service-class couples mentioned being so planful. Perhaps the college-educated couples were better prepared because they took somewhat longer before becoming sexually intimate than did the service class.

Sometimes the discussion of whether partners should think about birth control arose in response to observing their partner's behaviors. Jessica's partner, Martin, described how difficult it would be to be unaware that she was taking precautions to prevent pregnancy. "Well, I'd see her taking it, and what's great about her is she is a machine. Every day, 8 o'clock P.M. She doesn't even need a watch," he said. "She's very up front about taking the pill." James also commented that his partner, Monica, had been on birth control since he knew her, and lauded her regularity in taking it, explaining, "She's a pro. She hasn't missed a day. That's another thing I'm very attracted to about her, she's very organized like in her personal life." Those who were planners viewed taking precautions to prevent pregnancy as the right thing to do. As Lindsey commented, "Well obviously we've never had unprotected sex. He's a lawyer; I'm an academic. We're not exactly low-planning people, so we've never had unprotected sex."

Others couples discussed the need for contraception in the heat of the moment, a common behavior among both groups. Sometimes this was because the men presumed that their partners were already using birth control, though they were not always correct about this. Other times, the men mentioned that they habitually used condoms with new partners, or the women informed their partners that they should do so. Asked when they had first talked about birth control, 20-year-old Susan stated, "We've never really talked about it. I think it was just kind of, 'OK. Use a condom.'" Jeremy, who was completing his masters' degree at the time of his interview, said that his initial conversation with his partner, Karen, about birth control had been "Put the condom on!" the first time they had sex. Others do not even recall that much of a conversation. Kristina, a 24-year-old architect, said that before they were sexually intimate, "We didn't ever talk about it. We just kind of like assumed that both of us don't want this [pregnancy] to happen right now, so let's take care of it." Later on, she reiterated, saying, "We don't talk about it. We just do it."

A small number of couples reported that they had not discussed contraception until after they became sexually intimate. Carrie, a 24-year-old high school teacher, explained that at the time they were too much in the moment to stop and have a serious discussion:

> The first time we actually talked about that [contraception] was right after we had sex (*laughs*) because he didn't use anything. And I guess there wasn't really the, because I'd known him for a year and because I knew the type of person that he was, I wasn't concerned. But we didn't use [condoms], I was on the pill, and he asked afterward. And I was like, "Yeah, good thing, I guess!"

Nonetheless, several respondents commented on negative aftermaths associated with their conjectures about a partner's use of birth control or efficacy in taking it. Other men whose partners became pregnant

TABLE 4   METHODS OF CONTRACEPTION COUPLES WERE USING AT THE TIME
OF INTERVIEW

Method	Combined Sample		Service Class		Middle Class	
	%	N	%	N	%	N
Permanent sterilization	3.3	2	6.7	2	0.0	0
Hormonal contraception	39.3	24	33.3	10	45.2	14
Barrier methods	19.7	12	16.7	5	22.6	7
Fertility awareness method	1.6	1	0.0	0	3.2	1
Two or more methods consistently	16.4	10	10.0	3	22.6	7
Withdrawal only	3.3	2	6.7	2	0.0	0
Disagree on method	6.6	4	6.7	2	6.5	2
None	6.6	4	13.3	4	0.0	0
Currently pregnant	3.3	2	6.7	2	0.0	0
N	61		30		31	

early in their relationships mentioned that they had assumed she had
been taking precautions and therefore did not use condoms.

CONTRACEPTIVE UTILIZATION

At the time they were interviewed, most of our respondents asserted
that, as a couple, they were using at least some form of contraception
(see Table 4). And the method mentioned most often, by both groups?
Hormonal contraception, such as the birth control pill, the contraceptive patch, or the vaginal ring, was used by about 40% of couples at
the time of their interview. Barrier methods, such as condoms, were a
distant second, utilized by about 20% of the couples. Tied for the
third most common method were two radically different behaviors:
ten of our 61 couples used two or more methods, while another ten
couples either relied on withdrawal or disagreed on what they were
using or did not use any contraception at all. Essentially, these ten couples were unprotected or had low levels of protection as compared to
the ten couples who used two or more methods. Of the remaining three
couples who were using neither hormonal nor barrier methods to
prevent conception, two service-class couples indicated a partner had
pursued permanent sterilization, and one middle-class couple relied
on natural family planning. Last, two couples were pregnant at their
interviews.

Overall use of contraception, consistency of usage, and reliance on more versus less effective methods differed dramatically by social class. All college-educated couples reported utilizing contraception of one form or another to prevent conception. Almost half relied on the most effective hormonal methods, while nearly a quarter relied on condoms. Furthermore, nearly a quarter of middle-class couples relied on two or more methods consistently. Quite a few among this group described their fears of getting pregnant before they were ready to be parents. Jessica, a 30-year-old art teacher, explained, "I'm super-paranoid about accidents happening, and like I'm embarrassed to even say this, but I'm on the pill and we *still* use a condom." College-educated men also expressed the need to remain vigilant in preventing pregnancy. Kevin, a 27-year-old manager, expressed his desire to play a role, stating, "I think the pill's a great form of birth control, but it's what, only 99% [effective]. I guess it's that 1% that freaks me out, so that's why I chose to double protect." The middle-class couples reported being very consistent in utilizing birth control, and seldom mentioned lapses in usage or coverage.

Service-class couples, in contrast, were far less likely than their middle-class counterparts to use hormonal methods or to rely on two methods simultaneously. In fact, only half of the less educated couples reported using either hormonal or barrier methods at the time of their interview. Instead, they often admitted to nonuse, inconsistent use, or use of the least effective methods. Reliance on withdrawal as the sole form of birth control, for example, was exclusively mentioned by the service-class group. Although withdrawal is a legitimate method, in actual use its failure rate is quite high; in a given year, 27% of women relying on withdrawal who engage in the typical (inconsistent) use described by our respondents can be expected to experience pregnancy.[17] Adam, who did not want any more children, described his approach to pregnancy prevention by stating, "When we have sex it's like I pull out." Anthony, who described several pregnancy scares with his partner, Diana, attributed his daughter's conception to the fact that "I didn't pull out in time." Yet he continued to rely on withdrawal, as recent attempts at playing a role in pregnancy prevention by reminding Diana to get her lapsed prescription for the patch refilled, appeared unsuccessful. "I just keep after her, like every weekend before she goes in town like I remind her to do it," he explained, "but she keeps forgetting."

Our middle-class respondents reported taking advantage of a variety of strategies to remind them to take their pills that the service class did not reference. College-educated men were also far more likely to describe attempts to avoid conception as a team effort than were their less educated counterparts. Quite a few of the college-educated women described how they had programmed their phone with an alarm to remind them about the need to take their pill, or how their partner had done that for them. Justin said of Lauren, "She has an alarm set on her phone, 7:30. It goes off at 7:20, there's like a snooze, basically she hits snooze, which basically says, Okay, you have ten minutes to get your pills." Even if they were absent minded, then, this simple method kept them on a consistent schedule and enabled their partners to help them attain their desired goal of remaining child free. Fewer service-class women described this approach or had figured out how to be more mindful of taking their pills regularly. Crystal, a 21-year-old dancer who recently terminated an ectopic pregnancy, explained that while she had been on birth control pills, "I got kind of lazy, and I don't know what I thought, like, Oh, maybe nothing will happen." Sheryl also explained that while she had utilized birth control in the past, "I stopped for really no reason, because I'm bad about taking pills." But service-class men also did not use methods within their control. Several couples who relied on barrier methods also mentioned the challenges of remembering to refill their supply when they ran out. Randy, a 32-year-old mechanic, said that while they had used condoms all the time until a few weeks ago, they stopped when they ran out of condoms. His partner, Ming, corroborated his version, stating, "We always forget to buy the things."

Many family planning specialists do not perceive cost as a major barrier to obtaining contraception, due to the availability of Title X family planning clinics.[18] Yet about one-fifth of both service- and middle-class couples in our sample had at least one partner mention cost as a barrier to utilizing their desired method of birth control. Furthermore, cost was mentioned by women as a reason for lapses in birth control utilization or for reliance on less effective methods. For some women, frequent job changes or unemployment resulted in gaps in health insurance coverage, whereas others said their health insurance no longer covered their preferred method. Marta, who worked part time at a gas station, offered several reasons for why she stopped using birth control, though one reason was clearly the expense. "I lost my insurance with my hours cut," she said. "So I couldn't afford my birth control." Spencer mentioned that his partner, Brittany, was no longer using Depo-Provera, explaining, "She's not currently because she can't afford to, because she doesn't have insurance. She's just working at a pet shelter and a restaurant, so she doesn't have, like, benefits." For middle-class women, such reasons were often retrospective; Natasha, for example, said, "The only time I was off of it [the pill] was that small period when I was without health insurance when I was unemployed." But difficulties with insurance coverage took a variety of forms. Artie described how his partner had trouble getting her insurer to cover her particular pill, saying, "Well, she didn't want to pay for it and her health insurance was kind of screwing her out of it." Other respondents, such as Emily, a middle-class respondent who made her living as a pastry chef, also mentioned the fiscal challenges associated with her insurance coverage:

> Before we had been splitting the cost of the ring, because there's no generic. So the ring is 30 dollars a pop, with insurance. And that's a month. Without insurance it's 50 dollars a month. I know, it's insane. But it's the best thing for me. I cannot do shots. Now, my crazy health insurance, I have to get birth control through mail order now, because once you've filled so many times over the counter, they don't want to pay for it over the counter anymore. They just want you to pay for it in bulk, so they ship it to you in bulk. Well, it's a once-a-month thing, I didn't think it was going to be a problem, that is my only form of medication I take. So, I went to go pick it up, and it was 50 dollars because there was no copay anymore.

The additional 20 dollars a month was a financial stretch for Emily. After talking it over with Sean and discussing the possibility of going back to the pill, which did not work well for her, or relying on condoms, which neither desired, they came up with a solution. "So he's going to pay for it up front until I can get my paycheck and then we'll pay," Emily said, expressing happiness with Sean's assistance. Lack of insurance coverage, limitations in the contraception insurance covered, or changes in copays made it difficult for many women to afford to utilize the most effective or desired birth control methods.

Other kinds of costs also prevented women from obtaining the most effective kinds of birth control. Brittany wanted to get back on hormonal methods but explained that she needed to go to the gynecologist first, stating, "It's not really something I have money for right now, so I just keep putting it off and putting it off." Julie referred to a similar impediment, explaining, "I knew that I could be prescribed birth control, but I'd have to go in for an exam, and I'd have to pay for the exam out of my own pocket." Several men also expressed an interest in getting vasectomies but noted that they were not covered by insurance.

In fact, men's willingness to help pay for birth control often determined whether women used the most effective methods or less effective ones. Often, however, men were unaware that costs were an impediment for their partners. Chad's partner, Jackie, had recently suggested that she wanted to go back on the pill, leading him to muse, "I kind of wonder, too, if there is some, like, monetary stuff, she doesn't feel like she can afford it [the pill] at any given time." Brittany, who felt like she needed her partner to share the cost burden, was inching toward requesting Spencer to share costs but expressed reservations asking for help. "He hasn't offered to pay for it," she said, "so I think I'm going to get to a point where I'm going to ask him for half of it." Other women, like Emily, and Artie's partner, Brandi, continued their preferred method due to a partner's willingness to share expenses. In fact, cost sharing seemed particularly important for our service-class women; college-educated women's jobs provided better insurance coverage.

Even among service-class women who expressed awareness of the need to take precautions, what differentiated the actions of a small but important subgroup was their seeming lack of self-efficacy. Finding the time to make and keep appointments was often mentioned as a challenge, often attributed to the difficulties of juggling multiple jobs and school work. Stacy, a 21-year-old call center assistant manager who aspired to be a court reporter, had the best intentions of going to Planned Parenthood after experiencing a pregnancy scare. Yet she had not acted on her intentions for a considerable period of time, as she recalled:

> We had wanted to get me on birth control for at least a year, and I keep trying to go to Planned Parenthood, but every time I go something happens. I'll start my period, they're closed, they don't have a doctor in, I'm sorry, you can't have an appointment, there are too many people here, I've got to go to work. It's like, goddamn it! So I haven't got down there yet and had an exam.

Her actions clearly demonstrate the challenges she faced in organizing and regulating her behavior to achieve her goal of getting on birth control. But she was not alone, as our other stories make clear. Anthony's partner, Diana, had difficulty remembering to refill her patch prescription, Randy and Ming keep forgetting to replenish their supply of condoms, and other women had a difficult time taking the pill consistently. Another manifestation of lower levels of efficacy on the part of our service-class couples were instances where service-class men refused to participate in pregnancy prevention, mentioned by several of our service-class women.[19] Asked whether they had discussed birth control, Robert, whose partner, Vanessa, was forgetful about taking birth control pills, replied, "She basically just said I should start wearing condoms again. And I was like, 'No.' And she pressed the issue for a few minutes, and that was the end of it." Although middle-class respondents were not immune from memory lapses or method preferences, their greater ability to work together made contraceptive utilization more frequent and consistent. Though it was more often the women who maintained the regimen, many middle-class men reported being highly committed to preventing pregnancy. Andrew explained, "We have actually talked a decent amount about birth control. Because you know, both of us recognized early on that we are not going to have a child, hopefully, until we're ready."

Pregnancy Scares

Of course, even the best laid plans can go awry. While consistent contraceptive use can reduce the likelihood of getting pregnant, the probability of conceiving over time with regular sexual activity is not zero. Many of our respondents—particularly those with less than a college degree—relied on methods where the likelihood of getting pregnant in a given year was nontrivial. Nearly one in five women whose partner uses a condom will get pregnant over the course of a year (18%), as will over a quarter (27%) of women whose partner relies on withdrawal.[20] It is perhaps not surprising that many couples in our sample reported experiencing at least one pregnancy scare. Despite their reliance on more effective birth control methods (including utilizing two methods), far more of the middle-class couples reported experiencing pregnancy scares than did their less educated counterparts. Over 80% of the middle-class couples we interviewed—25 of them—mentioned being worried on at least one occasion that they were pregnant, compared with only 17 of the service-class couples. Regardless of social class, the nearly universal sentiment expressed by couples (particularly the women) who were worried they were pregnant was dismay.

Andre, whose partner, Stacy, provided the opening quote for this chapter, recalled, "We had one or two scares and you know, we'd just talk about it, the possibilities of what we would do." Despite these scares, however, they continued to rely on condoms. Asked if they had ever had a pregnancy scare, Howard replied, "I don't know. I'm sure everyone has." But his experience, according to his partner, had been a harrowing one for him. She explained, "I was switching birth control and I went two months without a period, so I freaked out that I was pregnant and I made him go to the store and he bought, I took all five pregnancy tests that he bought and they all came back negative. But we were still flipping out because it [her period] just never came. And then it came the next month," she said, concluding, "but I definitely freaked him out." Afterward Howard asked her not to tell him when she was late, given how stressful that experience was. While male partners were somewhat less likely to report pregnancy scares than women, those who did described them as experiences they did not want to repeat.

Among the service class, many had good reason to be worried about the possibility of pregnancy, based upon their narratives. On the whole, service-class couples who experienced pregnancy scares were often not using birth control at all, using withdrawal or engaged in inconsistent use of various forms. Spencer illustrated the gap between desire and behavior. Despite his strong interest in avoiding parenthood again, he mentioned that he and his partner, Brittany, sometimes had lapses in their condom usage. Describing one particular incident, he said, "It wasn't, like, super-scary, but it was just kind of like, the next day [after not using a condom] you're like, 'You know, we were a little fucked up last night and we should've used something and we didn't. And, you know, your period will be here in about a week, which means most fertile moment right now." Valencia and Jorge relied on withdrawal, mainly because (according to him) she does not like condoms. She described her worries, stating, "I was kind of feeling sick and stuff. I didn't miss a period or anything but I did go to one of those pregnancy decision places or I don't know what it was called and they did a test and I wasn't."

While most couples who reported either inconsistent contraceptive usage or no usage generally did not reflect on the risks these practices posed to parenting goals, in the course of discussing their scares some respondents realized that they should reconsider their birth control practices. Jorge explained, "I mean, like I told her I want to use protection, and I want her to have protection as well." Sheryl's realization came during her interview, midway through describing her one pregnancy scare with Adam. She exclaimed, "It's funny to say this, and not be on birth control sounds insane to me, and like I need to go get on some immediately." She then reiterated, "You know, I'm not on birth control right now." Whereas some of our respondents reported that experiencing a pregnancy scare (or two) encouraged them to pursue more effective contraception or to be more vigilant about utilizing their current method, others said they simply lapsed back into their old patterns of nonuse.

Even service-class women using effective forms of contraception, including hormonal methods, reported experiencing pregnancy scares. Sherry, talking about the time she thought she might be pregnant with her partner, Tyrone, said, "It was the worst feeling ever, like I wanted to throw myself down the stairs." The experience not only highlighted for her the very real risks of a pregnancy, but it also took a negative toll on their sex life. "After that we chilled out, as far as sex," she explained. "But once you have that scare, you're like, okay this is real, you know? This [birth control] isn't one hundred percent, and this can happen, these are the effects." Additionally, the pregnancy scare highlighted just how much distance there often was between service-class partners' views regarding pregnancy, childbirth, and abortion. Sherry explained how her views diverged from those of Tyrone's, who already had a child with a prior partner. "I mean, really it kind of split us up. Because I'm going one way, he's going the other way. I was leaning towards like, 'Well I can't have it [the baby],' and he's leaning towards, like, 'Well, you know, I'm 25 and I don't believe in that.'" Sherry was not sure if Tyrone was the right partner, and their parenting plans were more distant than immediate. Since service-class couples were more often not in concurrence regarding desires for children than their middle-class counterparts, a pregnancy scare sometimes revealed the fragility of their relationships.

Despite more consistent contraceptive usage, middle-class couples report experiencing pregnancy scares more frequently than did their service-class peers. What to make of these concerns? The middle-class cohabitors were not only more vigilant, but they also seemed more aware of cumulative risks and were unwilling to mar plans for the future with mistimed events. Furthermore, lapses in their contraceptive usage were patently different from those described by the service class. Most often, college-educated couples reported that they did not use a condom during the female partner's menstrual period or described a condom break. Nicholas explained that he and Rachel had forgotten that certain medications, like antibiotics, could reduce the effectiveness of hormonal birth control, saying "while she was on the patch, she was on some medication and it conflicted with the potency [of the patch] so she didn't think about it until we'd already had sex a couple of times, so we were concerned for a while." Audrey described how their pregnancy scare had occurred over a holiday weekend, which made it challenging to obtain a prescription for the emergency birth control they would have normally pursued. "We knew that the condom broke," she said, "and we were both scared to death." Middle-class pregnancy scares seemed to arise more often because the respondents were vigilant about avoiding unprotected sex, so that any break in protection was viewed as highly risky.

Unlike their service-class cohabiting counterparts, the middle class also had concerns about possible negative reactions to news of an unplanned pregnancy. Although they felt their families would be generally supportive, they worried that family members (particularly parents) would be disappointed in them and unhappy about the prospect of a nonmarital or "illegitimate" birth. Greg recalled Natasha's reaction to their pregnancy scare. "[She was like] Oh God. My mom's going to kill us!" Similarly, Amy, a speech therapist, said, "Both families would be mortified, just because we're Catholic and that is not cool. My mom would be ashamed if I was pregnant before I was married." While references to the stigma associated with nonmarital childbearing were not exclusively mentioned by the middle class, they gave much greater weight to such concerns, and, as we explore in a future chapter, have different ideas about the "next steps" they would take should they become pregnant.

PREGNANCY EXPERIENCED

A sizable number of the couples in our sample were already parents together. Others experienced pregnancies that they did not carry to term.[21] Nearly a fifth of the couples we interviewed—eleven—became pregnant over the course of their current relationships. A total of nine children were born to seven couples in our sample. Another six pregnancies were terminated through an abortion. Decisions to carry a pregnancy to term were generally drawn out and difficult. Only one of the conceptions within our sample can be described as at least somewhat intentional.[22] In general, the couples in our sample who got pregnant reveal the challenges to reducing nonmarital childbearing. Quite a few of those who became pregnant said that they were contracepting, though most acknowledged they were not doing so consistently or correctly. Their decisions about whether to carry out or terminate a pregnancy were not lightly made.

Of the five service-class couples who experienced a pregnancy, none were planned in the traditional sense.[23] Rather, all admitted that their conceptions were a surprise. Mark, who described Tracy's first pregnancy as unexpected, said, "I wasn't like 'I don't want to have a kid,' but I wasn't thrilled about it," he said. "It was wonderful to have a son and everything, but it definitely wasn't when and where I would have done it, which I think, I hate to say that but, that's probably how 80%

of all children are born." About his second pregnancy with Tracy, he stated flatly, "The second one wasn't planned at all." All of these couples' pregnancy stories revealed a lack of intentionality. Aliyah remembered dragging her partner, Terrell, with her to the Pregnancy Decision Center. She recalled his telling her,

> I don't know why you're making me go here. I know you're not pregnant. There's nothing wrong with you. Your period is coming. We actually were arguing in the office about it and the lady walked in and she said, 'You're pregnant. Your test came back positive.' And his mouth just dropped. He couldn't believe it!

Anthony also remembered his negative feelings upon learning that Diana was pregnant. He said: "I was just shocked. I was just like, 'Whoa! I'm really having a kid. This girl is still in high school, she's going to be a senior and having a child.' Like, I felt bad. I felt bad like I did something wrong." Diana said of his reaction to her news, "He cried. Like, not a happy cry. I think we both did."

In fact, abortion was discussed as a possibility among all five service-class couples who went on to have their children. For some, the discussion about what to do and whether to terminate the pregnancy went on almost up to the legal time limit (then 24 weeks). Whereas Mark and Tracy did not discuss the possibility of getting an abortion in their first pregnancy, he did suggest it as an option for their second pregnancy. "It was more tense," he explained, before going on to say that he had raised the issue even though he knew that "it wouldn't go." Tracy concurred that the second pregnancy was harder for both of them, saying, "It put a strain on our relationship at the beginning, but we worked through it." For some women—those who were not personally opposed to abortion—their decision about whether to have the child often were strongly influenced by their partners' responses to learning they were expecting. Maria mentioned that she took several pregnancy tests, but just could not accept the results and had been talking with her best girlfriend about whether to have an abortion. "Before I told him I had thought about it [an abortion], and that's what Heidi and I were kind of talking back and forth about, trying to figure out whether I really wanted to have kids, whether I was ready to have kids mentally, just everything in the whole ballpark." Her partner, Bill, responded positively to learning she was pregnant, which influenced her.

> He was fairly happy about it. He didn't seem to be disappointed, like you would see someone go (sigh), you know? He seemed to show genuine

enthusiasm, genuine care. He seemed to after that point handle me like fragilely but at the same time, you know, took care of everything and made sure everything was perfect and all that stuff. It just seemed to be fine and it did, it worked out fine. I mean everything turned out perfect for Katy and everything and she got a good daddy.

Aliyah mentioned that their partner expressed reservations about abortion, which ultimately swayed her thinking. As Terrell recollected, "Well, we discussed it maybe once or twice, about abortion. Yeah, I think she actually said, 'What do you think about abortion?' and I looked at her crazy, and she started telling me a little about school and finances and I was like 'All right.' I thought about it and I was like 'We ain't getting an abortion.'"

Although men's responses to pregnancy played an important role in the women's decision making, men often felt that their role was somewhat limited. Even though they could be supportive, the women were the ones making the ultimate sacrifice.[24] Diana, who was only 17 when she had her daughter, recalled:

At first, I think we really thought about getting an abortion, just because we were young. I mean we really looked into it. We did. We looked in it—not adoption, because I knew I couldn't do that. But we definitely looked into abortion because I was young.

Both Diana and Anthony said that it took almost three months before they determined to have the child. Asked why, Diana attributed her decision to the information gathering processes, explaining, "Well, just the papers that they sent us. And it shows the procedure, and I was just like, there's no way I can do that. So we didn't." Even after deciding to have the child, though, Diana said that she and Anthony felt unready.

Carly, who was expecting, described a similar drawn-out decision making process. Her partner, Vic, verified how uncertain they still were about their decision. He explained:

We talked about abortion. We went back and forth. We had at first decided to keep the child and then decided to get an abortion, and then sort of waffled there, where we didn't quite know what we wanted to do. And then we settled on abortion and then we changed our minds again and decided to keep it because we just sort of realized, You know what? We both sort of want it, you know? Even though it was completely the wrong time we still wanted it.

But Carly, who was just 18, still seemed very ambivalent about the decision and experienced frequent bouts of uncertainty about their choice.

"Like a couple weekends ago I was really depressed," she said, "and I was like, I don't think I can do this and crying and stuff." After more days of similar feelings, she talked with Vic. "And I was like, 'You know, I've been feeling like maybe I don't want the baby.' And he was like, 'I have feelings like that, too.' And we just like sat down and talked it out and everything. And we realized that we wanted it more than we didn't want it, and that we would make it work anyway." While many new parents experience a range of challenges, and adjusting to new roles is often difficult, the hurdles facing the children born to the parents we interviewed who were the least emotionally prepared may be greater than usual.[25]

The major way in which the two middle-class couples who got pregnant differed from their less educated counterparts was in their early embrace of their pregnancies. Describing how he reacted to Tabitha's news that she was pregnant, Edward said, "I was actually happy, because my mother had just passed and it was like, you know, the coolest thing because me and my mom were real close." Tabitha, who was working on completing her college degree at the time she got pregnant, did not think the timing was optimal but took it in stride, saying, "I was kind of shocked, because like I always knew I wanted kids but, you know, I was like I'd like to wait a year or wait till I'm married. But I mean stuff don't work out that way." Abortion was not an option for them, as she explained, "We don't believe in that [abortion], so we were having a baby." Peter described how he learned of his first child's conception. He and RaShinda were both working on their master's degrees and had only been involved for about a month when she told him she was pregnant. He states, "It's one of those things, you know, you haven't planned for and all that. But it was also a blessing to us, I think." RaShinda also wanted to keep the child, and neither approved of abortion. They went on to have a second child, which RaShinda described as another surprise, though Peter did not concur. In his words, "I think it was just kind of playing Russian roulette kind of a thing. We knew she was not using birth control pills, but at the same time you're like, 'If she gets pregnant, she gets pregnant.'" Both partners in these two couples were racial minorities. Although Tabitha, RaShinda, and Peter all felt that marriage before parenting would have been a more optimal sequence, consistent with middle-class norms, both couples individually expressed the belief that they would remain with the parent of their child(ren) permanently.

Of course, not all couples who experienced a pregnancy carried it to term. Six pregnancies that respondents mentioned ended in abortion. Of note was that in four instances only one partner referred to the abortion. In three instances, men mentioned their partner had an abortion that the woman described as either a pregnancy scare or did not discuss. Women may have been more concerned than men about possible stigma associated with abortion. Asked what he would do if his partner, Vanessa, were to get pregnant, Robert replied, "I would tell her this time she was going to have to pay for the abortion," grumbling that he had already paid for one about eighteen months before. Shane described a similar outcome for the pregnancy Sandra experienced. In one instance, it was the male partner who neglected to mention an abortion. Although Ron described Crystal's recent ectopic pregnancy and subsequent termination, only Crystal mentioned a prior pregnancy, stating, "This past time [that I got pregnant] I was very disappointed in myself, because just like eight months ago maybe I had an abortion."

Personal circumstances at the time of conception played an important role in why the couples in our sample opted for an abortion. The struggle and shame some women and men feel around the topic are reflected by the statements made by Max and Tameka, who experienced a pregnancy very early on in their relationship, when both were in their late teens. Max explained that Tameka was still in high school, and he teared up while talking, recalling, "I mean it was hard. That was probably one of the hardest things in our relationship and I mean something that we really felt, we don't even talk about it too much and so (*voice breaks*) it would not be an option at all." Tameka also stated flatly that she would never consider having an abortion again, though otherwise she indicated she would be fine not having children. Bill mentioned that he and Maria decided to terminate their second unplanned pregnancy, saying, "Actually, nobody knows nothing about it, except for her best friend and I think maybe one of my friends." But Bill went to great lengths to explain that they did not take the decision lightly:

> I had serious issues with being able to bring a third child in and you know, doing these things. So I mean we even after I said ok I would agree to it [an abortion], it still didn't, it wasn't something that just happened. We sat and talked about it quite a bit and went round and round about the pros and cons, the whys and why nots, the what ifs and everything and then we decided to go ahead and go through with having an abortion. You know, it still bothers me a little bit now, but you know, realistically I'm a practical person. There's an awful lot of people in this world who are brought in here, don't want to be here, and contribute zero to society, and I don't see the point in bringing another life into the world that is already coming in shorthanded, is going to put an entire, the other four people who are already here

out further and strain the relationships that are there already. It just, it didn't seem to be a very viable solution, so that was the situation.

All of our respondents who mentioned that they had pursued an abortion with their current partner were from the service class. While middle-class respondents did rely on more effective birth control methods than did their less educated counterparts at the time of their interview, and many mentioned consistently using two forms (birth control pills and condoms), their behaviors may have arisen from prior experiences. Five middle-class men and four college-educated women had experienced an abortion with a previous sexual partner. Only two of the service-class women reported that they had terminated a pregnancy with a prior partner.

What differentiates many of the middle-class men from their service-class counterparts is a strong strain of both regret and subsequent determination to play a larger role in ensuring that birth control is utilized. Both Jonathan and Janelle mentioned that they had pursued an abortion with a prior partner and knew about the other's experience. As Jonathan explained, "Both of us have been through that before. I've gone through an abortion with an old girlfriend, and she's been through an abortion, so both of us learned our lesson on that one. So yeah, we're both pretty careful about it. They wake you up, basically." Asked what would happen if he and his current partner, Emily, were to discover they were pregnant, Sean mentioned, "I think about that a lot, because I, I got my high school girlfriend pregnant." Although he states that if he and Emily were to get pregnant they would get married and have the child, he realizes how different his life would be if his girlfriend at the time had determined to have the child. "Every once in a while, when I hear about somebody who had kids really young, single parents, I think to myself, God, my life would have been fucked!" Sean said. He did not have a say in that partner's ultimate decision. "I don't think it was a matter of discussion, like where she was considering having the kid. It was just like she told me and said, 'My mom's taking me to get an abortion.' That was it." Travis, who was 18 when his high school girlfriend had an abortion, also said that he had no say in that decision, but that he and his current partner, Katherine, had seriously discussed what would happen were they to discover that she was pregnant. "So from early on," Travis stated, "Katherine and I had already talked about it that if, you know, it happened. Both of our parents want grandkids. We're both, we both can handle kids and we financially can handle kids, we mentally can handle kids. So we've already decided, you know, if it happens, we're just going to go forward with it and just probably get married very quickly." This sentiment, that a pregnancy would result in a speedy marriage, highlights another reason why fewer middle-class cohabitors share children.[26]

Not all the middle-class men viewed their prior pregnancy experiences in such a light. Soliman said that a previous partner had gotten pregnant. While he said he paid for the abortion, he seemed to have doubts that he was actually the father. Peter, who had two children with his current partner, RaShinda, also mentioned that a previous girlfriend had gotten an abortion. Neither of these men approved of abortion, but neither desired to take responsibility for using condoms and taking part in pregnancy prevention. Soliman mentioned that his partner was on the pill but that he did not trust the pill, and therefore also practiced withdrawal, while Peter also left responsibility for contraception to his partner, RaShinda, despite the evidence that such behavior was difficult for her.

Most of the six women who had pursued abortions from a prior relationship were in their late teens or early twenties at the time, and several described the relationships as being temporary or not serious. Jackie, for example, was 18 when she got pregnant, with a short-term boyfriend who had moved away across the country a few weeks before her discovery. Alone and scared, she determined an abortion was the best option. Janelle, at 21, was a little older, but still in college when she became pregnant; Lauren was also just finishing up college. Three other women described unusual circumstances—getting pregnant while still drug addicted and worrying about the harm to the fetus; rebounding after a divorce at a young age and getting pregnant in a fling; or getting pregnant with an ex-husband before they were married and not wanting to become parents prior to the wedding. Most of these women—five of the six—described being very cautious about ensuring that another pregnancy did not ensue, with all of them utilizing hormonal methods. Only one of these women mentioned that she and her partner were not utilizing birth control at the present time, though she also acknowledged the very real risks she and her partner were taking.

WHAT WE LEARNED ABOUT COHABITORS, CONTRACEPTION, AND FERTILITY

Our findings suggest that more and less advantaged young adults draw upon different personal resources as they maneuver their way through romantic relationships. Distinctions in how service- and middle-class cohabitors viewed the importance of planning and timing, which pre-requisites are important prior to becoming parents, as well as their adherence to sequencing norms regarding the ordering of marriage and childbearing and contraceptive behavior clearly set these young adults on different trajectories. The college-educated couples expressed greater consensus regarding their parenting plans or whether to remain child-less. They also generally demonstrated the self-regulation necessary to prevent conceptions. As a result, the middle class adhered more strongly to the belief that births should—and could—be "planned." For them, this meant "delayed."

A subset of the service-class cohabitors, in contrast, demonstrated a much more laissez-faire approach to deferring pregnancy. Though most desired to defer childbearing, they often did not demonstrate high levels of contraceptive efficacy. They were less planful in approaches to preg-nancy prevention, often were unable to prioritize activities in order to achieve the goal of remaining childless, and were more fatalistic about their ability to prevent pregnancy. As a result, service-class couples less often utilized contraception, were less likely to rely on the most effective forms, or let usage lapse. Service-class women's attempts to put more of the onus for contraception on male partners also were sometimes met with resistance, as service-class men generally viewed fertility preven-tion as the responsibility of women rather than as a joint pursuit.

But while both service-class men and women demonstrated less effi-cacious behavior than their middle-class counterparts, they also faced more barriers that challenged their abilities to be effective in preventing pregnancy. Service-class women had poorer insurance coverage or worked in jobs that did not provide access to their preferred birth con-trol method. The upfront costs of paying for a doctor's appointment or shelling out the copay for some of the newer, more expensive (and more effective) birth control methods were seen as too much of a financial burden, given limited and unpredictable earnings. Finally, more couples in the service class manifest signs of poor relationship quality, perhaps due to their more rapid relationship progression and generally challeng-ing financial situations, as well as indicators of poor mental health and substance use. In other words, social class affected the strength of the relationship between efficacy and pregnancy prevention. As a result, even the most efficacious service-class women, like Brandi, often expe-rienced more challenges to pregnancy prevention than the most effica-cious middle-class women. Small wonder, then, that less persistent service-class women are less efficacious than their equivalent middle-class counterparts.

These findings provide some tantalizing hints as to why efficacy differs across social class. In addition to their social class advantages, the college-educated individuals in our sample, both men and women, have clearer social scripts regarding the appropriate location and time for childbearing, as well as incentives (such as the promise of career advancement and large weddings) to defer childbearing. Their goals—to solidify careers, travel, save some money, and have some time alone with a spouse before becoming parents—reinforce what were once normative sequencing behaviors of marriage prior to children. Even among those uninterested in marriage or childbearing, incentives to be efficacious contraceptors reinforced deep-seated behaviors. Among the service-class couples, on the other hand, pathways toward successful adulthood are harder to detect.[27] Educational attainment was a slow and often protracted process, few had clear employment paths, and some had accrued considerable amounts of debt. Furthermore, their trajectories into adulthood started younger and with less parental financial and emotional support. Service-class respondents had frequently moved out of the parental home at 18, and relationships with parents were often described as fraught with tension and resentment. A handful of service-class women reported feeling overwhelmed by the demands of their lives: juggling multiple jobs, struggling to accrue school credit, parenting across households, as well as dealing with partners who are sometimes less than supportive either emotionally or financially. Making the effort to prevent pregnancy, even when it was the last thing desired, ended up being just one more thing to do. It is the experience of this minority that illuminates why conception rates are greater among service-class women.

The experiences of those who conceived (or whose partners did) also highlight how life trajectories differed across the service and middle class. As we indicated, a larger number of our service-class couples were already parents. In describing their decisions to bear a child, many expressed the belief that even though the timing had not been optimal, having the child was the right thing to do—the "correct" option. Describing Diana's response to getting pregnant at 17, Anthony said, "She stepped up to the plate." They therefore demonstrated a rather different ideology about planning than their middle-class counterparts who reported experiencing pregnancies as teens. A handful of our middle-class men—Sean, Travis, Jonathan, to name a few—could have been parents had their partners not obtained an abortion. And several of our middle-class women also reported a pregnancy with a prior sexual partner that had been terminated. The opportunities available to that small subset of our middle-class respondents were conditioned on decisions made (sometimes by them, sometimes by a partner's parents) earlier in their lives. They had not always been the efficacious contraceptive users they were at the time we interviewed them. Among the service class, past life experiences seem to reduce confidence in their abilities to chart their own courses and plan desired outcomes, like parenting or marriage. It is also challenging for service-class respondents to either escape from or deter the adverse outcomes associated with cumulative disadvantage that stems from financial strain. Our middle-class respondents, in contrast, appear to benefit from more of the scaffolding necessary to enable them to achieve their desired ends, even when there were missteps along the way.

While we have gained a window into the experiences of cohabitors who become pregnant, our sample is a selective one. It does not tell us anything, for example, about those couples for whom a pregnancy ended their relationships—or was an impetus to marriage. Nonetheless, there are lessons to be learned from the in-depth stories of the nine couples who became parents together, as well as those who conceived but chose to terminate the pregnancy, either with their current partners or a prior one. Forgetfulness and misunderstanding of the most effective use of contraceptives are perhaps more easily solved than some of the other issues that arise for these couples. Greater education about how contraceptives work or how to select the optimal method given costs and benefits could go a long way toward preventing more unplanned pregnancies. So would providing contraception at little or no cost. Some of these couples would also benefit from better communication skills, which could be provided in high school programs designed to strengthen relationship skills. Without addressing such issues, our prognosis is that the United States will continue to see diverging fertility outcomes for America's more and less advantaged young adults.

What is clear is that how our couples responded to their fertility experiences reflected and also shaped other dimensions of their lives. Some of this is revealed in couples' discussions about what ensued after a pregnancy, or what might, the content of which we highlight in Chapter 7. Respondents expressed rather different views about whether marriage would be considered in the case of a pregnancy, and why this might (or might not) be the result of an unplanned conception. Whether cohabitors' prior experiences shape such perceptions, and how discussions of the future play out, are the subjects of our next two chapters. Our results suggest that whereas fertility experiences often pulled our less educated couples apart, among the middle-class couples, pregnancy scares might have had the opposite effect, drawing them closer together or moving them along an already predetermined trajectory. How our couples experienced their living arrangements in part accounts for these distinctions, as did their plans for the future, as we explore in Chapter 6.

6

For Better or for Worse?

Perceptions of Cohabitation,
Marriage, and Parenthood

Nineteen-year-old Diana was reaching the end of her rope with Anthony. Although they shared parenting responsibility for their toddler, Kaley, at the moment she expressed no interest in marriage. "When I think of wedding rings," she explained, "I just think of them as handcuffs that are pretty." Cohabitation for her was preferable, because, in her words, "It's like if you're dating or whatever we are, if there's something that you want to do you can do it, because you're still your own person." But lately, Diana had begun to feel more constraints, even without a ring on her finger.

Both Diana and Anthony said that initially they had been happy with the path they chose, explaining that moving in together had some advantages. For Anthony, living together "makes me feel more mature, more responsible," he said, "like I am actually doing something right." And Diana saw the financial advantages of cohabitation, and liked the idea that Kaley was able to be with both parents all of the time. Nonetheless, the two also said that the negatives of living together could outweigh the positives. Anthony sometimes took Diana for granted in ways that he said he wouldn't if they were still just dating, and that both the romance and their sex life had gone downhill. He also blamed sharing close quarters for their more numerous arguments. Diana felt that she had lost her freedom. She explained, "I don't really feel independent, and that's the thing that gets me a lot."

That Diana was feeling ambivalent about her relationship was clear throughout her interview. She had dreamed of being married before having a child, but Anthony had made his feelings very clear on the subject. He was not ready to tie the knot until he was certain this relationship would be permanent, and he was not sure of that yet. Anthony explained that living together was better than marriage because "We wouldn't have to go through all the trouble of a divorce, you know? It's not that commitment scares me or anything, it's just that it [marriage] just seems like a hassle." Over time, Diana's views of marriage changed as well, even though she sometimes wished she had an engagement ring. She explained that getting married would mean that the two would be more stuck in their relationship, with even more intense pressure to make it work. In contrast, she said, cohabiting had its advantages. "We know that we can leave whenever we want, and that's nice to know— that you aren't stuck there because you can't leave," she said. In fact, at the time of her interview, Diana seemed to be making a phased move away from Anthony. She and Kaley were spending half of each week with her parents, who lived several hours away.

Asked if her experience living with Anthony had changed the way she felt about marriage, she said, "Yeah, it definitely has. Definitely. I would much rather do this (cohabit) for the rest of my life than probably be married. Being married, it's very in-depth, and it's very, you really devote yourself. And we do that, but it's just like, I don't know, it's really hard to explain." For her, marriage symbolized being mature and settled. "When I think of married," she clarified, "I just think old and I think forever, and it's something I want to do, but, just, we're young you know, so . . . " In fact, Diana had come to believe that marriage operated differently for others in situations unlike hers. She preferred to live with a partner while she finished school, Anthony got his career started, and they bought a house, rather than have a fancy wedding. Diana explained, "I think the big weddings are kind of for the people that date for a year, and then they get engaged after that year, and they're like engaged for a year and then they get married." But that was not her situation.

College-educated Evan and Julianna, on the other hand, were "those kind of people." Evan, who worked in sales, and Juliana, who had recently completed her master's degree and was searching for a position in health care, initially met at his sister's birthday party. Juliana had been friends with Evan's sister and brother-in-law for quite some time, and as Evan tells it, "It's kind of funny, because the day Juliana and I met, my sister and her now husband said that we were going to get married." They began dating six months after that meeting and moved in together thirteen months later. The time line was just as they wanted. Evan explained, "I had always wanted to be with someone for a least for a year before I moved in with them. Same for, like, getting engaged. So that was like my goal." Rather than feeling prematurely pushed into moving in together, as Anthony and Diana felt they had been, Juliana explained that moving in together just made economic sense, especially since they were spending nearly every night together anyway. Although they had not talked about a time frame, and Evan joked that Juliana would have to wait for at least five years before they tied the knot, the two had marriage on their minds at the time they moved in together. "At that point I kind of knew that we were pretty much set. I was getting older, I wasn't getting any cuter," Evan explained, laughing, "you know, the whole deal."

For Evan and Juliana, living together was an improvement over dating. In contrast to Diana, Juliana still felt that she had her freedom. Her life changed a bit, in that she now included Evan in her plans. But, she added, "He goes out with his friends and asks if I want to come, and I go out with my friends and ask if he wants to come. We never ask each other if we can go out, but we always try to include the other person. But we definitely know that we have the freedom to have separate lives." In other words, she felt strongly that she was still autonomous. Evan echoed her sentiments. For him, however, living together had changed things for the positive, by making him more financially responsible. He said, "Putting stuff down towards our future is more important to me now then just being able to go out to a bar and blow a hundred bucks. Now I'm like, 'Hey, I can put that extra hundred toward the principal of the house,' knowing that her and I as a team can now start paying off these things and set ourselves up better in the future." In other words, while they still felt that they had their freedom to go out separately, they also thought about investing in things that would benefit them as a couple.

Given that cohabitation was an improvement in Evan and Juliana's already positive relationship, it is not surprising that the two became engaged two months after moving in together. Asked how marriage would be different than cohabitation, Evan said, "I don't know that it would be. I view marriage more as a, like kind of what they say, it's an outward symbol. My feelings towards her will not change, like I have those feelings now. It's just more of everybody on the outside can see that we are married. I don't think our decision making will change any." Like Diana, Juliana thought of marriage as a binding union but saw that as positive rather than negative. She described marriage as "knowing that you are there for each other. You have to work things out; you can't just leave. . . . So I think it's that binding commitment in front of everybody that says, 'I'm in this and I'm good to go.'" Beyond the fact that she thought marriage was "something special," like Evan, she was not worried that their relationship might degenerate. Asked what would change when they tied the knot, she replied, "I keep thinking that it can't be any better. I really don't know what could possibly change once we are married. I mean, we've been living together for a year already and nothing's really changed from when I moved in a year ago. I don't know how July 10th would be different from July 9th."

Both Evan and Juliana were looking forward to being parents someday but thought it ideal to be married first. Asked if he thought people should be married before having children, Evan replied:

> Yes, just because a child puts so much stress on a relationship that you have to know that you can rely on that person before adding that stress. I mean, going through a wedding, getting engaged is enough stress, enough to figure out, alright is this really going to work? Can we really do this in good times and bad? With a kid, you're always tired, constant attention, no time for each other. So you have to know that you have that foundation there.

Juliana agreed, with both adding that, if she were to become pregnant now, six months out from their wedding, they would want to move their marriage up prior to the birth of their child. She explained, "My dress is two sizes too big right now, so I could probably be pregnant and wear it, [but] we'd probably get married sooner." Asked why that would be her preference, she laughed and said in a mock-aghast tone, "Because you can't have a baby out of wedlock!" She then added, more seriously, "I think that a child needs its mom and dad and I don't think that there's any room for escape at that point."

In this chapter, we examine the beliefs that couples like Anthony and Diana and Evan and Juliana have about the differences between dating and cohabitation, as well as between cohabitation and marriage. We look further at how their views are linked to beliefs about having children outside of marriage, both in general and for themselves. This provides us with a window into the role that cohabitation serves in the lives of service-class and middle-class cohabitors. We argue that differences in the attitudes the more and less advantaged have toward the benefits and drawbacks of marriage, as well as the appropriate location for bearing children, in part explain the diverging behaviors of young adults from different social class backgrounds.

Our middle-class respondents, for example, generally viewed marriage as more desirable, both for themselves and for their (future) children, than did the service class. These initial views were reinforced by what ensued at each successive stage of the relationship. Although many college-educated cohabitors noted that moving in together did not change things, they more frequently said that living together made life easier and better, and extrapolated that to marriage, than did their service-class counterparts. Among our less educated respondents, in contrast, each successive phase of relationships often seemed fraught with additional challenges. College-educated respondents were also more conventional regarding the sequencing of marriage and parenting. Finally, the tempo to shared living and plans for what happened subsequently were dramatically different for our more and less educated respondents. Because they were involved for longer prior to moving in with their partners, our college-educated cohabitors had greater opportunities to vet their relationships for the long run. They also had clearer scripts for how relationships should unfold, from dating to living together to marriage and childbearing, with acknowledged tempos for various stages. Taken together, these attitudinal differences, in part, explain why college-educated cohabitors more often are headed down the aisle, while service-class cohabitors are biding their time.

WHAT DO WE KNOW ABOUT YOUNG ADULTS' FAMILY BELIEFS AND BEHAVIORS?

News headlines regularly trumpet declines in the percentage of married Americans. A Pew Research Report, for example, showed that in 2012, a record number of Americans—about 20% of those 25 and older—had never been married.[1] The declining proportion of married American adults is portrayed as a sign of a decline in "family values." The organization Focus on the Family frequently decries the "marriage crisis" and along with other associations argues that the breakdown of marriage will lead to the collapse of society.[2] As to why young adults are delaying marriage, they have fewer clear answers, often suggesting that young people today are more selfish and that they no longer wish to be "tied down." Yet surveys of what young adults think about marriage consistently show that most still value marriage as a social institution. The majority do hope to marry in the future and do hold commitment to a partner in high esteem.[3] Do marital delay and the increase in cohabitation mean that today's young adults no longer want to wed, or are there other factors that might be getting in the way of young people's ability to "tie the knot"? Does this divide—between what young Americans say about marriage and what they do—reveal their *real* preferences? Or might other factors better explain what is influencing young people's attitudes toward marriage?

On the whole, family attitudes among young adults have become more liberal. Acceptance of permanent singlehood, voluntary childlessness, cohabitation, and unmarried childbearing has clearly increased over time. From 1988 to 2002, for example, the proportion of Americans who believed that marriage and children were necessary for a happy life declined significantly.[4] Attitudes toward cohabitation have become more accepting as well. In the early 1980s, 45% of Americans disapproved of cohabitation. By 2009, 57% of young adults found cohabitation acceptable; only 24% disapproved of living together without marriage.

Most research shows that attitudes about the desirability of marriage and acceptance of premarital cohabitation do not differ significantly by social class.[5] However, views regarding the acceptability of divorce have shifted over time. In the 1970s, women who were college graduates had the most permissive attitudes toward divorce, but by the early years of the 21st century, four-year college graduates had the most restrictive attitudes.[6] In fact, women with only a high school degree or some postsecondary education but no four-year degree had become far less likely to agree that divorce should be more difficult to obtain than did their college-educated counterparts. Some suggest that the greater acceptance of divorce expressed by women with less than a college degree is due to their greater uncertainty of achieving a good marriage, given increases in economic insecurity experienced by both less educated women and the men that are in their marriage market.[7] Even as highly educated women were expressing increasingly restrictive attitudes toward divorce, women with lower levels of educational attainment were loath to make divorce harder to obtain and were also becoming less likely to marry. At the same time, their likelihood of cohabiting increased, and they increasingly viewed living together as one way to "divorce proof" a marriage.[8]

Nonmarital childbearing is another area where there have been changes, but more so in behaviors than in attitudes. The proportion of all births to unmarried women increased dramatically in the closing decades of the 20th century and in the early years of the 21st century. As of 1989, 27% of all births in the United States were to unmarried women; by the end of the first decade of the 21st century, nonmarital births accounted for over 40% of all births to American women. And over half of those new parents were cohabiting at the time of the birth.[9] At the same time, acceptance of nonmarital births has increased much more slowly than has actual behavior.[10] Furthermore, less educated Americans—who are most likely to have nonmarital births—are most likely to view births outside of marriage as immoral.[11] The highly educated, in contrast, express more tolerant views about the ability of single women to successfully rear children.

Do growing social class differences in attitudes toward marriage, divorce, and parenting outside of marital unions shape the likelihood that young adults from more and less advantaged backgrounds will get married—or eschew the institution? Certainly our previous chapters suggest that the experience of living together differs greatly between couples from more and less advantaged backgrounds in ways that may influence subsequent behaviors. Determining the causal relationships between attitudes toward marriage and actual behavior, though, is challenging. There is abundant evidence that unmarried adults with more positive attitudes toward marriage are, in fact, more likely to tie the knot.[12] We argue that the actual process of living together shapes attitudes about what marriage might be like in ways that reduce marriage among some groups more than others. We also note that service-class and middle-class couples have qualitatively different relationship skills when it comes to expressing trust and resolving disagreements. In other words, the context shaping living arrangements influences how relationships are subsequently experienced. Although we cannot draw conclusive causal inferences, our results strongly suggest that the actual experiences of living together shape cohabiting individuals' views of whether (or not) to progress in their relationships to engagement and marriage.

FROM DINNER DATES TO MOVING BOXES: THE DIFFERENCE BETWEEN DATING AND COHABITATION

Asked about how things changed between dating while living apart and cohabiting, respondents mentioned a number of factors. Some referred to differences in the quality or quantity of their sex lives, others mentioned how they had disappointed grandma by moving in together, while a few, like Anthony, shared the realization that they felt more like adults now that their toothbrushes resided in a shared holder. While our respondents described numerous facets of their lives together, one class distinction was crystal clear. Service-class individuals more often identified ways that cohabitation was worse than just dating. Middle-class respondents, in contrast, more frequently noted that either nothing had changed or that life had actually gotten easier once they moved in with their partners. For the middle class, then, the overall ease of the transition from dating to cohabitation encouraged them to consider taking the next step. For our service-class respondents, on the other hand, the negatives that often accompanied moving in together made them even more reluctant to move their relationships to the next level.

Of course, not all of our service-class respondents experienced the transition from dating to moving in negatively. Service-class couples brought up numerous ways that the move-in had improved their lives. Some couples enjoyed getting to know one another better, having more sex than they had when living apart, or the additional financial resources that cohabitation allowed many to access. Perhaps because they moved in together at a considerably more rapid pace than their college-educated counterparts, the service class more often mentioned that cohabitation had the clear advantage of allowing them to spend more time with their partners. Jerry, who managed a frame shop, explained, "It's nice to spend time with someone and always having them there. It's good if you just want to relax and watch a movie with someone. It's a lot less lonely. I lived by myself for a year, which was really fun, but, you know, it's always nice to have somebody else there doing what you want to do."

The service-class couples we interviewed often had less family support and fewer financial advantages than our middle-class respondents. For many of them, then, moving in with their partners was a clear way to harness both additional financial and emotional support. Mark, a stay-at-home father, explained:

> Life can be a burden, and like any burden it's easier shared. You have a bad day, you come home and you can talk to somebody about it, you know? If there are money problems you have two people to solve the issues. Although sometimes that can be one more person necessary for a good fight . . . but for the most part, I think living together makes life easier because you can share the burdens and share the pleasantries.

Similarly, Josh, a part-time library clerk, said, "Well, it helps to have someone pay the bills as well as help out around the house. It's good to have someone else to live with just to talk to." Others noted that it was nice to have someone to take care of them when they were sick or even just to commiserate with when they were in a bad mood.

But even when service-class individuals explained the advantages that cohabitation provided that dating could not, just under the surface were hints of trouble in paradise. Service-class respondents were more likely than their middle-class counterparts to mention that living together was a more committed union than was dating, for example. In half of the instances when the service class discussed the greater commitment offered by cohabitation, however, it was in the context of being worried about the sexual fidelity of a partner. That is, they suggested that moving in together made it easier to ensure that their significant other's potentially wandering eye did not get the best of them. This was mentioned most often by service-class women. Beth, a nanny, said, "If I were [just] dating him I would probably feel insecure about myself and our relationship, because I wouldn't be able to check his collar when he comes home or smell the perfume of some other chick on him." Rhoda, an administrative assistant, explained that were she and Sam not living together, "We probably wouldn't be as close as we are now, because there are a lot of nice young ladies at his job, you know, and he mentions them, so I worry that if we were just dating that he would probably be dating other women. But since we're living together I know that we're just seeing each other." When asked the best thing about living together rather than dating, Vanessa said, "I guess you don't have to wonder where the other person's at. He's there (*laughs*)." Contrast this to the middle class, who also frequently mentioned that living together was more committed than dating. Rather than discussing sexual fidelity, however, they talked more about the deepening of positive feelings toward one's partner. Janelle, who owns a yoga studio, said that were she not living with her partner, things would be "very different, because since we've been living together, I mean it's really become like this (*folds fingers together*)." For the service class, then, while cohabitation may have the advantage of putting one's partner on "lock down," the fact that some feel the need to do so in the first place does not bode well for the state of their unions.

On the whole, service-class cohabitors brought up the negatives of living together relative to dating far more often than did the middle class. With reference to a few of our service-class individuals, this makes sense. Moving in, often quite quickly, with a partner you do not fully trust, hardly sets the stage for a successful relationship. But other elements of living together, such as an increase in arguments or a shortage (rather than an increase) in resources may deter some couples from wanting to formalize their relationships. Fourteen service-class individuals (versus only three middle-class cohabitors) noted that with shared space came more arguments. The content of these disagreements ranged from struggles over the household division of labor to deciding how going out with the guys or gals needed to change after moving in together. Patty explained that for her, the worst part of moving in together were the arguments about finances and struggles over who would do the housework. Among the most distasteful realizations of her new living situation was, in Patty's words, "The fact that I feel like I'm turning into Josh's mom and having to do all that. When we were dating I didn't have to worry about if he was coming up with money for his rent, because I didn't live with him, and I didn't have to care if he wasn't cleaning things if I was going home to my own apartment." Moving in with a partner, however, created new issues which required couples to negotiate who would do what.

For others, general proximity increased disagreements. Harry, who did not like conflict, attributed the increase in arguments after he and Marta began cohabiting to the fact that they were together more. Asked what he viewed as the worst things about living together rather than dating, Harry replied, "Um, just the fights. I don't like the fights. They get bad sometimes." Probed about how it would be different if they were dating rather than living together, Harry suggested that the arguments would not be as frequent, because "we wouldn't be around each other so much. We probably get on each other's nerves more often." Others did not directly raise the fact that more feuding had occurred since moving in, but explained that they either struggled over sharing limited space with their partners or felt as if they were stuck spending too much time together and had lost much of their freedom.[13] Service-class respondents reported this "stuck" feeling far more often than did our college-educated respondents.

Whereas the common adage that "two can live as cheaply as one" suggests that living together will benefit couples economically more than living apart, not all respondents saw it that way. Service-class respondents, far more often than their middle-class counterparts, mentioned that living together was more financially costly for them than dating and living apart. In addition to losing personal space and freedom, 40% of the service-class individuals noted that moving in together had actually hurt them financially, due to the expectation that they would help support their (poorer) partners to a greater extent than ever before.[14] Jake, who was in computer support services, explained, "I do think that I would probably have a good deal more money if I were living on my own," adding, "because, you know, Stephanie might not be around quite as often so I would not have to buy groceries for both of us, I would not have to pay for quite so many things." Although Harry, who had worked at a variety of low-paid service jobs, was unemployed at the time we interviewed him, he also thought he would be better off financially if he were not living with Marta. Asked why, he explained:

> Well, because I spend all my money on [Marta's] kids. After I pay the bills, I buy stuff for the kids. I'm always buying stuff for the kids, and if me and Marta were just dating, I don't think I'd buy stuff for the kids as much. At least, I don't think I would. I'd probably still be spoiling them, but probably not as much. I wouldn't have all her bills, 'cause before I met Marta I didn't have any bills except for my hospital bills that were already on my credit, so now all my money goes to bills from her previous marriage.

Like Jake, most respondents did not really mind helping out their partners, in large part because they expected the favor to be returned or they felt that they were repaying a past debt. As Brandi said, "It might be a little better [if I lived alone], but I've helped him. He's the same way with me, I mean, we don't ever consider ourselves owing anybody money. We just help each other out, basically."[15] Still, if things are going this poorly during what should be the honeymoon phase, and one might be better off financially living alone, some may question the wisdom of taking the relationship to the next level.

In fact, several respondents, mainly service-class men, alluded to the fact that it had become clear that this relationship was not the right one. Nonetheless, a shared lease was keeping the relationship alive—for now at least. Ron, asked how his life would be different if he was dating but not living with Crystal, quickly replied, "If we were dating, we probably wouldn't be together anymore, because I would probably be dating someone else." He elaborated, saying, "I wouldn't probably spend time dealing with her bullshit anymore, as far as not coming home, getting drunk, passing out in somebody's house, passing out here, making excuses, like, 'I fell asleep in my car.'" Crystal also attributed the decline in their relationship to moving in together:

> We probably wouldn't have gone through half of the problems that we've gone through, because I think if I would have kept my distance, if both of us would have kept our distance, like I don't know, it's like once I started staying there it was almost like he expected that I come there like after work and stuff you know, and you start to feel like you're not like independent

anymore. Like now I have to worry about what he's going to think. So it probably would have been better if I wouldn't have stayed with him, if I would have stayed by myself or with my mom.

For couples like Ron and Crystal, things had gone so badly after moving in that a separation seemed inevitable. But because living together did impose some constraints, it made it more difficult to end what to both of them was a poor match.[16]

Most of our middle-class respondents, in contrast, reported that the transition from dating to moving in had progressed quite smoothly. Some discovered that the experience of living together really was not that different than their shared experience as daters had been, perhaps because they had taken more time to get to know their partners and had already been spending several nights a week at their partners' houses before officially moving in together. Aaron, for example, dated Emma for ten months before the two moved in together. He explained that if he and Emma were not officially living together, things would not really be that different, as they would still be staying over frequently:

If we weren't living together, there'd be a lot more coordinating but we'd probably still be staying in one another's places, because like I said, right from the beginning I think we were, like, very comfortable with each other. We have some arguments, but we really don't have prolonged arguments and we don't ever throw appliances at each other, we don't break things or scream at each other. You know, there isn't really that kind of thing where somebody has to storm out or anything like that, so I guess I would assume that one way or another we would be, if not living in the same house together, that we would still be doing what we were doing before that, staying with each other.

Kate, an internship coordinator, likewise explained that her life really had not changed since moving in with Paul:

I'm still going out with the girls and that hasn't changed since we lived together. It has just maintained the same, I guess. It's weird. Like we're home and we're together, but I feel like we're doing things separately, too, which is good. So I don't feel like we're smothering each other or anything like that. So I mean in terms of like if we were just dating and I was living alone, I would probably still be doing the same things.

Some respondents even felt that living together was far better than dating and living apart. More middle-class respondents (twelve, compared to 2 among the service class) said that moving in together actually made their lives easier or was more convenient. Asked how life would be if they were still dating rather than living together, Jared, a mechanical engineer, stated, "I think it'd be a lot more hectic. There would be a lot more driving involved, you know? Every night one of us wouldn't be home." Lindsey, a professor, explained that if the two of them each lived alone, things would be more complicated.

> Well, it would be a time suck. That is one of the great things about living with each other is it's so much less of a time suck, right? You don't have to worry about like the end of the evening. When we were not living together, when we were long distance, I mean that was sort of the feeling for both of us is that you lose all of the normal life things. There's all that sort of easy stuff you get to do, like wake up together in the morning, brush your teeth together, you talk and work out and stuff. If you're dating, you don't get any of the day-to-day casual contact, so everything is sort of high pressure. Everything is "the date." Everything is the "We're doing something together now," not just hanging out. You can't do the just hanging out and watching TV thing, because you don't have time for that. You have to be making out on the couch. So I think it is much more relaxed than if we were actually dating.

If cohabiting changed things at all for our middle-class respondents it was generally for the better. Such experiences may also mitigate fears about the prospect of tying the knot.

IS IT WORTH IT? HOW MARRIAGE MIGHT BE DIFFERENT FROM COHABITATION

Individuals were asked about how they thought marriage might differ from living together. Given the negative changes many of the service class have already experienced, it is perhaps not surprising that, on the whole, the less educated were far more wary of the changes marriage might bring. This is in sharp contrast with the views expressed by many of our middle-class respondents, who more generally looked forward to the social and emotional changes they anticipated would result from getting or being married.

As with the transition from dating to moving in together, service-class respondents do not see the transition from cohabitation to marriage as being entirely negative. A large number expected, for example, that being able to do taxes jointly or the possibility of being on a partner's car or health insurance policy would save them money in the end.[17] Nonetheless, all that glitters is not gold. Service-class individuals more often anticipated that marriage would positively change things about themselves or their partners. But these transformations seemed unlikely. Some hoped that their partners would somehow magically be able to hold a steady job, while others wished that partners would suddenly become more emotionally supportive. Patty, an 18-year-old barista who struggled with having to do the bulk of the housework and economic providing, mused about what she thought might happen should they get married, saying, "I think Josh would probably try a lot harder to make the money that he knows he needs to, and I think he would try a lot harder responsibility-wise to keep up his end and probably to help just in general a lot more." Valencia hoped that if she and Jorge got married he would express his love for her more often but also that "I guess I hope that if we were to get married he'd be more understanding of how messy I am, stuff like that." Even if some of these service-class couples do make it down the aisle, the expectation that a ring will change fundamental aspects of who they (or their partners) are seems a set-up for disappointment.

Furthermore, service-class respondents also anticipated negative changes that would come with marriage more often than did their middle-class counterparts. Indeed, marriage often seems to hold more undesirable than positive possibilities for them. While some of our less educated respondents held out hope that marriage would be, as Patty mentioned, part of the "push to actually, you know, be a responsible adult," others disparaged the "adult lifestyle" expected of married couples. Service-class individuals were almost twice as likely to say that they saw the "marriage lifestyle" (which to them frequently meant "growing up" or giving up their individualism) as something they would much rather avoid. In response to our question about how marriage would be different from cohabitation, Mitch, a chef, explained, "I've never been married so I can't really answer that question, but people that I know who have gotten married, there's like this stress factor that enters into it. It seems like they view that you have to grow up now or something. You can't be you, can't be yourself, who you were when you weren't married, that you have to change all of a sudden." Similarly, Jackie, a social work paraprofessional, explained, "I think that marriage just means to me, like, 'OK, my youth has officially ended, you know, and now I'm officially a grown up.'"

Along with growing up, the service class feared that they would have to act like "husbands" and "wives," or even parents. Several evoked expectations that with marriage came an embrace of traditional gender roles, as Stacy explained:

> People who have gotten married, I think, are like, "You are my husband, I am your wife, so we should act as husband and wife act. You know? I should do this certain chore, like the ironing. The woman does the ironing, and you

are my man." And they act so, like, programmed, instead of acting the way they've acted towards each other for the past two, three years that they've been dating. They act like a husband and a wife, and for me, like, I'm living with Andre, but I'm not married to him, so I still think of myself. People who are married are like, "I must forsake all of my own hopes and dreams because I'm with this person and we are a union."

For some, like Chad, who installs phone systems, this pressure to change comes from family and friends. He explained, "I imagine people like kind of actually viewing marriage with more like intensity, kind of more intense outside eyes, like, 'So you guys going to have kids now? [Are] you going to . . .' You know, and just, like, people putting more pressure on stuff, paying more attention to the mechanism, the inner workings of our relationship. Whereas now we just live together, so people are just kind of like content to leave us alone." Shane, a retail worker, blamed the media for this image of what a married couple is supposed to be like, referencing the television shows he was watching in the 1980s and 1990s as impossible role models of married men and women that he did not want to emulate.

As Stacy alluded to above, some of these stereotypes make service-class women, in particular, leery of marriage. Service-class women often expressed concerns that marriage had a certain set of expectations for wives. In fact, most of these women already lived in households where they had taken on the majority of the housework, even as they, too, worked for pay. A number were both the primary earners and the primary homemakers in their relationships. They worried, then, that getting married would mean that their partners expected them to become even more "wifely" at home. Valencia, for example, explained, "I guess I think if we were to get married like it would all of a sudden actually be my responsibility to cook and clean and keep him happy. But when we're not married it's like, 'You know what? I don't care. You can eat whatever you want' (*laughs*)." Rhoda, an administrative assistant said:

> I feel like with marriage it's like a ball and chain, now that I think about it. It's like you have to answer to this person and you got to tell this person where you're going, what you're doing. I guess the views of marriage, the way we were raised, it's like if you are married, you've got to do it. Women have to do it. They don't want to cook? They've got to do it. Men sit around and do nothing all day. I just figure with the way I want to do things, I don't like the idea of marriage. I'm more comfortable with living together.

Sheryl mentioned both men's and women's roles in her ideas of marriage, though it is noteworthy that "male jobs" are much less routine and time-intensive than the "female jobs." The 29-year-old waitress explained that in marriage, "Women are doing the cooking, the cleaning, and all this." Asked what men are doing, she said, "Fixing the car, taking the car in. What do guys do? (*laughs*) I don't know. Putting up the storm windows. Mowing the grass. I don't think that those roles are placed as intensely when you're cohabiting." Terrell was the lone service-class man to mention that should he and Aliyah marry, she would expect him to do more "manly" jobs. Asked what Aliyah would expect him to do if they were married, he said, "I guess fix up stuff more. I don't fix nothing. I'm not a handyman. I don't like to get dirty (*laughs*)."

Many service-class individuals mentioned fears that marriage meant that they were trapped. Such feelings could lead, in their opinion, to arguments (or additional arguments) with their partners. Nearly half (n = 28) of our service-class respondents mentioned that marriage was confining. Explaining how cohabitation was preferable to marriage, Stephanie stated:

> I could get up and leave if I wanted to. And that freedom is valuable to me. I don't like being tied down. Sometimes even having the dog makes me feel too tied down, because she's a responsibility. And I'm young, I don't like responsibility. So, that kind of ties into that, you know, living together as opposed to being married.

Beth, a nanny, explained that if she and Mitch were married, "I would feel extremely trapped at this point. Even though I share a lease with him I know that I have the opportunity to leave and there's nothing legal binding us at all. I mean, if we were to get married I would probably feel trapped legally, financially even more, just simply because I am not going to be able to get out of that. I don't have the money to buy that, the divorce papers." She added that there would be more social pressure, as well, to stay married should they tie the knot, saying, "I feel that if we were to be married, like people would look at us in a different light as far as 'Oh, you guys are married,' especially my parents. My mom would say, 'If you're married you should try to work things out' kind of thing." The idea of marriage being a snare was mentioned primarily by women, which flies directly in the face of popular wisdom which says that women cannot wait to tie the knot, while men must be dragged down the aisle.

Middle-class respondents also sometimes mentioned that marriage could be constraining, though they more often did so in a lighthearted way or in the same breath they also mentioned positives of marriage, such as greater security and commitment. Middle-class men, in particular, often noted that getting married would make others in their lives happy. In their minds, little would change day-to-day once they were wed. But they expressed the belief that their parents, grandparents, or friends would be thrilled and that they would get more social recognition for their relationships. For example, Matthew, a 30-year-old architect, explained that as he has gotten older, marriage had come to mean less to him than it did in the past. Nonetheless, he hoped to marry his partner someday. When asked why, he said, "I just think it's an ingrained societal thing. I've always thought that graduations, weddings, they're not for you. They're for your parents. So that ceremony, when it finally does happen, it will be for my mom, it will be for my dad. It's not for me." Sean, who sets up art installations and had just started planning his wedding with Emily, explained that he looked forward to other people viewing their relationship as more serious. Elaborating on what that meant, he explained:

> The way that other people react to you when you're married is a big thing, because when you introduce somebody as your girlfriend and you've been living together for a couple of years, people don't know if that means this is somebody you just met a month ago. When you introduce somebody as your wife, then it's like, "Hey, this is the person I'm going to spend the rest of my life with," not "This is the person I'm seeing right now." That's a big difference, and I think it's going be a really good feeling when I first get to introduce her as my wife.

Middle-class individuals, then, felt that there were social advantages to being married that their service-class counterparts rarely mentioned.

In addition, middle-class cohabitors anticipated that marriage would result in even more positive emotional changes than the transition to cohabitation had yielded. They frequently mentioned that marriage was more permanent than cohabitation but saw this as a positive thing (rather than a constraining one) that would increase their already loving feelings toward their partners. The idea that marriage was more permanent than cohabitation was the most common concept that arose as college-educated respondents discussed the difference between the cohabitation and marriage. For the middle class, "permanence" referred to stability, increased closeness, and a stronger incentive to make the relationship work. Words like "trust" and "deeper commitment" were frequently mentioned, and many thought that they would grow closer as a married couple. Emily, a professional baker and Sean's fiancée, was asked what marriage meant to her. She said, "It means stability. It means unconditional everything. Unconditional everything like across the board. It's not that everything's going to be, you know, flowers and wine but it'll be, it'll be closer." Similarly, Travis, a CPA, explained, "I think we would have a little more trust of finality, that, you know, we're here and we're not going anywhere. I think that's the thing that marriage would add—that permanence that I think living together doesn't have." Such expressions stand in stark contrast to the views expressed by our service-class respondents, who voice the belief that marriage is more of a snare.

FIRST COMES LOVE, THEN COMES . . . MARRIAGE? OR CARRIAGE?

How service- and middle-class couples and individuals feel about the optimal location for bearing children provides the third piece of our puzzle. Before asking whether they, personally, would want to get married if they became pregnant, respondents mentioned their general views about nonmarital childbearing. Gender differences in how nonmarital childbearing was perceived in general were stark. The majority of our female respondents, regardless of social class, believed that it was better if marriage preceded childbearing. This sentiment was expressed by equal numbers (n = 16) of service- and middle-class women. Valencia, the one service-class woman to have met her partner at church, explained that people should defer childbearing until after marriage because marriage provided greater stability than cohabitation. "It would be, not better financially but just knowing that most likely you might stay together," she said. "I mean, you're not really obligated to [stay together] when you're not married. You can just kind of leave up and go. When you're married you have to go through the whole divorce, and it's just a much bigger mess that you have to go through." College-educated Alisha explained that marriage helped build a better foundation for children. "I think getting married first would be better," she asserted. "I think that children need to see that kind of strength and commitment." Carrie, a middle-class teacher, added that cohabitation was a solid relationship for her but that it was not quite the same for children as a marriage would be. "I could almost consider what Brad and I do like very close to being married," she explained. "But I think that marriage is that promise or that step that is just saying that you'll be together forever. I'm sure somebody could make the argument that you really didn't need the marriage part of it to have that, but obviously I think it would just be a much more stable environment for a child to understand that your parents are married." For women, the stigma and challenges of single motherhood are greater than those faced by unmarried fathers, leading to their stronger sentiments that it was better to be married before having children.[18]

While men were less likely than women to view marriage as a necessary prerequisite for childbearing, service-class men were the least likely to adhere to that norm. Many had already become parents without marriage, or they did not foresee being able to marry in the near future. Only about a third of service-class cohabiting men believed that marriage before childbearing was optimal. Harry, who lived with Marta and her two children from a prior marriage, explained, "I don't think you have to be married to be a good parent," going on to clarify "as long as you're there for your children when they need you, and you let your children know you love them." Similarly, Josh, a library clerk, said, "I think a child can be raised by two nonmarried people just as well as can two married people, because I don't think having a little piece a paper that says you are married really changes things *that* much ultimately, at least it shouldn't." Middle-class men far less often agreed with that sentiment.[19] Nearly half of the middle-class cohabiting men believed that parents should be married before having children together. Caleb, a musician and recent college graduate, said that he felt people should have children within marriage, because "it seems like a more solid foundation with the mother and father definitely there and tied into a bond of marriage. Even if they're not getting along that well, they're still there for that child." Aaron, an office supply store manager, described marriage prior to bearing children as "the logical sequence."

When it came down to what our respondents wanted for *themselves,* even larger contrasts emerged. Personal rather than global attitudes about unmarried parenthood may result in a greater number of middle-class couples heading to the altar. While about a quarter of the middle-class respondents expressed the belief that couples did not have to be married before having children, most quickly mentioned that they, personally, wanted to be married before becoming parents. Drew, asked if he felt that people, in general, should be married before having children, said, "That's kind of old-fashioned to only be that way," elaborating that "these days I don't think it's that big of a deal." But, when asked what he would want for himself, Drew said, "I would like to be married first." Asked why, he stated, "Just old-fashioned beliefs, like I mean I'd like to have that structure. I'd like to date, then get engaged, then get married, then have kids, then die, die old (*laughs*)." Sabrina, a middle-class cashier at a gourmet grocery store, also explained that great families came in lots of forms. She said, "There are single moms who do a great job, you know, and there are single moms who don't do a great job or single dads you know, and I think it just depends on the relationship that the children have with their parents and the parents' relationship with each other. I don't think you have to be married to be happy." However, asked to clarify her own preferences, she said, "I wouldn't look at my friends and be like 'Ooh my god, you're not married,' but I want to be married." The service class was less likely to express personal desires that differed from their global attitudes toward marriage before childbearing.

Another major difference between our service-class and middle-class respondents was the solution they proposed should they get pregnant unexpectedly. Among many in the middle class, marriage was still very much the expected outcome to an unplanned pregnancy, something that was far less often mentioned among less educated cohabitors. So-called shotgun marriages were quite common in earlier decades, but as cohabitation became more normative the likelihood of marrying before a birth declined. Yet many of the middle class, the men in particular, seemed oblivious to this new reality, with most stating that an unexpected pregnancy would speed up a marriage. Asked if they would get married if his partner, Juliana, found out she was pregnant, Evan responded, "Yup, no question." Greg said, "We'd just do what we need to do, you know, since we're getting married anyway it wouldn't be a great big deal." College-educated women, on the other hand, were more anxious about what would ensue. Asked what would happen were she to get pregnant, Kristina, an architect, responded: "Oh God, I don't know. I just, I definitely think I'd be crying. I'd be scared. I'd be freaking out. I'd be like 'Oh my God what are we going to do?' I'd definitely be like, 'OK, if you're going to marry me, marry me now!' kind of thing." Some of the middle-class cohabitors pointed out sheepishly that while they had in the past disparaged others who got married because they were pregnant, they would hope for that very outcome. Tara, a 28-year-old computer programmer, said, "We probably would get married, though when I see people on TV doing that, like they're walking down the aisle, I'm like, 'What's the point?'" before going on to say, "We'd probably try to get married."

Service-class men expressed greater ambivalence about jumping into marriage as a result of an unplanned pregnancy. Asked if he had considered marriage before his first child was born, Mark, whose partner, Tracy, was pregnant with their second child, replied, "Just because she was pregnant? No. That would have been silly." Shane went into great detail in explaining why diving into marriage as a result of a pregnancy was a bad idea:

> I wouldn't consider marriage for the sake of the child. I know a couple that got married *only* because they had a kid together. And they are *so* unhappy with each other and this kid is going to grow up in *such* a bad environment because of that decision. I fear for this child's future, because they, the parents don't get along. They argue and scream and throw stuff at each other.

Middle-class men also question whether marriage would be "the logical step" should an unplanned pregnancy occur, though this was most evident among those in poorer-quality relationships. Jack, a 24-year-old financial planner, felt that a pregnancy would force the question of whether he and his partner, Audrey, would marry or not. "I guess if she was pregnant now, it would probably, maybe definitely force the envelope or make our relationship progress to some sort of next level," he said. "I don't know if that would be marriage, but definitely push, possibly, that envelope," before reiterating that his biggest concern would not be becoming a father but having his hand forced on "whether we should get married or not." One other college-educated man, Mason, was also loath to be pushed into marriage, though he wanted to be a father. As he explained it, "I'm not saying I would break up with her because she got pregnant. I'm saying I'm not going to throw a ring on her finger either. I'm not going to say, 'Well, I've got to do the honorable thing and marry you but I don't love you.'" Yet among our college-educated respondents, such responses were rare.

Finally, several women, particularly among the service class, expressed reservations about marrying because of a conception. For many of these women, they did not want to feel like they were forcing their partner's hand, as Mason stated above, but rather preferred to get married because of the "right" reasons—their partners loved them and were ready to take that step. Natalie, a 24-year-old secretary, typifies this sentiment. While she herself would definitely prefer to be married before having a baby, if she sensed any unwillingness from her partner to marry beforehand, she would pull back, as she stated. "But if he was like, 'I'm not ready' or anything, I wouldn't be like, 'No, we have to,' you know? I would just be like, 'OK.' You know? Yeah, I'm not, I wouldn't be like, 'No, we have to!'" College-educated Emma was also ambivalent about whether she would want to get married in the face of a pregnancy. "I don't know about that," she mused. "I don't want to be asked to get married because

I'm having a baby. I would prefer that it be a reason of you would like to be with me, not because there's a sense of responsibility or of traditional mores." Because middle-class men more often adhered to the belief that they should be married before having children, and many of their relationships were progressing toward marriage, our results suggest that class differences will persist as to whether children are born within a marital or nonmarital union. In fact, nationally representative studies of union transitions among cohabiting women who experienced a conception reveal that by the time the baby was born, the majority of college-educated women were married. That was far less likely among pregnant cohabitors with less than a college degree, who more frequently remained cohabiting when they gave birth.[20]

WHAT DID WE LEARN ABOUT SOCIAL CLASS DIFFERENCES IN COHABITORS' ATTITUDES TOWARD COHABITATION, MARRIAGE, AND CHILDBEARING?

How our respondents experienced different stages of their relationships, from dating to moving in and beyond, are clearly shaped by many factors, but our results highlight the importance of social class as a crucial mechanism. As we note in previous chapters, the experiences our cohabitors had prior to moving in together, their reasons for entering into shared living, and how they negotiated emerging aspects of their relationship clearly shaped their views about what the future held. Furthermore, because we interviewed those who were already living together, rather than following couples throughout their relationships from the very start, our respondents were at differing relationship stages. Many were not yet ready to wed but willing to consider it in the future.[21] Others, however, were engaged, and quite a few were actively planning their weddings, while a few had one foot out the door, thinking about or in some cases, even discussing, how to separate out their lives. Diana, for example, who we profiled at the beginning of this chapter, struggled between balancing her desire for independence and maintaining a stable family for Kaley, and was creating her own sort of "trial separation" a half a week at a time. Evan and Juliana, in contrast, were planning their wedding, as we learn more about in the next chapter. In fact, our middle-class cohabitors were far more likely to envision marriage in their near future than were their service-class counterparts. We argue that their more positive experiences, at various stages of their relationship, condition this willingness.

Of course, finances likely play a role in the more positive experiences and attitudes of our middle-class respondents. Cohabitors' economic situations often put the kibosh on relationship progression into marriage. But these fiscal difficulties often preceded the start of the cohabiting union, and in fact, among the service class, accelerated transitions into shared living. As we demonstrate here, moving in together often caused more headaches than did just dating, particularly for our service-class couples and, notably, for our less educated women. These challenges caused some of our respondents to presume that getting married would only make matters worse. Contrast this with the experiences of our college-educated cohabitors, who took longer before moving in with their partners and generally had enough resources to live apart. Their slower entrance into shared living may have helped winnow out poorer matches (though some clearly still remained). It also allowed the middle-class cohabitors more time to discuss future desires, as well as observe how their partner acted with regard to money, contraception, and disagreements. An additional factor, communication skills, also played a strong role in the successful relationships of the middle class. As we see in this chapter, as well as in our discussions of housework fairness and contraceptive responsibility, the college-educated couples compromised more, argued less, seemed to engage less in magical thinking regarding the capacity of their partners for change, and worked together more frequently to come to consensus. It is perhaps not surprising, then, that our college-educated cohabitors express more positive views toward their cohabiting experience, as well as the future likelihood of marriage. For many of them, cohabiting provided advantages over dating, and the future or their relationships looked even brighter when they considered marriage. Add to that the fact that the college educated feel more strongly about having their children within marriage, and it is not surprising that more of our middle-class couples seem poised to formalize their unions.

What then, do we make of this? We are certainly not arguing that marriage needs to be (or should be) the goal of every couple. Young adults today have more opportunities for new forms of relationships than did even their parents' generation. Many may choose not to marry, or to put it off until midlife. But it is clear that unless both the entrance into and experience of cohabitation changes for the service class (or that the sequencing of marriage before childbearing radically changes for the middle class), we are likely to see a continued bifurcation in the relationship progression of more and less advantaged young adults, where cohabitation continues to be a step toward marriage for the college educated and more of a relationship limbo for their less educated peers. Of course, even if they express less than positive attitudes toward marriage, individuals may decide to wed for other reasons, as some of our respondents have already made clear. They may seek to legitimize their unions in the eyes of others or want to make their partners happy. Chapter 7 explores how couples negotiate one of the penultimate challenges toward transforming cohabiting unions into marital ones: the proposal.

Waiting to Be Asked
or Taking the Bull by the Horns?

Gender and Social Class Differences in Marriage Talk, Proposals, and Wedding Planning

Children's rhymes about romantic attachments in adulthood naively presume, as in the well-known playground chant, that young adults will follow what once was the normative sequence into adulthood: first comes love, then comes marriage. But where does cohabitation fit in this sequence? For many of our respondents, particularly among those in the middle class, cohabitation was just a new intermediary step between love and marriage. Over two-thirds of the college-educated couples were either engaged at the time we interviewed them or were having serious conversations about getting married. Although some service-class couples were also planning on tying the knot, and a handful had even gotten engaged, far fewer were in agreement regarding marriage or had concrete wedding plans. Not all our respondents were ready to discuss marriage. Furthermore, a small number rejected the institution of marriage, as they did not see how that "piece of paper" (the marriage certificate) would make any difference in their lives. Service-class couples were better represented in this group, as well. Cohabitation was far more likely to serve as a precursor to marriage for middle-class couples than for the service class.

What factors contribute to these divergent pathways? Building on the findings of our previous chapters on the division of responsibilities for housework and contraception, we find that there are important gender and social class distinctions in how women and men discussed relationships and negotiated desired changes. Socially accepted "scripts" for intimate relationships generally afford men greater power than women to further intimate unions. They do this by assigning the desires of the male partner more weight in relationships, and also by naturalizing and romanticizing male enactment of these roles. Nowhere is this male prerogative more evident than for the topic of proposing. While cohabitation generally lacks common and agreed-upon rules, and allows men and women dissatisfied with traditional gender norms the opportunity to "flip the script," relatively few of the couples we interviewed were comfortable doing that when it came time to the penultimate step dividing those couples who were engaged to marry from those who were not—proposing. As a result, among most couples contemplating formalizing their unions via marriage, traditional gender roles remained rather firmly entrenched. Men were expected, for the most part, to be the one to propose that the couple get married, with the women accepting the man's offer of marriage.[1] As Laura, a 23-year-old waitress, explained, her partner would have to propose, "Because that's the man's job. The man is supposed to do it." Asked what her job was, she replied, "To say yes. To wear the ring."

Our college-educated women, however, demonstrated greater agency in other aspects of negotiation, being better able to negotiate a more egalitarian division of housework, for example, and greater participation and support in methods to prevent pregnancy. Did their advantages in these realms spill over into relationship progression? Even though college-educated women did not disagree with their service-class counterparts regarding who should propose—men—their role in moving this stage of the relationship forward differed in important ways from their less educated counterparts' attempts. Middle-class women were generally more assertive in advancing their relationships than their service-class counterparts, particularly if engagement was their objective. Middle-class men, though often initially reluctant to discuss engagement, frequently ceded to their partners' desires or expressed personal readiness to take the next step.

Nathan and Andrea had gotten engaged shortly before we interviewed them. Asked how they had gotten to that point, Andrea noted that while Nathan's energies were directed toward buying a house together, she was more focused on where their relationship was headed. She said, "[I asked him] 'Do you see us getting married someday?' and he said 'Yes' and I was just like, 'OK, in the near future or is it something that's going to be happening within the next year or so?'" Nathan proposed a few months later. Service-class men, in contrast, more often resisted moving the relationship forward. Jerry mentioned his plans to propose to his partner, Natalie, but when asked when they would get married, replied, "I'll probably put that off as long as I can." Bill recounted how his partner asked him to get married, and then asked again after a year and a half went by. Asked about his reaction, he replied, "I told you, you know, nothing's changed. I'm not going to get married until I get done with school." Unlike Nathan and Andrea, our service-class men often expressed confidence in their ability to control the tempo of relationship progression.

Of course, both gender and class variation exist in how our couples progress in their relationships or tread water to remain in place. Some men were more eager to raise the topic of marriage than were their girlfriends, and not all women were comfortable expressing their desires for a shared future with their partners. And, as we discuss in the Chapter 6, some couples did not foresee a future with their current partners at all. Nonetheless, middle-class women were far more proactive in their negotiations for the future of their relationships and their male partners more amenable. The result, we show, is that while service-class women frequently found themselves, in the words of more than a few of the men and women, "waiting to be asked," middle-class women more often took the bull by the horns and established a time frame for engagement.

WHAT DO WE KNOW ABOUT RELATIONSHIP PROGRESSION AMONG CONTEMPORARY COUPLES?

Glossy magazines at supermarket and convenience store checkouts frequently regale shoppers with stories of celebrities who meet, get engaged, and married (and often divorced) all within a six-month time span. But for the vast majority of American couples, the decision to tie the knot is not one taken lightly or entered into hastily. While sexual relationships may unfold rapidly and quickly transition into shared living, subsequent advancement to discussions of marriage and, perhaps, engagement, is often a more protracted process. One study of cohabitors in New York City found that many couples had not even begun discussing engagement until they had lived together for at least a year.[2] Others suggest that cohabitation had taken the place that dating used to play in the courtship process.[3]

When couples who are living together do start considering next steps, discussions of a permanent future do not always proceed smoothly. Such conversations can be risky. What if partners do not envision the same type of future? And even if couples see a shared future together, partners may have very different time lines for things like engagement or marriage. Expecting the next step to occur too soon may frighten off one partner, but waiting too long means risking that an impatient partner will move on. The ability to get one's partner to focus on conversations about the future, to ward off a partner's desires to discuss "next steps," or to simply assume that a particular decision or task is primarily under the jurisdiction of the male (or, occasionally, female) partner all demonstrate a form of relationship power.[4]

There is perhaps no step in heterosexual romantic relationships where men have more power than in proposing marriage. As we note in prior chapters, relationship scripts generally favor men when it comes to advancing intimate relationships. Notwithstanding a failed social experiment in the 1920s by jewelers to sell a "male engagement ring," the common social script is for men to do the asking while women wait to be asked.[5] In fact, female proposals are most often presented as a joke, derisively called "flopping the question," or even shown as impossible. In the popular television show *Friends*, for example, Monica attempted to propose to her marriage-shy beau, Chandler. This could have been a groundbreaking moment in television. Producers instead chose to play it for laughs. As she got down on her knee to "pop the question," Monica began crying so hard that she could not continue, eventually wailing, "There's a reason why girls don't do this!" At that point, Chandler "took over" and proposed to her. As long as the proposal is widely accepted—by both men and women—as a near-exclusive prerogative of men, men will retain the right and control over whether to move relationships forward when they see fit or fail to advance the relationship to the next stage.

While historically there were very clear reasons why men were tasked with proposing—in an era when men were expected to provide economically for families while women performed domestic and childbearing tasks, men needed to be able to demonstrate their ability to support a family—many of these justifications for male dominance in decision making regarding family relations are being challenged.[6] As we note earlier, the majority of women are now employed in the paid labor force, and at the time we were conducting our interviews about a third of women earned more than their partners.[7] These transformations suggest that women have more bargaining power in their relationships than they did in the past and may therefore be more likely to propose marriage.

In order for women to propose marriage, men would have to be amenable to having a partner propose. But power dynamics within couples may not be as one-sided as such unilateral decision-making models suggest. Even though men and women can have different interests as individuals, they may come to realize that to optimize the well-being of the couple, compromise is required. In other words, sometimes one partner may be able to persuade the other that a step—such as engagement or marriage—should be taken for the good of the couple, even if one partner is perfectly content to remain cohabiting.

While gender may matter less now than in the past, the evidence indicates that social class matters as much or more when it comes to relationship progression into marriage. For less educated men, the prerequisites for marriage—a stable job, the ability to support a family—may seem impossible to attain or difficult to sustain. And as is discussed in the prior chapter, service-class women also express concern that marriage may mean that their partners expect them to shoulder a larger portion of the already onerous "second shift."[8] In contrast, college-educated cohabitors have more positive attitudes toward marriage than their less advantaged counterparts, often expressing the belief that marriage would be even better than living together. And the evidence bears out that they are more likely than their less educated counterparts to take the leap and tie the knot.[9]

Much of the evidence, including what we present in earlier chapters, suggest that women—or at least college-educated women—have more bargaining power in their relationships than women did in the past. Nonetheless, challenging established gender norms can be an uphill climb. After all, when norms—such as those surrounding relationship advancement, housework performance, or pregnancy prevention—advantage men, men may not be interested in change. They might simply refuse to cede control over the important decisions in their purview, stall negotiations, or convince their partners that gender roles are natural or inevitable.[10] This results in maintaining gender inequality, especially if women feel uncomfortable pushing for change. But middle-class men often felt like they *should* participate more in domestic work, even if they didn't split things 50–50. These men also frequently played a more central role in family planning than their service-class counterparts, as well as men in the past. Does that mean that men—middle-class men, in particular—are then more amenable to being persuaded to take a step toward formalizing their union, or do they continue to assert that they alone decide when relationships will progress? When women desire something (such as engagement or marriage) more than do their partners, are they able to convince their partners of the rightness of their position? And do cohabitors overturn norms regarding proposals? Our findings regarding these questions are both refreshing and depressing.

PLANNING FOR PERMANENCE?

The decision to live together often elevates societal expectations that marriage is being considered. Yet among our respondents, very few had explicitly discussed plans for marriage prior to moving in together. Talk of the future, and whether marriage is in the cards, became more frequent once couples were sharing a home, though such discussions range widely in both content and seriousness. Some individuals were strongly opposed to marriage, while others were not yet sure their current partner was the one or were not ready to broach the issue. How these talks progressed, the roles played by men and women in forwarding or impeding these discussions, and what ensued over time suggest that women in cohabiting couples—particularly college-educated women—are challenging conventional female roles, even as the behaviors of both men and women continue to reinforce men's dominant role in relationship advancement.

Fuzzy Math, or How Few Couples Have Future Plans upon Moving In Together

If the role of living together is to serve as a trial run or "practice" for marriage, then one might expect couples to have at least begun to discuss the possibility of a long-term future together prior to establishing a shared residence. That was not the case for most of those we interviewed. Only two couples—one service class and one middle class—mentioned being engaged prior to moving in together, while a few individuals recalled discussions of marriage with their partner that their partners did not mention.[11] In fact, couples were more likely to talk about never getting married than to talk seriously about marriage.

Though small in number, six of the couples we interviewed count themselves among those who reject marriage as an institution.[12] Four service-class couples said they had always known that marriage was never in the cards for them, even before their current relationship began. Partners agreed that they were not interested in marriage and had raised the topic early on in their relationships. Mitch, a 25-year-old chef, explained, "I think we discussed marriage like probably the first date we had or something, just because I wanted to get it out in the open that I didn't want to get married ever, not unless [it was for] insurance or tax purposes, something like that." Luckily, Mitch's partner, Beth, felt the same way. "He discussed marriage with me and I said, 'I don't believe in it so don't be stressed out about it, you know? I'm not waiting for a ring to be on my finger.'" Stacy recalled a similarly blunt discussion with Andre when they first got involved.

> But I told him the first day, the first day, before we even had sex I told him, "Look. If you want to date me, that's cool. I want to date you, too. . . . But I'm not having your puppies and I'm not getting married, so if you're looking for marriage or puppies you better look to somebody else. It's not me. I'm not that girl."

This level of frankness leaves little room for partners to misunderstand future intentions. The decision not to marry was arrived at more gradually by the two middle-class couples. Dean and Lindsey had been together for nearly two decades, and Dean explained that there had been several turning points in their relationship when getting married would have been a natural step.

> I mean there were a couple of instances where it seemed like it was going to be obvious to get married, like after we both had graduated from college and were both going off to graduate school. You know, it could have been when we, when Lindsey got her Ph.D. and was starting a career. You know what I mean? There were a couple of different instances, and I honestly can't remember when we decided we weren't.

Their decision was made over time, as neither partner ever pushed the subject of making a change (that is, getting married). But for the second couple, the man had always known that he did not want marriage, while his partner only gradually came to accept that she would never marry as long as she wanted to remain with him. Derek explained that he had never been interested in marriage, but that his partner was not always on board with his views. Derek then revealed how he arrived at a compromise that worked for him: he would be willing to have a child if she would be willing to forgo formalizing their union. He said about this transition, "I mean, it's certainly been an ongoing discussion over the course of the relationship, up until a couple years ago. I think we sort of settled that we weren't going to pursue that, and I think that's when she started thinking about having kids, sort of a transference of sorts." His partner, Kathleen, indicated that she had initially hoped they would get married, but no longer did, thereby demonstrating Derek's greater ability to get what he wanted in their relationship.

Marriage rejecters mentioned a variety of reasons why they would not wed. Most commonly, they explained that having experienced a parental divorce kept them from tying the knot; others noted that since they were not religious, marriage held no real meaning for them, or that they did not want institutions meddling in their personal lives. Lindsey explained:

> One [reason we don't want to marry] is political—we don't like the institution. So I guess like the social control thing, I don't think it actually succeeds the way it is supposed to succeed. I don't want the government telling me what to do, don't want religion telling me what to do, so [I'm] against it more or less politically . . . I mean all of the traditional reasons for getting married, we don't buy into any of them.

Finally, these marriage rejecters noted that getting married wouldn't add anything to their relationships. Shelly, a waitress, noted that marriage would not improve things, because, in her words, "We're still in the same relationship." Derek simply stated, "I can see a lot of reasons why marriage would make our relationship worse and I can't see any that would make it better." Nearly all of these marriage-rejecting couples intend to remain, in Lindsey's words, "permanently nonmarried" to one another.

Whereas these six couples stated that they had discussed never marrying, another four couples got engaged without ever having discussed marriage. As a result, the male partner's proposal was a total surprise to the women—which suggests that the men were sure of how they would be received. Mark decided to propose to Tracy as a lark, after a brief long-distance relationship, during her first visit to Columbus to see him. Jonathan jokingly said that his decision to propose surprised even him, as neither he nor Janelle were interested in marriage or children. Janelle, asked when discussions of marriage had come up, replied, "It never did. I was shocked! We NEVER talked about marriage." Asked why she was so surprised that Jonathan proposed, she replied, "Well, I knew we'd be together forever, I just didn't think that we'd be married. I thought we would be very unconventional, so I was a little bit shocked that he was conventional, because I would have never pushed for that." Asked why he had proposed, Ray, a 30-year-old bookkeeper replied, "It was something that I knew that she wanted, it was a way for her to see that I was committed to her and we were going to, you know, be together."

Not Yet Ready to Raise the Issue and May Never Be

Because so many of our respondents had moved in with their partners early on in their relationships, quite a few had not even broached the topic of a future together before they began cohabiting—nor since. Several noted that they preferred to "live in the now." Describing his disinclination to discuss future plans, Adam said, "We were kind of like a day at a time thing, just play it by ear, you know? If things work out, then they work out. I try not to think too far in advance when it comes to relationships, because you never know what can happen." Susan also revealed her disinclination for planning ahead when asked if she and Eugene had discussed the future when they moved in together. "Not really," she said. "We still don't really. I mean, because it's the future, you don't know really much about it. It can change."

Others felt that they had not been together long enough to raise such a serious topic as marriage. Asked what kinds of plans they had discussed before moving in together, Chad laughed, explained that they had moved in together very quickly, then said, "It just didn't make sense to do all the marriage stuff at that point, you know?" His partner, Jackie, was far more interested in talking about travel plans than wedding plans. The service-class cohabitors who moved in rapidly often suggested that couples should live together for at least a year, if not longer, before raising such serious topics. Eugene explained, somewhat defensively, "I mean, I have plans of marrying her," then clarified, "but I don't really want to discuss it right now, just because it has been less than a year since we've been dating. I want to know her more than I do now."

Another group mentioned that they had not discussed marriage because they were not yet sure that they had made a permanent love connection. Sherry, who had been involved with Tyrone for under a year, stated, "I definitely want to get married, probably in the next four years, you know, but it's not on my mind for some reason right now." She also expressed reservations about whether Tyrone was "the one," stating, "Like, he's the person for now. I don't know, it makes me sound *so* horrible. He's the person that's filling that right now. I don't feel like it's just there yet, like I don't know that he's the one yet. I don't feel it, uh uh." Finally, for others, such as the individuals profiled in the Chapter 6, marriage talk was avoided because they were certain that they were with the wrong match. Mason, for example, referred to his future with his partner as "a black hole," conspiratorially saying that he hated the sound of Kiersten's voice. Such respondents demonstrated little interest in talking about whether marriage was in their future.

Testing the Waters

Although not all couples had discussed marriage, the majority of couples we interviewed—over two-thirds of the service-class couples and nearly three-fourths of the middle-class ones—said that the topic had come up, in one way or another. For some, that took the form of "jokes" or casual conversations that allowed individuals to slowly gauge their partner's receptiveness to making shared plans; others mentioned pointed conversations about when and how the couple should marry. In general, women brought up these conversations, often indirectly. In a few instances the man was the first to raise the topic of becoming more serious or proposed without ever having discussed marriage with his partner. Nonetheless, the overwhelming pattern that emerged among couples who had discussed marriage was for the woman to initiate the conversation. What kind of response greeted those who brought up talk of the future, whether they persisted in their enquiries, and the ultimate outcomes highlight the importance of thinking about the gendered ways that unions progress over time.

For many, initiating discussions about the future of the relationship was fraught with discomfort. Raising the topic of marriage was seen by many women, regardless of their social class, as playing to gender stereotypes, "showing their hand" too nakedly, or not following the rules (with little enquiry into who had established these rules). In fact, several women commented that for them to raise the topic was to push the envelope in a way that was risky or unbecoming. Service-class Brandi explained, "It was just kind of like an off-subject, you just don't ask, you know?" Asked why, she responded, "I didn't want to put pressure on him to think that just because we live together that this is like forever." Dawn's restraint was driven by previous experience. "I tried not to talk about marriage," she explained, "because I talked about it with my last boyfriend, and it just really didn't make things very good." Middle-class women also discussed their fears of "breaking the rules." Kristina, a 24-year-old architect, believed that talking about marriage might make her partner run for the hills. "Women just learn that you don't say certain things," she explained. Carrie expressed the belief that it was up to the man to raise the future, stating, "that's just something that I've never really liked to push or talk about unless they bring it up, because I don't want to seem pushy or overwhelming, or anything like that." Women's concern that marriage talk will be unwelcome reveals how gender norms—particularly the notion that it is men's prerogative to raise the issue of marriage—are well known to all. Indeed, some women who wanted to raise the topic of marriage actually felt unable to do so. Few men expressed similar concerns about bringing up talk of marriage, though some, like Justin, also mentioned not wanting to show their hand too soon. But no men mentioned feeling stigmatized about raising the issue of marriage, or being perceived as desperate or needy, as the women feared.

Despite these concerns, over time many of our respondents plunged in and began discussing their thoughts about the future. Such gambits were usually met in one of two ways. The first approach was for a partner— usually but not always the male—to shut down future forays into the topic or express unwillingness to further such a conversation. Josh, a 20-year-old part-time student and library worker, mentioned Patty's attempts to talk about the future. Asked if he had wanted to further that discussion he stated, "Have I wanted to? Not really. I'd talk to her about it but, it would not take very long before it would start making me feel uncomfortable if, like, it started like going in a direction like talking about planning getting married." Anthony, whose partner, Diana, had dropped hints about getting engaged, remained uninterested in discussing the topic, stating, "I don't know, I'm just comfortable with the way things are right now, and I don't see any reason to change them. I mean, we share a joint bank account, everything is in both of our names. I don't know, maybe someday." Aliyah revealed the female perspective on men's reluctance. Asked if she and her partner, Terrell, discussed a future that included marriage, she replied, "I usually have to force him into talking about it," a story that Terrell confirmed. When she raised their future together and the possibility of marriage, he told her, "Well, I ain't ready, I don't want to talk about it."

Quite a few middle-class men also expressed recalcitrance in response to their partner's probes. Edward said that after they had attended his brother's elaborate wedding, his girlfriend wanted to talk about marriage. For Edward, this conversation was unwelcome. He commented, "I don't like doing all that stuff. That's stress. Marriage is not for guys." Paul expressed a similar desire to avoid marriage discussions, explaining, "You've got to understand, I try not to talk about this stuff at all." In fact, the best example of men's ability to shut down conversations they are not ready for is demonstrated by Jack, a 24-year-old financial planner who had been dating Audrey for over four years, though they had only recently moved in together. "Call me a jerk," said Jack, who clearly resented Audrey's attempts to advance the relationship, "but you know, 'You can walk,' that's what I say. I mean, like, don't force my hand. So if you really want a decision, the decision is going to be you are walking."

A handful of women also expressed reluctance to discuss marriage, though this was far less common than it was for their male counterparts. These women typically had previously been married, were responsible for children that lived with them, and the primary breadwinners in their relationships. They were also disproportionately drawn from the service rather than the middle class. For these women, marriage posed more of a risk than a reward. Marta provided an example of how marriage discussions made her feel trapped and how she had stopped her partner from constantly raising the topic. "About a year ago," she explained, "he [Harry] stopped demanding that we had to be married, because I told him that if we had to be married, then I was going to break up with him, because I couldn't promise that," explaining that she'd not been divorced for very long.[13] Fewer middle-class women expressed a disinterest in marriage, though some, like RaShinda, commented that such talk made them feel pressured.

One key way in which the responses of our middle- and service-class respondents differed is that the less educated were more likely to accept their partner's admonition to "wait and be patient." In other words, service-class men were better able to cut off conversations that they were not ready for than were their middle-class counterparts. Shane, who worked part time stocking shelves for a clothing store, had been living with his partner, Sandra, for nearly two years. He described how Sandra gradually stopped bringing up marriage. "Eventually she realized that I was so undecided and, like, not ready that she just kind of backed off without saying anything like that," he explained. "She just kind of stopped pressing the issue. So I'm pretty sure it's something she still thinks about, and it's probably still on her mind. But she hasn't been bugging me about it."

In fact, service-class men were confident that their partners were eager to get engaged but felt that they needed to control the pace of relationship progression. Stan declared about his partner's eagerness to get engaged, "Oh, she's waiting for, itching for that," a sentiment echoed by quite a few of the service-class men. Dawn chafed at her lack of power to convince Eric to propose already. "I just feel like he wants to, he wants control of the situation," she lamented. "He wants to do it when *he's* ready for it." Although she admitted that finishing school before getting married was the right thing to do, she also wished that a proposal was more imminent, as she felt the prospect of school completion was quite far away. "I don't know, the way he's going, he might be another two years," she grumbled, mentioning that he was already in his sixth year of school. She concluded, "I'm just waiting for my boyfriend to ask me."

Middle-class women, however, were more willing to keep asking for what they wanted, compared to their less educated counterparts. The college-educated couples tended to have lived with their partners for shorter amounts of time, often entered into their unions at later ages, and had clearer notions of how they wanted their relationships to unfold. Furthermore, they felt more confident bringing up the topic of marriage to determine if their partners were on the same page, persisting in such conversations as well as occasionally setting ultimatums. Bree, a confident 25-year-old auditor, indicated that she had given her boyfriend clear markers of what she wanted. When they graduated from college, for example, she told him that they were either exclusive or they were over. "He loved that," she said, sarcastically. She also set the time frame for getting engaged. Taylor, her fiancé, recalled that ultimatum. "She just simply stated that, 'You know, after this lease is up, if we're not engaged then it's time to live on my own, and then we'll still date and that sort of thing, but I just feel if you're not ready, then I don't know when you're going to be ready.'" Asked if she was prepared to actually follow through with her implied threat, Bree said:

> Yeah, I think so. I mean I didn't want to think about it, but I was pretty sure that he would. I was just trying to kick him in the butt a little bit, you know? And I really didn't think it would come down to moving out, but I think I would have followed through with it.

None of the women in our service-class sample (or their male partners) mentioned giving their partner an ultimatum or even a broad time frame for when they would like to get engaged. While this may be a function of our sample—we only interviewed intact couples, and those where an ultimatum was issued may no longer be together—these results are consistent with the findings regarding college-educated women's confidence in negotiating other aspects of their lives, such as housework and contraception.

Furthermore, college-educated women were more often able to convince their partners to do as they wished. Taylor, for example, agreed with Bree's assessment of what was needed. "I was all right with it," he stated, "I mean, it was fair enough, honestly, and a lot happened between then and now." In fact, more of the college-educated couples revealed that either both partners were ready for discussions of marriage to take place or one partner had persuaded the other to engage in marriage talk. These couples exhibited more of a back and forth process regarding relationship progression. While women remained more likely to initiate discussions about where the relationship was headed than men, there was far more male participation in the subject, rather than naked power plays or simmering disappointment or resentment, than among the service class.

Sometimes, discussions of the future progressed relatively seamlessly. Jared, a 24-year-old engineer who at the time of his interview was in the midst of wedding planning with his fiancée, Alisha, revealed how his partner had initially broached the topic of their future. "She started the conversation," he recalled, "the 'Where's the relationship going?' conversation." Then he stated, "We pretty much both inched into 'Yes, I want to marry you one of these days.'" Middle-class partners Sean and Emily also had a relatively easy transition into talk of marriage. He described one such conversation while they were camping. "We were just sitting by the campfire at night and had a pretty long, serious conversation about marriage and us being married." Emily also mentioned that relationship talk, recalling, "We went camping and uh, I'm like, 'Where are we on marriage?' You know, 'Where do we stand?' Just to make sure we're on the same page, we are, you know, going down the same road. And he was like, 'You know I have been thinking more about it.'" Although Sean indicated that he had not necessarily viewed himself as a marriage guy, he explained his willingness to have such a conversation, saying about Emily, "This is the person I'm willing to live my life with for the next 30, 40 years, which I had planned anyway, so why not do it officially or on paper?" While Sean didn't seem to need much convincing, his amenability to marriage talk made it easier for them as a couple to determine that they were on the same page.

Other couples mentioned a fair amount of kidding about marriage and a somewhat slower back and forth before getting more serious about the topic. Evan, a salesman, asserted that he and his partner, Juliana, joked more than anything else, stating, "It's not like we sat down and said, 'Where is this going? Are we going to get married? What's your time line?'" But the two would walk past a jewelry store and check to see if the other wanted to go inside, as a sort of barometer to sense where the other stood. Juliana said that she eventually upped the ante. "I dropped not so subtle hints about things all the time, like 'So, that's a really nice ring' (*laughs*). Just really obvious, like wedding on the brain. The bug definitely got me, and I was ready for it." Fortunately for her, Evan was ready for it too.

Several of the men actually mentioned that they proposed mainly because of their partner's desires. Service-class Jerry, for example, knew that Natalie wanted to be married. At the time of their interview, Jerry was planning their upcoming vacation, which included his proposing. He admitted that the proposal was for Natalie's benefit. "I'm always still kind of against it," he said. "I still, even though I am going to propose to her, it's more for her gratification. I mean, I don't think it's necessary to get married, like that whole matrimony and stuff. I'm not really that religious of a person and . . . I don't really want a wedding." Martin also said that his engagement with Jessica was more for her and her family than for him, as he said, "We could have kept on living together forever and I wouldn't have felt like, 'oh, we're behind.' I mean, I felt that if we got married that was cool, but if we ended up being the people who were dating for 30 years I wouldn't care, because I would be with the person I want to be with, and I don't really care how we're arranged." Such sentiments are similar to the sentiments expressed by Edward and others opposed to marriage, that the institution was largely for women. The main difference is that these men, most of whom were middle class, were willing to take that leap with partners.

How Long Does Testing the Waters Take?

Our respondents expressed different notions of what constituted appropriate relationship tempos, which may contribute to why our middle-class cohabitors were more likely to progress into engagement with set marriage dates than were service-class couples. College-educated cohabitors often mentioned specific time frames for adequate testing of relationship quality. Discussing what he foresaw happening in the future, Paul said, "It [marriage] is part of the deal, as far as I'm concerned. If this works out, if we can cohabitate more or less peacefully for a year and a half, I'll give it a shot." Middle-class women also had specific time lines in mind regarding appropriate relationship lengths. Andrea, a 25-year-old social worker, had dated Nathan since high school; they had been living together for a year. "I think I am the one who initiated it [talking about marriage]," she said, "probably because we've been together almost four years and I just was needing some kind of acknowledgement that this was going somewhere." Many other middle-class respondents expressed the belief that after cohabiting for about a year (in addition to the time spent dating), couples should be ready for the next step.

Service-class individuals, in contrast, more often mentioned what needed to be in place before an engagement could occur. Eric, who currently worked part time as a security guard while attending school, explained, "We know we're going to get married someday, we're just waiting to get our careers going, I guess." Other service-class men concurred that concerns over future employment and job stability were holding them back. Max, who had been involved with Tameka on and off for several years, and was hoping to complete his associate's degree to solidify his position in the Columbus school system, said, "Now we're at the point where it's like, OK, I know that's what I want to do [get married]. So I'm just working on my financial situation and schooling and things like that." Both service-class men and women wanted to be earning more, to have decreased their debt, completed school, or saved money for a house or a wedding before getting engaged.[14] The cost of engagement rings also featured in these talks; men sometimes said they had to save up for a ring, whereas women mentioned the pressure their partners felt to buy a "nice enough" ring. Employment instability among the less educated as well as inadequate resources were often used to justify why couples were not advancing their relationships. It is perhaps not surprising, then, that we observed far more engagements among our middle-class respondents.

PROPOSALS AND ENGAGEMENTS

Perhaps nowhere do normative gendered expectations appear more strongly than in expectations for marriage proposals. Among the couples we interviewed, men are overwhelmingly expected to be the ones to propose marriage. This puts quite a weighty burden on men. Many, however, were quite territorial about their prerogative. While a few men seemed tickled by the idea of a woman proposing, others viewed such a possibility as a joke. Furthermore, several women disparaged or denigrated women who would resort to such a measure.

Men sometimes said that they would be open to a woman proposing. This acceptance was often only hypothetical, particularly among men who were not interested in marriage, or was mentioned by men who had already proposed. Josh, for example, asked about which partner could propose, responded "Uh, whoever wants to propose," a sentiment his partner, Patty, echoed. But as indicated earlier, discussions of marriage made Josh nervous, so he avoided them. James had already asked Monica to marry him but said if she had asked him, "I would have been blown away, yeah, I would have said yes. I would have been pretty tickled pink about that, her asking me. I mean, that's not something that normally happens." She, however, had expected him to do the proposing. Other men also embraced the possibility that women could propose. Simon was one of several men who said, "I think it would be cool if she would (propose), though. That would be awesome. I do think, you know, in today's society that it would be all right for either one." But most of these men also said that they would be the ones doing the proposing, most often because their partners wanted to be asked. Simon's partner, Laura, for example, expressed the belief that proposing was "the man's job." Even women who were generally less conventional frequently said that they were traditional when it came to getting engaged, or, in the words of Andrea, "That's just something a boy does." A small group stated that though the woman might want to ask, she would defer to her male partner. For a few, this was so that the man could prove that he was ready for marriage. Asked why the onus was on him, Jake replied, "I'm the one with the marriage hang up, so I think she'll wait till I'm ready." For most, though, it was a result of adherence to normative gender roles—by either the man, the woman, or both.

A look at who proposed among the couples in our sample that were engaged at their interview highlights the power of normative gender scripts. A total of 18 couples in our sample had gotten engaged over the course of their relationships (though three had broken off their engagements but were still living together and contemplating their futures). The vast majority of their proposal stories—16 of the 18—followed a normative script, with the man asking the woman to marry him and the female partner accepting his proposal. As we mentioned above, in four cases the couple had not discussed marriage prior to the man proposing. During our interviews, quite a few men talked about the background work they had done, without their partner's knowledge, before popping the question. Service-class Jerry planned an elaborate vacation abroad for his proposal to Natalie, while Mark "tricked" Tracy into picking out her own engagement ring under the guise of helping a friend choose one for his girlfriend. "Even if I hadn't wanted to get married," Mark crowed in recollection, "it would have been worth being married for the rest of my life just to be able to tell everybody, 'I pulled that off!'" College-educated men were equally designing. Jared arranged for a ring from his grandmother to be reset, and also reserved a horse-drawn carriage to meet him and Alisha at a high-end restaurant after dinner, while Nathan rigged the Halloween pumpkins they were carving so that Andrea's contained the engagement ring. Men described their furtive attempts to hide what they were doing from partners with great satisfaction. Doing something novel or memorable no doubt also put a fair amount of pressure on men. But most relished telling their engagement stories.

Although men were generally expected to be the one to propose, their female partners often "helped things along" quite directly. Seven women (six of whom were college educated) explained that they strongly encouraged their man to propose. Middle-class men in general did not seem overly bothered by these hints about getting engaged. Many felt that they were ready for that step and also mentioned that having their partner express such strong desires for their proposal let them know that their reception would be positive. Sean recalled how his partner. Emily. allayed his concern on that front. "One thing that she had said a long time ago," he recalled, "was 'No pressure.' I think the first time she said 'No pressure,' it was 'but if you ever do want to ask me, the answer would be yes.'" That still, however, was not enough to allay Sean's qualms about how to do a proposal the "right" way, which required Emily to more clearly set the parameters of what, to her, was an acceptable proposal. "I was still kind of nervous just of what to do," Sean explained, "and you know, we talked about how would she want me to propose and I said 'Do you want some sort of big thing, you know, a grand gesture?' And she said, 'You don't have to do anything—asking's fine.'" For male partners, knowing they could expect a positive (ecstatic) closure with their question made the somewhat daunting proposal process easier.

Women sometimes did more than just help things along. Two service-class women actually did the proposing. Vic explained how Carly had "accidentally" proposed:

> We were just sort of discussing it [marriage] in general terms, and she didn't say "Will you marry me?" but it was close. And I looked at her and I was like, "'Did you just ask me to marry you?" and, she said, "Uhhh . . . no. Did you want me to?" and I was like, "You can, you know?" So I said yes, and then she was like, "That's not how I wanted it to be!" So then I asked her right after that, but she was like, "No, you have to do it for real. *You* have to do it!"

Carly viewed this conversation more as a discussion than a proposal. She indicated that she had mentioned wanting to share Vic's last name, as they were expecting a baby. "I did want us to share a name," Carly said, "and so I brought it up and he was like, 'Well, OK.' And then, you know, he agreed. So it wasn't like, we didn't propose to each other or anything. It was kind of, like, talk about it." She went on to say that he threw out a date to get married right away, but they then decided to defer getting married until after their child was born, for "practical reasons." Maria also proposed to Bill, on Valentine's Day:

> We were eating dinner, because we had a candlelight dinner for the two of us. I looked at him and I pushed the ring [box] across and he opened it and inside there was a little sign that said "Will you marry me?" And he just, like, said "yes! (*teary voice*)," and then he put the ring on. But he hasn't worn it since, because I asked him to put it away till we actually got married, because he felt weird. Honestly, he was like, "Well, if anybody's gonna wear the engagement ring it should be you."

While she was happy that she acted, her fiancé was less satisfied. Describing why he did not wear the ring she gave him, he said, "I don't know of guys having engagement rings or anything." None of the middle-class couples mentioned that the woman had proposed, though several—like Bree—had set a clear time frame for their partners to propose to them. Karen, who also gave her partner, Jeremy, a time frame for proposing, recalled, "I said, 'You have to do it before the end of August.'"

Quite a few service-class women, in fact, stated that they would like to propose but did not because of the expected response from their partners. Dawn was quite impatient to get engaged, having lived with Eric for two years. Asked if she would consider proposing, Dawn replied, "I would've already done it if he would have let me. 'Cause I've threatened to propose to him a few times. He's like, 'No, the man does it (*in a deep voice*).'" But she was also aware that her reception would be less than positive if she were to take the bull by the horns and propose. "I mean, he made it very clear to me that he didn't want me to do it and kind of hurt my feelings," she continued. Eric confirmed that Dawn broached the subject more than he liked. Asked how she did so, he recalled, "She's like, 'You better watch out or I'm just gonna propose to you.' I'm like 'Well, if you do I'm gonna say no!'" As a result, Dawn has turned the prospect of a woman proposing into a joke, stating, "What girl really wants to be the one that has to propose, 'Will you take me as your wife' (*in a pathetic voice and then laughs*)?" Several service-class men mentioned how preposterous they viewed the idea of a woman proposing. Spencer commented about the possibility of his partner, Brittany, proposing, "It would be hilarious!" Terrell said that Aliyah threatened to propose all the time. Asked what he would do, he responded, "It would be funny. I probably would laugh! I would laugh, and then I would be like, 'Come on, girl, get off your knees. Stop playing around.' Then I would eventually go do it for real—the real way, how it's supposed to be done." Service-class men in particular expressed opposition to women's proposing. Robert, who never wanted to get married, expressed the belief that it was "not really her place to make the decision." Andre, also a marriage rejecter, said that if they ever were to marry he would be the one to propose, because "I'd just like to do it the quote-unquote right way, I guess." While some of these men did admit that there was not just one way, they still strongly believed that there was a best way. As Ron explained, "It's not how it's got to be, but it's how it *should* be." Even if women desired to take control of their relationship's progression, they needed the consent of their partners. For most of these couples a woman's proposal would be disappointing or (as in the case of Aliyah) treated as a joke. In the face of such derision or outright rejection, these women are left waiting for the man to do the asking.

Middle-class men less often expressed the belief that a female proposal would be funny, but some college-educated men joked with their partners about how long they were going to have to wait to get engaged. Evan said that when he and Juliana started talking about the future, he let her know that he was in no rush. "I had always told Juliana that she was on the seven-year plan, and she was okay with that," he recalled, clarifying that he told her it would take that long because "that was kind of my way of testing her of how long are you really willing to wait and how much do you actually like me kind of thing." But Evan proposed several months after they had moved in together. Other college-educated men seemed more receptive to having a woman propose. Soliman thought that if a proposal were to happen that it would come from him but then went on to say, "I hope she does. That would be cute." Paul, a 28-year-old political lobbyist, also mentioned that he would really like it if his partner proposed, because it would be nontraditional.

But quite often, middle-class men who said they were open to a woman proposing also preferred to be the one doing the asking. Justin, whose partner had floated the idea that she would ask, indicated that while he would say yes, he would prefer to be the proposer, stating, "I'd still want to ask her, but I don't think I'd be offended if she asked me, either."

Asked why he wanted to follow what he called the more traditional route, Justin explained, "I just think that weddings, proposals, engagements, all that, it just goes so far back. It's in hundreds of movies and just everything we've ever learned is the man asked the woman to marry him." Nathan clarified why he was the one to propose to Andrea, rather than waiting for her to ask him. "I wouldn't have a problem with saying yes," he explained, "except for I think it's the guy's job, not to be chauvinistic and old fashioned. But I think I would have felt kind of like a putz if she would have proposed to me."[15] Negotiating egalitarian lives given long-standing expectations shaping what men and women "should" do is challenging, even for those in alternative living arrangements.

Women, especially middle-class women, also believed that initiating a proposal flouted normative gender conventions, with quite a few stating that doing so would leave them feeling unfeminine. Karen, who worked as a research assistant for a children's health organization, was getting impatient with not being engaged and recalls telling her partner, Jeremy, to get a move on. "I said, 'If you don't do it by a certain time, I'm just going to do it.' But I don't mean that, because I don't want to do it, because then I'll feel like masculine, and I don't want to feel masculine." Asked why she would feel masculine, Karen replied, "Because society tells you that the guy is supposed to ask the girl to marry him. Even though I've definitely been the initiator in some of our other circumstances that are traditionally, I think, male roles, this is just a big one. And because everyone will ask, 'How did it happen?' and I don't want to say, 'Well, I did it.' I can't, it would kill me, I think." Other women felt torn by their desire to be proposed to, admitting that it ran counter to their closely held desires to be equal partners. Katherine, who worked as a research coordinator and was considering applying to graduate school, explained: "I guess I just have that old-fashioned view that he should be the one to do it. It doesn't make any sense. I mean, I'm a liberated woman. I guess I should be, you know, open to doing that [proposing] myself." But she just could not convince herself that she should ask, stating, "Like I said, I know it's stupid and irrational, but part of me still wants to hear the proposal from him, and I know that's dumb but I can't help it."

The Meaning of Being Engaged

While proposing is a major step in the progression of relationships, the stage of being engaged may also signify something important to the outside world—or not, as the case may be. Whereas many of the couples we interviewed described how they were preparing for their wedding, others had not begun to plan a formal ceremony—even after the passage of considerable lengths of time. The way our engaged cohabitors discuss what ensues after the proposal suggests that the meaning of engagement actually differs for those from service- and middle-class backgrounds. The steps that our respondents were taking to prepare for weddings, or the justifications they provided for why they were not doing much, culminate in the ultimate distinctions between our more and less advantaged couples.

As we indicated previously, only five service-class couples reported being engaged at the time of their interviews, compared with twelve of our college-educated couples.[16] While the majority of our middle-class couples (particularly the women) reported on plans for their wedding, often in great detail, four of the five service-class couples had been engaged for considerable lengths of time with little evidence of much progress toward getting married. Mark and Tracy had been engaged for over five years at the time they were interviewed and were expecting their second child. Mark, who was the couple's designated planner, was more than willing to talk about what kind of wedding he would like and what time of year he preferred for a wedding, but when asked when they might get married, replied, "I have no clue." After mentioning that he and Julie were engaged, Ray replied to a query about the timing by saying, "Let's see. We've been together seven years. I think we got engaged after being together for two years." Asked if they talked about marriage much, Ray answered:

> Oh, marriage is always talked about. We get our friends, our family, everybody is always asking us, "Well, when are you guys getting married?' It's constant, and we just agreed we're not going to let outside things interfere with our own decisions or change our decision as to when we're going to do it and how we're going to do it.

Neither Ray nor Julie had a specific time frame in mind for when a marriage might take place. Maria and Bill also did not mention concrete wedding plans, despite being engaged for several years. "We've kind of discussed some of the details," Maria explained, "but nothing concrete." Only one of the service-class couples had a near-term plan for getting married; Vic and Carly had hoped to get married before the birth of their child, but had already put off that plan once and were now contemplating marrying after the child was born.

The vast majority of the middle-class couples, in contrast, were counting down to their wedding days and had already done a good deal of the preparatory work. Ten of the twelve engaged middle-class couples mentioned their wedding dates, or had narrowed them down to a season and year and were working out details. Even those who had only recently become engaged had discussed a time period they were contemplating. Jonathan and Janelle provide perhaps the starkest contrast to our longtime-engaged service-class cohabiting couples. Jonathan was quite pleased with their quick progression:

> We got engaged I think in July or something, and she had the whole thing planned in like a week. And we get married three months later. A lot of people have these kind of long-drawn-out affair things. We don't. We were always, you know, like let's just get this over with.

Nathan also was matter of fact about the relatively quick transition from engagement to marriage, saying, "We got engaged October 26th and we'll be married next October 14th, in Columbus, Ohio." For most of these engaged couples, their next step was very clear. Asked where she saw her relationship heading in the future, Amy, who was getting married that summer, replied, "Straight down the aisle!"

Why such dramatic differences in transitions following engagement? Our service-class respondents frequently mentioned financial challenges that made it difficult to plan for a wedding. Julie kept circling back to economic hurdles that hindered her and Ray from progressing on the wedding front. Describing what happened after they got engaged, Julie explained:

> Initially, like the first week, I was like "Oh, O.K. We'll get married in about a year." But I think when it set in, we were like "We have no money." His family, you know, is very blue collar, factory worker type family, and my mom wasn't remarried and she was just a secretary. But I still had these images, because when I grew up we had a fair amount of money, so I had just always assumed I'd have such and such kind of wedding, and one thing came up after another. We decided we were going to move back [to Ohio], that took precedence, school, you know. It just kind of snowballed into pushing it further and further back.

With further probing, it became evident that unrealistic expectations were at part to blame for their stalled engagement. Julie had initially started planning a wedding, beginning with finding a dress. But she had no idea how much a wedding cost, the dresses she fancied were not cheap, and she envisioned an exotic honeymoon in Fiji. In the ensuing years, she lowered some of her initial expectations. Asked what it would take for them to get married, Julie replied, "Our income would have to increase enough for us to start saving for a wedding. That's basically what it comes down to." But saving up was a challenge. "We save," Julie explained, "and then we have car problems. Then we save, and somebody is on their death bed in Wisconsin, you know, so nothing [saved] that ever is anything. Usually it's used up one way or another." Still, Julie held fast to her high standards. Although her dream wedding no longer included a honeymoon in Fiji, she now imagined having family members go to Hawaii for a week, and combining the ceremony and honeymoon. Asked for a ballpark estimate of what she thought a wedding would cost, Julie replied, "For that kind of wedding with a honeymoon and all that? I'm thinking probably $15,000."

But it was not just unrealistic expectations of what a wedding should be that hindered our less educated couples from transforming their engagements into marriages. All of the engaged service-class couples with children mentioned various disincentives to getting married. Three of our five engaged service-class couples either shared at least one child or were expecting, and all mentioned that getting legally married would reduce the economic benefits they received from being unmarried parents. Carly and Vic, together less than seven months, were nearing the end of her first trimester. Both mentioned that they had set a wedding date but decided to defer for a while. Describing their decision-making process, Carly said:

> Vic's not that big on marriage, and neither am I. But we kind of, we had decided to get married. We were actually supposed to get married a week from today. Yeah. And we were going to be married and everything, we're engaged. And I'm on Medicaid, and they'll drop me if I get married, because we'll make too much. Yeah, we'll make too much together, and that's how we're paying for the birth and everything. So, we put it [marriage] on hold. . . . So maybe like after the baby's born we might get married, but . . .

Carly then trailed off. The other couples who shared children also mentioned that there were more benefits to being cohabiting parents, at their income level, that dissuaded them from getting married. Tracy attributed their lack of movement on the wedding front to a variety of factors, but kept returning to financial reasons to account for why she and Mark remained cohabiting, musing, "I think one of the things that might be holding us back is we get penalized a lot financially for being married," clarifying that they would pay more in taxes. Maria also said that for her and Bill, financial justifications predominated.

There are times when I would love to be married, you know, when you're seeing the weddings happen around you and you're looking around. I mean, when is ours going to happen? You know? And then it turns back to, well, financially we really can't do it. I mean, we could go to court and get married, but like I said, I'd get more [for financial aid] out of school being single than I do the other way [married]:

Several college-educated couples also mentioned financial challenges when discussing their weddings, and most were quite aware of wedding expenses. Unlike their less educated counterparts, however, our college-educated engaged couples described how they determined to move forward regardless by economizing. Nathan and Andrea both took on second jobs to make some money to put away for the wedding. Sean, whose fiancée, Emily, was a pastry chef, revealed that she would contribute in her own way, explaining, "Emily's making the [wedding] cake, which is great."[17] Others economized by planning small events. James and Monica were planning on getting married over the winter break during his first year at law school. Asked what kind of wedding she was thinking of, Monica said:

> Not elaborate. I want to get married on the beach, like on the Oregon Coast, and he's like, "Yeah, that's sounds good to me". . . . Like, I'm not a huge wedding person. I just thought it'd be better, like a romantic, small, on the beach thing. That's what we want to do.

James concurred, saying, "We're not looking at spending more than four or five hundred dollars, though, so it works out. Just rent a little place and go out to the beach, you know?" Jonathan and Janelle were getting married by a judge, with only family members in attendance. But they were having a reception, which Janelle described as low key. "Saturday night we're having just 50 people upstairs at Monarch Bistro in the Village, so just a little party. I mean, I'm borrowing my wedding dress. It's so easy." For these couples, being married took precedence over a large, extravagant (and expensive) event.

Yet another distinction between our more and less educated engaged couples was the role played by family members in covering the wedding costs. Service-class couples rarely mentioned family member involvement in forwarding their engagements into weddings, though additional questions revealed that few thought their parents would contribute much. Rather, family members nudged them to get married but did not seem willing or able to provide any instrumental help to that end. Our college-educated couples, in contrast, frequently mentioned the importance of family in covering wedding costs. Furthermore, while it was traditionally the woman's family that bore the brunt of the wedding costs, our middle-class couples frequently declared that both sides of the families were contributing to various wedding features. Sean indicated that Emily's parents could not afford a big wedding, before going on to say, "That's a pretty big issue. My parents said that they would help out with it, I mean to get it to a point where it's nicer." Taylor and Bree both said that their parents were splitting the costs of the wedding. "Both of our parents gave us an equal amount," Taylor stated. "It's kind of surprising, but that's how it worked out because that's what they volunteered at first." Sometimes, other relatives helped as well. Asked who was paying for their wedding, Kevin said, "We're paying for some things. Her mom is paying for the church and the reception. My parents are paying for the flowers. Her brother is buying her wedding dress. My aunt and uncle are buying our wedding cake." Asked how this division had happened, Kevin said, "So, I mean it was just people volunteering to pay for stuff. I'm like, 'OK!' But I'm paying for the DJ, limos, and honeymoon. And then Amy's all the favors and all the little stuff you don't really think of, she'll take care of that." His fiancée, Amy, concurred, saying, "So a lot of people are doing things like that for their gift for the wedding, which has helped out a lot." These couples are nested in families that can provide the resources to enable them to wed, something that does not emerge in the wedding discussions of our service-class respondents.

Few of the college-educated couples in our sample were planning large weddings, but even in these instances, norms were somewhat upended because the groom's family often bore a sizable share of the cost. Alisha ran through a huge list of what she had already checked off:

> We have the church; we have the reception hall; we already have the contracts signed. We have the flowers; we already have the DJ, we have the photographer; we have the girls' dresses. My dress is already ordered and on its way. We have my veil; we have my crown; we have his tuxedo already ordered.

Alisha and Jared were planning a wedding for 350 of her and Jared's friends and family members. Asked how they were paying for this wedding, Jared explained, "My parents, her Dad, her step-Dad, and us." Pressed as to how the costs were being shared, he stated, "I'd say it's probably going to be 75 percent my parents, 25 percent the rest of us." Jared's father was from a large family, which he explained accounted for the size of the wedding. As he explained, "I'm from a celebratory family, you could say. We like to get together." Taken together, the middle-class couples' excitement to take the next step, willingness to economize, as well as considerable amounts of family support, set our engaged college-educated cohabitors on a different trajectory from the engaged service-class couples.

WHAT DID WE LEARN ABOUT COHABITORS' DIVERGING RELATIONSHIP DESTINIES?

As in other dimensions of life, we see dramatic differences in how service- and middle-class couples negotiate relationship progression. College-educated women more often promote discussions of marriage than either their male partners or their service-class counterparts. The middle-class women in our sample were simply less willing to, in the words of many of our service-class men, "wait and be patient." And while middle-class women more frequently raised a time frame for what many saw as "the next step," their male partners abetted their desires by also being willing to discuss the topic. This was not always the case initially, but our middle-class men seemed more interested in keeping their partners happy—even if that meant the dreaded "M" talk—than were service-class men. Not only were they more receptive to their partners' suggestions, but they were better established in terms of careers and finances. Furthermore, both the men and women in middle-class couples frequently mention time frames they hold for when relationships should progress to the next step. That is, their scripts for how and when a relationship should progress were often much clearer than those of the service class.

Even though middle-class couples more frequently progressed toward engagement and concrete wedding planning than did their service-class counterparts, class distinctions do not emerge in how such a step (engagement) was expected to transpire. The majority of men and women, from both the service and middle class, believed that proposing was the prerogative of the man. While some men expressed more openness to their partners' proposing, in reality, that rarely happened. Women often felt that they wanted to be asked, whereas men thought that proposing was *their* right and were unwilling to cede it to women, especially as it might come sooner in the relationship than they desired. And the men who mentioned that they would welcome a female proposal were often already engaged, and had themselves done the asking, so they were fine with the idea only in theory. In other words, although our college-educated women were more likely to raise talk of marriage, and often suggested a time frame for when a proposal should ensue, for both middle- and service-class women the ball still remained in the man's court. Even men willing to share that burden were often partnered with women wedded to traditional notions of who "should" propose. The result is that the process of becoming engaged remained very gendered. Men were expected to do the asking, and women largely waited to be asked.

The key factor differentiating our middle- and service-class couples, then, is college-educated men's willingness to propose. Among those we interviewed, far more of the college-educated men had asked their partners to marry them than had service-class men, despite having been cohabiting, on average, for shorter periods of time. Not only do middle-class men mention being more economically ready for this next step, given their career trajectories, but they are clearly more willing. In fact, many of them viewed their next steps with their partner with anticipation, as something that will add to their well-being and enjoyment of life. The majority of our middle-class couples commenced wedding planning soon after becoming engaged, and most set wedding dates for a year to two years following engagement. The process of transitioning from cohabitation to engagement to marriage is much more clearly demarcated for the college-educated than it is for our less educated cohabitors. Engaged middle-class cohabitors have far more of the trappings that demonstrate a wedding will ensue (had set a wedding date, purchased a wedding dress, rented a hall, pruned a guest list) than their service-class counterparts.

Our middle-class women hold considerable power to convince their partners to take this next step, perhaps because their male partners are willing to be persuaded. Service-class men, in contrast, frequently shut down conversations about the future they were not ready for, demonstrating the ability to impede relationship progression held even by men in relatively weak economic positions. When their partners persisted in talking about marriage or engaged in trial proposals, they treated them dismissively, demonstrating yet another area where communication skills among the service class lead to lower relationship satisfaction, particularly for women. Here, service-class women were left with the prospect of either ending the relationship or waiting it out. These women are complicit in this dance; even among those who attempted to forward the relationship, few mentioned a willingness to accept the alternative should their forced choice not go the way they wanted. Once a male partner shut down a conversation about advancing the relationship, the negotiation typically came to an end.

But while challenging a well-established gender norm is very difficult, the middle-class women we interviewed demonstrated that it is not impossible. The relationship dance of the middle-class cohabiting couples was one of greater mutual discussions of both partners' desires and time lines for the relationship, contained both more give and take and, at times, a stated willingness to end unions if partners proved not to be on the same page. This difference may result from middle-class women's better prospects, in both the partner and the job market. Perhaps in the not so distant future, these shifts will lead to alterations in the engagement process; that, however, will require that both sexes be comfortable with women being more assertive.

Cohabitation is an arena where normative gender roles are often contested, if not necessarily changed. Because cohabitation is incompletely institutionalized, there is more of an opportunity for women to flip the script or at least modify it a bit. Of course, creating change is a difficult task, even for men (or couples) actively pursuing more egalitarian relationships. Our findings suggest that although contemporary cohabiting relationships are more egalitarian in belief than in practice, an important subset of women increasingly feel empowered enough to act on their own desires on various fronts within their relationships. But the very group willing to modify conventional gendered behavior continues to believe in normative institutions such as marriage. The end result for middle-class cohabitors will often be marriages of relative equity. The future of our service-class couples, in contrast, appears far less likely to lead to equal unions or lasting marriage. But this is not just, or even mainly, due to the fact that couples cohabited. Rather, the processes undergirding their relationships, from where and how they met and progressed into being a couple, to the pace at which they moved in together and the reasons underlying that transition, to how couples discussed (or didn't) the division of domestic labor, birth control, and the future, contribute to the diverging outcomes of the college-educated and their more moderately educated peers, more generally.[18]

In Chapter 8, we discuss what our findings mean for the future of relationships, marriage, and the growing disparities between the family-building processes of the more and less educated. We review our findings, detail the important ways that couples from more and less advantaged backgrounds communicate, negotiate, and resolve differences, and ask what role cohabitation may serve in weakening or strengthening the institution of marriage and conventional gender roles. We conclude with an assessment of how the increased prevalence of cohabitation has altered American's relationships.

8

Cohabitation Nation?

The Role of Gender and Social Class in Relationship Progression

Cohabitation is often portrayed in the news media as a stepping stone toward marriage. Our goal in this book is to explore how cohabitation—the "new normal" stage in courtship—unfolds differently for today's young adults from the service and middle class, as well as how those processes are gendered. While living together often segued into engagement and marriage-planning for our middle-class couples, few of our service-class couples were progressing toward that end, or if they were it was at a much slower and bumpier pace. Disparities emerged from the very start of their new relationships and frequently set our service-class and college-educated couples on radically different trajectories. Service-class couples tended to move in together relatively early on in their new relationships, frequently because of financial difficulties or housing need. Rapid transitions into cohabitation often set the stage for high levels of relationship conflict, communication differences, and contraceptive mishaps, sometimes making the disadvantages outweigh the benefits of cohabiting. Among our college-educated couples, in contrast, the move to shared living generally occurred more gradually and was often viewed as an improvement over dating and living apart.

Cohabitation allows couples to simulate what marriage might be like—though the most economically strained respondents were often experiencing the most fiscally challenging, low quality, and poorly matched unions. If shared living provides a trial run for marriage, it is no wonder that many—both men and women—express doubts about whether "wedlock" is the right step to take. Given our findings, we argue that at least among the less educated, cohabitation is weakening the institution of marriage, because it reveals how arduous it can be to remain together "for better, for worse, for richer, for poorer" when it seems that the future holds more economic deprivation than wealth.[1] Among our college-educated respondents, in contrast, better financial trajectories combined with supportive family, friends, and community led to a brighter view of the future. As a result, rather than challenging the institution of marriage, cohabitation is part of the process. Norms regarding the optimal location of childbearing remained broadly accepted, with marriage expected to precede childbearing. Men accepted marriage as part of the progression into adulthood. And college-educated women continued to attach great importance to marriage, even while valuing independence.

Rapidly changing gender roles are, in part, implicated in these growing class differences. Fighting against established gender norms (such as customs that only men may propose or that contraception and housework are a woman's responsibility) can be an uphill battle. Such social norms typically empower men, because overturning them requires active cooperation and willingness to change on the part of both partners. Many of our couples aspired to more egalitarian relationships. But acceptance of women's greater role in decision making was stronger among our middle-class couples than among the service class. College-educated women exhibited more agency than their less educated counterparts, on various fronts, and middle-class men were more receptive to their female partners' opinions and desires than were service-class men. College-educated women, for example, more frequently initiated talk of moving in together or marriage. Traditional gender divisions were generally more firmly established among the service class, and less educated women often expressed frustration about their inability to attain their desires. As a result, gender conflict emerged more consistently among service-class couples. But on some fronts, gender norms remained solidly entrenched. Both men and women assigned the prerogative of initiating dating and proposing marriage to men. Women who sought to take control of their romantic lives often did so indirectly, or "set the stage" and then left the final step to their male partners. Many of the women we interviewed were able to persuade their partners to do as they desired. But most couples seemed to feel that the man had the final say.

Our study has implications for contemporary debates about marriage, new family forms, and gender equality. Many of the changes that distinguish the family-building patterns of the more and less educated are driven by differential access to resources—decent earnings or stable wages, health insurance coverage, housing support, and educational capital—that are the foundation for stable relationships. The service-class couples we interviewed were also far more likely to be living with children than were our middle-class couples, something that tends to make the household division of labor more unequal and decreases relationship satisfaction.[2] Our focus on relationship processes, however, allows us to suggest additional reasons beyond structural explanations as to why marriage remains the norm among college-educated young adults who cohabit while for the less advantaged, marriages are less common and more unstable. Nonetheless, the divergent trajectories of the more and less advantaged couples are not inevitable. We conclude by discussing policies that might help stabilize relationships, allow young adults to take more time in selecting romantic partners, and increase the likelihood that relationships will be formalized in marriage, if that is their ultimate goal.

MIDDLE-CLASS SATISFACTION, SERVICE-CLASS WOES

Why are college-educated couples headed down the aisle, while relationships among service-class couples are stalled, or in some cases, headed out the door? As we have noted, the financial underpinnings shaping the experiences of our two groups clearly differed in important ways. Our less educated respondents had fewer resources on which to draw as they navigated their relationships than did their college-educated counterparts.[3] But material circumstances alone cannot adequately account for the differences we observed. Nor were cultural orientations that dissimilar; both groups valued good relationships. Rather, we argue that the strategies utilized within relationships by our service- and middle-class respondents, and the cultural toolkits men and women drew on to solve problems, helped create and reinforce different class trajectories. Social class differences in the accumulation of relationship-enhancing skills begin early in life and increase over time.[4] Compared to their middle-class counterparts, service-class cohabitors often failed to demonstrate mastery of important life skills increasingly central in both contemporary relationships and the work world: communication, cooperation, and negotiation.[5] As a result, not only did our middle-class cohabitors have more in the way of structural supports, but they also exhibited more of the "soft skills" required to help them reach for and achieve what they desired. We distilled three important factors that differentiated the relationship experiences of our service-class and middle-class cohabitors.

Communication Skills

For starters, our middle-class cohabitors demonstrated greater facility with the give and take that is an important part of ensuring couple-level satisfaction in relationships than did our service-class couples. In plain language, our more advantaged cohabitors simply had better communication skills. One particularly notable aspect of the discourse of our more highly educated respondents was college-educated women's confidence in asking for what they wanted.[6] This was evidenced in various ways among middle-class women, from their ability to ask for more help with the housework, discuss their desires to utilize more than one contraceptive method to allay fears of unintended pregnancy, or initiate discussions of where their relationships were heading. Middle-class cohabiting men were more receptive to their partners' requests, such as taking on more of the housework when asked, than were their service-class counterparts. These men frequently acknowledged that such appeals were "fair" and reasonable in the context of maintaining positive relationships.[7] There was far less evidence of direct discussion, negotiation, and compromise among our service-class couples. Rather, service-class men continuously demonstrated their interpersonal power, in terms of the performance of housework, their assumption that pregnancy prevention was the woman's job, and in shutting down discussions regarding the future of their relationships. Less educated women were left to concede to their partners' decisions or leave the relationship, and several acknowledged that this negatively affected their relationship satisfaction and feelings of being valued. Because communication is such an essential part of any relationship, it is therefore not surprising that middle-class men and women expressed much greater levels of relationship satisfaction and were more likely to be engaged or talking about marriage than were their service-class counterparts.

Perhaps the clearest demonstration that communication skills diverged across our social class groups was when couples, or one member of a couple, began the process of assessing where the relationship was heading. College-educated women were often quite intentional in getting partners to discuss their futures together and to consider whether (as well as when) an engagement or a wedding would happen. Middle-class men frequently were on the same page in thinking about the future and marriage as their partners, though some did attempt to shut down such serious conversations. And if college-educated women were not getting what they desired from their relationships, they seemed more willing to walk away from their current unions. Even though service-class women often hinted at wanting to be engaged or grumbled about wanting a sign of commitment from their partners, they demonstrated far less agency in directly asking for what they wanted, and far less satisfaction with what they ended up receiving, than did college-educated women.[8] While men ultimately still retained the prerogative—and what both men and women seemed to consider an inalienable right—to forward the relationship through a proposal, we find an important subset of women who increasingly feel empowered to act on their own romantic desires. But these women are disproportionately found among our highly educated women.

Support from Family and Friends

A second way in which our service- and middle-class couples differed was in the extent to which their social networks supported their unions. Our college-educated respondents reported receiving substantial amounts of social and sometimes economic support from family and friends at numerous relationship stages, something which was mentioned far less often by the service-class couples. Our findings provide some tantalizing hints as to where social class discrepancies in union outcomes (such as marriage) start. The middle-class couples we interviewed often met in college or were introduced through strong interpersonal ties—such as a best friend or sibling. Not only did this increase their chances of partnering with someone from a similar social class background but the meeting locale also signaled future success—higher occupational status and earnings. Purchasing several cocktails at a swanky bar downtown or subscribing to an expensive gym membership said something about their prospective mates' cultural and financial capital. Service-class cohabitors, in contrast, often met in more anonymous settings, such as dive bars or free online venues, locations that were often described by our respondents themselves as somewhat risky; these relationships generally received lower levels of social support or approval from their family and friends. Research has found that strong ties may facilitate the development of more trusting bonds and further relationship progression.[9] Weak ties diversify the kinds of people with whom individuals interact, which can result in lower levels of perceived social support for their relationships.[10] Service-class couples were often of different racial or ethnic backgrounds, or differed in their parental status or age group, which some said influenced how parents or close friends perceived their relationships.

The social and friendship networks of our couples also provided examples of life trajectories that differed by social class. Both service- and middle-class cohabitors mentioned that attending a wedding often spurred them to think about or discuss marriage. But attending weddings occurred far more frequently among our college-educated couples, given that marriages are far more likely nowadays among those with college degrees. The middle-class couples had far more practicing models to emulate. Our service-class couples more often mentioned friends getting divorced or breaking up than marrying.[11] We also see evidence that middle-class respondents continued to receive familial encouragement, as well as fiscal support, to move a relationship along into an engagement and then marriage. The parents of our college-educated couples often formed quasi-in-law relationships with their children's partners and provided "gentle nudges" to encourage couples to take the next step. Others volunteered to pay for a part of the wedding (such as the cake or the gown). In yet another nod to changes in roles expected of men, several of our engaged college-educated men mentioned how their parents volunteered to share the financial burden of a wedding, signaling their approval of this step in the relationship.[12] Even though our service-class respondents sometimes joked that a parent was nagging them to marry, very seldom did they indicate that such nudges came with offers of financial assistance. While young couples with more in the way of family support—both economically and emotionally—are better able to wed, our service-class couples, who are largely on their own without a safety net, were loath to dive into marriage without such backing. Lacking the assistance received by many middle-class couples, service-class respondents worried that they would not be able to make a successful go of marriage.[13]

Planning Ahead

The third factor that distinguished our service-class couples from their college-educated counterparts is that the middle-class couples seemed more often to be "planners."[14] Their future versus present orientation is demonstrated on various fronts, from their sense of timing about relationship progression, to intentions to delay fertility until the time was right, to discussions about the sequencing of particular events (such as weddings) around employment transitions. The college-educated, particularly the women, often had distinct time tables in mind about when certain events should take place. Having a blueprint for how they wanted their lives to unfold provided many of our respondents with benchmarks that they used to measure their life progress. Many of our college-educated respondents, for example, had an implicit sense of how much time they wanted to elapse before becoming sexually intimate, and quite a few mentioned feeling like there was a "right" amount of time to be involved before considering cohabitation. Furthermore, when couples were asked about their future plans, the middle class had readier answers regarding when a proposal "should" occur. Many middle-class individuals also mentioned wanting to be married for a period of time before having children. Finally, among most of the college-educated couples that had gotten engaged, there was a clear plan for a wedding, to take place within a year to two of getting engaged.[15]

Our service-class respondents less often articulated clear plans for their lives, as individuals or as couples. Their difficulty planning may be a reflection of how constrained their lives actually were. For example, many sought to defer serious talk of marriage until after they had attained particular markers they deemed to be necessary prerequisites— school completion and obtaining a stable job. But many had been attempting to attain a degree for considerable lengths of time and were uncertain when they would finish. One of our service-class women most desirous of getting engaged mentioned that her partner, Eric, wanted to complete his degree first, then noted that he'd already been working on it for six years and had another few to go. In fact, quite a few of our service-class couples were still seeking to take those last few classes that would provide them with the long-sought-after credential in their late twenties and early thirties. Other service-class respondents wanted to find their "dream jobs" before tying the knot but had only hazy ideas of what those were or how they might find them. Given their circumstances, our service-class respondents often ended up reacting to events, such as an unexpected pregnancy, rather than setting a plan and following it through to its culmination.

Perhaps nowhere is the difference in planning more evident than when it comes to pregnancy and parenting. Whereas most middle-class cohabitors reported having ongoing discussions of contraception, used the most effective means of prevention, and often utilized multiple forms of protection, many of the service-class cohabitors were more laid back about pregnancy prevention, even if they did not want to become parents. Men from service- and middle-class backgrounds also expressed different views about whether marriage should precede childbearing, with college-educated men often quite adamant in their preferences to be married prior to becoming parents. Middle-class men and women both mentioned a desire to be married for a while before adding children to the mix. Many service-class men, in contrast, felt emotionally ready for fatherhood, if not marriage. Whereas the college-educated wanted all of their ducks in a row before becoming parents, service-class men in particular seemed more comfortable taking things as they came, even if that meant that events were out of conventional sequence or were not optimal outcomes. Some service-class men even explained that if pregnancy happened, it was meant to happen—casting themselves as captives of fate rather than masters of their destiny. Our middle-class respondents were cognizant that not all always went according to plan, but they expressed confidence that they could modify their behaviors while keeping to their plans—for example, by moving up a wedding to ensure that their child was born to married parents or taking precautions to prevent mistimed pregnancies.

THE INTERSECTION OF ECONOMICS AND VALUES

In the initial chapter of this book, we reference the work of Charles Murray, who argues that the fortunes and futures of the moderately educated are diminished by eroding cultural values, short-term gratification, and inadequate parenting.[16] We have argued that while structural constraints challenged our service-class cohabitors in their pursuit of stable relationships and economic well-being, attitudinal differences played an important role as well. But we do not believe that the majority of our service-class respondents exhibited the "weak wills" that Murray writes about. Neither do we blame their parents for their behaviors.[17] In fact, we would challenge Murray to try making a go at a middle-class existence while juggling near minimum-wage jobs, without considerable familial support.[18]

Rather, by peeling away the layers of our respondents' stories, we have revealed how structural disadvantages often interacted with behavioral factors to make attaining desired life goals more challenging for our less advantaged respondents than for our more educated ones. Service-class couples who demonstrated behaviors similar to their college-educated peers, for example, still experienced greater challenges to attaining their goals. Many were not academically oriented during high school, choosing instead to enter the labor force. But with few job skills, most soon realized that more schooling was required. Most of those pursuing additional schooling in their early twenties or later frequently did so, however, without receiving much guidance or financial assistance from parents. Not all of our college-educated respondents recalled being studious in high school, but those with college-educated parents nevertheless assumed that additional schooling was the next step after high school and generally received assistance, both in terms of know-how and finances, to attend college.

Significant class differences can also be observed in preventing unintended pregnancy. The majority of our service-class women reported being relatively vigilant about utilizing birth control but generally had less access to the most effective (hormonal) methods than their college-educated counterparts, often because of the nature of their jobs. But the stories told by our middle-class respondents also revealed that unanticipated outcomes—such as unplanned pregnancies—were often resolved quite differently among those who went on to obtain college degrees than among our service-class respondents. Whereas Diana and Anthony moved in together and had their baby during her senior year of high school, both Sean and Travis mentioned that their pregnant high-school girlfriends had abortions. This resulted in very different life course trajectories for those men—college attendance and completion, subsequent engagement to a different partner, and plans to defer childbearing until after marriage.[19] Finally, for many of our struggling service-class couples, particularly those with children, existing tax policies served as a disincentive to formalizing their union via marriage. In particular, marriage was thought to reduce access to student loans, ultimately making a college degree more difficult to attain.[20]

There were, of course, service-class couples in our sample that exhibited poor decision-making skills and had difficulties remaining employed. Many worked consistently, though at jobs with very high turn-over rates. The couples that exhibited the weakest attachment to the labor force or the most fatalistic attitudes about their future often struggled with mental health issues or addictions. Sometimes these issues were being treated, but frequently they were not. Our middle-class respondents had better prospects for dealing with adverse mental health situations, largely due to their employment-based health insurance coverage, and many of the women worked in health-related industries. In general, however, we believe that the actions of a relatively small number of our service-class respondents should not be viewed as representative of the whole group.

Communication skills, ability to plan, and family support are not always absent among service-class respondents. Nor are such skills uniformly bestowed upon those who graduate from college. Rather, the factors of growing up poor, class-based parenting styles, and available financial resources are all associated with levels of efficaciousness.[21] That said, there is likely something about having a bachelor's degree that reinforces preexisting cultural and economic advantages. A university education exposes young adults to ideas of egalitarianism and seeks to instill problem-solving and critical thinking skills.[22] It may not be surprising, then, that college-educated young women are more assertive and their male partners willing to exercise greater self-regulation under the guise of fairness, if not feminism.[23] Advantage, furthermore, begets additional advantage. The college educated more often came from married-parent families, and their parents had relatively high levels of educational attainment and earnings themselves.[24] What that means is that not only did the college educated see more successful models of relationships while growing up, but their parents had greater financial means to help them attend college as well as smooth their paths to marriage. Finally, being successful in college requires time management skills, the ability to prioritize tasks, fulfill requirements, and execute a plan.[25] We find that our college-educated cohabitors extended those skills into their personal lives—determining whether and when a relationship should continue or end, formulating a plan, and then taking the necessary steps to attain their life goals. The economic challenges and uncertainty facing our less educated respondents, in contrast, often undermined the ability to engage in planful behavior so commonplace among our middle-class respondents.

THE FUTURE OF COHABITATION

It is unclear what role cohabitation will play in family formation in the future, as it is something of a moving target. It remains an incomplete institution. To be sure, cohabitation has diffused across the population. It is now quite prevalent among the college educated and has become the normative union formation pattern among the less educated. As a result, the number of individuals who have ever cohabited has grown at an incredibly rapid pace over the past few decades. But the roles, obligations, permanence and stability, and disposition of cohabiting unions are unfolding unevenly across the U.S. population.

We anticipate that the proportion of college-educated cohabitors will continue to grow, as living together outside of marriage becomes increasingly normative and acceptable. If the patterns revealed in our study persist, cohabitation will serve as a precursor to marriage for most of the college educated who enter into a cohabiting union, with a relatively small group of the most advantaged remaining in cohabiting unions for extended lengths of time. It is among the moderately educated or less that we expect to see the greatest shifts in the role played by cohabitation. This is the group that most often mentioned housing difficulties and financial necessity as reasons for why they moved in with their partner, as an alternative, as it were, to dating and living apart. We interviewed our respondents before the 2008 start of the Great Recession. The financial difficulties caused by a continued decline in blue collar jobs for men, the subprime mortgage crisis, rents rising at a much faster rate than wages, as well as high levels of nonmarital births disproportionately impacted the service class.[26] As a result, we expect the proportions of service-class adults who cohabit, or engage in serial (repeat) cohabitation, to grow. But perhaps more important, we expect that cohabitation may also increasingly serve as a substitute or alternative to marriage among the less advantaged, especially if it remains as difficult to attain the standard of living deemed necessary to "tie the knot."

As cohabitation becomes even more widespread, how might gender roles change in these unions? Many of our respondents viewed cohabitation as a way to avoid some of the traditionally gendered constraints of marriage (the "ball and chain" discussed by Rhonda, or what Diana saw as "fancy handcuffs"). And in fact, studies of cohabitors from the 1980s and 1990s found that cohabitors engaged in more egalitarian sharing than did their married counterparts.[27] But the movement toward more egalitarian gender roles seems to have plateaued in the mid-1990s, at the same time that cohabitation was becoming increasingly commonplace.[28] Cohabitors of today hold somewhat more conventional attitudes toward gender than those who rebelled against patriarchal and traditional roles in the late 1980s and early 1990s. Nonetheless, our results suggest that gender role ideology among cohabitors differs by social class, especially among men. College-educated men held greater expectations for equality on the domestic front than did their service-class counterparts. Our findings indicate that conventional gender norms are more often challenged and changed among middle-class couples, and that college-educated men and women were more comfortable doing the negotiations necessary to achieve egalitarian relationships.

Despite evidence to the contrary, the majority of young adults see living together as the optimal way to "divorce proof" relationships and ensure that they are good for the long run.[29] Yet media portrayals of cohabitation as the "new normal" still essentially utilize a middle-class-centric lens. Many news stories feature cohabitors whose relationships progress rather seamlessly from dating, to cohabitation, to marriage. Our *Glamour* blogger, for example, whom we profiled in Chapter 1, dated her partner for two years before they moved in together, got engaged soon after, married, and then honeymooned in the Caribbean. The odds are that she and her partner will live happily ever after, thanks to a good education, a decent income, and a network of friends and family to support her union. While middle-class cohabitors like her are, in general, in a good place, the relationship outlook is much bleaker among the moderately educated service class. Of course, not all cohabitors, particularly among our service-class couples, aspired to marriage. A handful considered themselves "permanently nonmarried," which they viewed as a perfectly fine alternative to traditional marriage. Still, most of our service-class respondents expressed a desire to get married someday. For many of them, cohabitation often seemed to be a kind of limbo, and, for the unlucky few who would prefer to separate but could not afford to do so, living together even may be a type of purgatory. Their cohabiting unions were less likely to transition into marriage, and often resulted in unintended pregnancies or births. Their relationship challenges reverberated across multiple generations, and shaped intimate trajectories and life opportunities for adult partners and their children. So it is important to contemplate what might help those among the service class achieve and maintain relationships as stable and rewarding as those that their middle-class counterparts attained.

Improving Relationship Satisfaction among the Service Class

One cannot check out at a grocery store without seeing numerous lifestyle magazines, many claiming to provide the keys to a successful relationship. Headlines like "10 Tricks to Blow His Mind" or "The Chicken Dish That Will Make Him Propose" may be useful for some.[30] But we do not believe that tips for individual kitchens (or bedrooms) will be enough to help achieve real change. Therefore, we would like to advance some suggestions for how public policies, federal and state laws, and social institutions can help strengthen contemporary relationships and yield greater security for today's young adults.

Many cohabitors assert that they value marriage and expect to marry in the future, but are not in a good enough financial positions to contemplate legalizing their union at the present time. Large numbers also mentioned that well-paying jobs are few and hard to find. Numerous scholars have argued that the decline in jobs for less educated men has been particularly damning for marriage rates among the service class. Always more gender-traditional than their middle-class counterparts, less educated men may be clinging ever more tightly to the last vestiges of the breadwinner role—not sharing in the housework while maintaining control over the tempo of relationship progression—even as their ability to be good providers has diminished. Work was historically a way for moderately educated men to prove their worth. But in our current service economy, there is less opportunity to fulfill such a role, due to the decline of jobs that pay "breadwinner" wages. At the same time, large proportions of service-class women are working for pay, even if they have children, in order to help make ends meet. Many resent their male partners' unwillingness to share more of the work at home and are increasingly seeing marriage as a bad bargain for them.

What can possibly be done about the economic challenges facing today's young adults? In recent years much attention has focused on how adults, even those working forty hours, are not earning enough to ensure a basic standard of living, thereby leaving individuals (and their families) to rely on government programs for supplementary assistance.[31] Our respondents were often earning more than the minimum wage but still struggled to make ends meet. They often were burdened with education loans and credit card bills, the high cost of rent, and frequent turn over in jobs as they pursued something better or juggled multiple pursuits. Even if they were childless, full-time near minimum-wage jobs did not pay enough to allow them to make ends meet.[32] Advocates for a living wage, one that can meet basic needs to maintain a safe, decent standard of living within the community where a person resides, have argued for the passage of local ordinances that will adjust minimum hourly earnings to a standard deemed more adequate for family survival.[33] In the past few years, the push for a living wage has spread across the country, with some states and municipalities setting minimum wages above the national requirement.[34] Seattle, for example, recently moved to an $11 per hour minimum wage.[35] New York is set to raise the minimum wage to $15 per hour for all state employees by 2018, while Boston raised the minimum wage for home care workers to $15 per hour.[36] But passage of such ordinances face numerous challenges from businesses concerned about their bottom dollar, who argue that such high wages will increase unemployment by reducing their ability to hire workers. Furthermore, most such laws have been limited to narrow employee segments and do not cover the vast majority of our respondents, who work in a variety of low-paid jobs. Nonetheless, the debate over what constitutes a living wage, in conjunction with growing attention to income inequality, has resulted in a growing political constituency seeking to address the need for what used to be termed a "family wage."

Housing costs are also a frequent source of concern for our respondents, though more so for the less educated than among those with college degrees. Experts suggest that households spend no more than 30% of their income on rent, but in 2006, nearly half of Ohio renters were exceeding that standard.[37] Our respondents were no different. In 2005, when we were in the middle of conducting our interviews, the median cost of rent in Columbus, Ohio, was $803.[38] On the basis of their reported household incomes, approximately half of service-class couples and five of our middle-class couples would have found themselves significantly burdened by the cost of rent. Many of our couples economized by living with additional adults—roommates, friends, even siblings. This was quite common among our service-class couples, fourteen of whom reported initially sharing their home with another adult. Other couples found themselves further challenged because they also had children, which required more space; fourteen of our service-class couples (not necessarily the same ones as those who lived with others) had children of one or both partners living with them at least part of the time, as did four of our middle-class couples.

The need for affordable housing among service-class young adults is considerable. But the building of affordable housing has largely stalled.[39] Although mainly seen only in the largest cities, incentivizing local developers to build more studio and "micro" apartments throughout the country would likely hold great appeal, especially among millennials who prefer to rent rather than buy.[40] Still, this would not provide a solution for couples with children as such small spaces frequently have occupancy limits. Furthermore, several of our respondents resorted to moving in with a partner because finding a roommate was too challenging. While dating apps have proliferated over the past decade, there has been little expansion in providing services for those looking to match with a compatible roommate. Sites do exist, but those who have not attended a residential college may be less aware of them. Then again, many of our couples may question the feasibility of maintaining separate apartments and paying individually for rent, utilities, and other living costs if they are spending most of their free time together and could economize by living together.

Housing costs were not the only factor expediting the move to shared living among the service class. Unexpected pregnancies precipitated the transition to shared living among several of our younger couples, while a few more discovered they were pregnant shortly after moving in together. Yet another way to help service-class couples achieve their personal, professional, and relationship goals would be an increased emphasis on encouraging the use of long-lasting contraception, as well as ensuring that accessing the most effective forms of contraception are easy and convenient. In *Generation Unbound,* Isabel Sawhill advocates giving young adults ready access to LARCs (long-acting reversible contraception), which include IUDs and implants. Those who actually *want* to start a family must take steps to get pregnant, rather than taking steps to prevent conception. The result of providing such an option has been evaluated in several locations. The Colorado Family Planning Initiative provided birth control at no cost to young, low-income women, with LARCs included as an option at various family planning clinics statewide. The initiative resulted in reductions in fertility rates among 20 to 24 year olds, as well as declines in the abortion rate.[41] The St. Louis CHOICE Project also offered no-cost reversible contraception to participants for several years, with a goal of increasing the utilization of LARCs such as the IUD and decreasing unintended pregnancy in the area. Participants in the study were substantially more likely to choose long-acting methods than were teens and young adults nationally, and the mean annual rates of pregnancy, birth, and abortion among CHOICE participants were far lower than rates for sexually active women of similar ages nationally.[42] The evidence suggests that educating women about long-acting reversible contraception, and providing it at no cost, reduced unintended pregnancy and abortion rates substantially. Would such an approach work with the cohabiting women we interviewed? The evidence indicates that it very well could, given adequate education and, of course, ensuring that it was affordable (or providing it at no cost).

The enactment of the Affordable Care Act (ACA), with its goal of covering contraceptives as preventative medicine and requiring insurance providers to cover contraception with no copay began a process of reducing the barriers to contraceptive usage experienced by many women like those in our sample. Yet questions remain regarding how accessible such coverage will be. Health insurance is still often employment based, which presents a challenge to young women who often cobble together several part-time jobs in order to make ends meet or work at jobs where taxes may not be paid (as was the case for some of the women employed as nannies). While Title X clinics were available to all of the women in our sample, in recent years political pressure to cut back on funding for such clinics have posed challenges to their continued existence. Over half of Ohio clients served in Title X-supported centers utilized Planned Parenthood clinics; recent years have seen immense political pressure to eliminate the federal funding Planned Parenthood clinics receive to fulfill their mission, which will likely leave many young women searching for contraceptive care.[43]

In Ohio, women who lacked health care coverage could take advantage of the Medicaid expansion as of 2013 (available for women with incomes below 138% of the poverty), as well as expanded access to private insurance. Medicaid would have aided over half of the service-class women we interviewed, who alone or with their children made less than the threshold in the mid-2000s.[44] But while the passage of the ACA means many more women have access to health coverage, doctor's visits often still require payment up front, depending upon the amount of the insurance deductible. And, calls to "repeal" (and sometimes "replace") such legislation following the 2016 elections put the future of health insurance, particularly for the service class, in doubt. Furthermore, recent Supreme Court rulings exempt some employers from covering contraception, meaning that while some women will have excellent access to birth control, others will continue to struggle to access safe, effective reproductive health services. In addition to reducing the financial strains for couples that result from unexpected pregnancies, better access to long-acting contraception might give service couples more time to get to know one another before feeling the pressure to move in together, by reducing the likelihood of unintended pregnancies. The results of the 2016 election cast doubt on the promise of contraceptive access and affordability for all women of reproductive age, something our findings suggest will disproportionately impact low-income and service-class women.

COHABITATION NATION

Most Americans aspire to having loving, long-term relationships and strongly believe that love is the main foundation of marriage. The majority of young adults who have never been married say they would like to get married and start a family at some point. But today's young adults are not rushing to the altar, and the U.S. marriage rate is at an all-time low. Our study provides a window into understanding the factors challenging the formation and progression of relationships among American young adults. The insights provided by the 61 couples we interviewed, who offered us an insider's perspective into their lives, highlight the challenges facing young Americans in the early years of the 21st century.

Growing levels of inequality are shaking the foundations of American society, including marriage and the family. In a more unequal society, it is perhaps inevitable that the families formed by young people from more and less advantaged backgrounds would also be diverging. Our evidence suggests that the relationship outcomes of young people with more advantages, such as a college degree, a supportive family, and good job prospects look far more rosy than do the family prospects of young adults from more economically constrained backgrounds. While many gender norms remain firmly entrenched, college-educated women's assertiveness, and their male partners' willingness to compromise, at least to some degree, generally leads to a relatively high degree of satisfaction within their unions. But the successful trajectories of their relationships began before these couples ever met. The private safety net that middle-class families often provide for their adult children may not ensure their finding love and happiness in partnership, but it certainly does ease the way and make finding secure and stable relationships more likely. The majority of our college-educated couples followed what was once a normative relationship progression with an intervening modern twist—cohabitation. For most of these couples, cohabitation was but a stopover on the way down the aisle.

But for young adults from less advantaged family backgrounds, family support for their relationships and lives was scant, and public supports limited. Their attempts to navigate the vicissitudes of life made forming stable relationships challenging. Cohabitation was initially attractive and even advantageous for less educated couples, who often relied on the economic boost that sharing the rent provided. But the long-term risks of shared living were higher. Service-class men's more traditional attitudes toward gender seems to lower relationship quality. These couples were less likely to share domestic chores equitably, less likely to jointly negotiate plans such as engagement and marriage, and more likely to experience unintended pregnancies—all of which posed risks for the long-term success of the relationship. Furthermore, these men generally could not earn a "family wage," further exacerbating tensions and deferring transitions into adult roles. As a result, far more of these couples remained living together for considerable lengths of time. Many had experienced the dissolution of their parents' marriages, and those who had children were also setting the stage for yet another generation of disadvantage.

Short-term economic uncertainty undermines long-term relationships, stability, and commitment. It diminishes aspirations for the future. That was clearly evident among the young adults we interviewed. Even those who described the early stages of their romance with dewy eyes quickly fell back to earth when bank accounts ran low, hours at work were cut, or household chores piled up because of time away from home juggling work and school. Relationships can provide individuals with nurturance and support, but love alone is not enough. Good economic fortunes seem to be an increasing prerequisite to help facilitate transitions into marriage among those interested in that goal. What this means is that, for the moderately educated, cohabitation has become a waiting room, and many of its occupants wait indefinitely for a time when their financial situations allow them to either marry or separate.

So, what to make of this great divide? Despite rising shares of young adults moving in with their romantic partners, we see no evidence that cohabitation in the United States will become similar to living together in Canada or Western Europe—as essentially the equivalent of marriage. For one thing, American's religious underpinnings make it unlikely that marriage will lose its place as a sacred or special type of union any time soon. Even if they are not religious, though, many American young adults, including most of those we interviewed, believe in marriage as the pinnacle of a love relationship. For most, even if marriage was not currently achievable, it was aspirational. Greater institutional and political supports may be necessary to help launch many of our less economically advantaged couples on the pathway to marriage, by helping them earn a degree or expanding the number of jobs that pay a living wage. But for most, the desire to marry was already firmly entrenched. Continued inattention to the factors that prevent many young people from achieving their marital desires, however, will serve to further weaken marriage and strengthen cohabitation as an increasingly attractive alternative.

Interview Guide

Probes are in *italic*.

I. FAMILY HISTORY

I'd like to start off by getting a brief history of your family as you were growing up.

1. Where were you born? Tell me what your family was like growing up? Were you living with **both** parents? How did it change? *People to cover: biological parents, step-parents or parent's partners, siblings, step-/ half-siblings, grandparents who lived with/cared for them.* **Pay particular attention to marital history of parents.**
2. When you were little what kind of family did you picture having when you grew up?

II. CURRENT LIFE: SCHOOL AND WORK HISTORY

What were you doing after you turned 18? And what are you doing **now?**

1. Did you continue SCHOOL? How far would you like to go? How do you pay for it?
2. What about WORK? What kinds of jobs did you have? *What are things you yourself feel are most important in a job? Why? What do you see yourself doing in the future? What things have led you to want to be a ____? If you could arrange things just the way you wanted, what would you prefer to be doing—working at your present job, working at another job, or not working at all? Why?*

3. Where do you see FAMILY fitting into your life? What do you want as far as family goes? *How do you intend to balance work and family?*

4. Do you have any plans for CHILDREN?

5. What about MARRIAGE?

6. What would you say is your #1 PRIORITY right now?

III. DATING HISTORY/RELATIONSHIP PROGRESSION

We're going to talk now about your relationships.

1. Have you ever lived with anybody else?

2. How did you meet your partner? Where was it? When? (*Try for month, year*) Who initiated dating?

3. How did you spend time together? How often in a given week?

4. How long had you known each other before you decided to move in together? Who brought up actually living together? (*PROGRESSION: Was it initially staying over a few nights (#), more than a few? Whose place? What about clothes, space? How quickly, in their words, did the relationship progress?*)

5. SO, WHY DID YOU DECIDE TO LIVE TOGETHER?

6. Were there other things going on at the time that influenced your decision?

7. Where did you two first live together?

8. Did you and your partner discuss any plans for the future when you moved in together? *If Yes, WHO brought it up? Did you both agree in WORDS?*

9. Did you discuss marriage? *Did you want to? If Yes, WHO brought it up?*

IV. RELATIONSHIP EXPECTATIONS/SATISFACTION WITH COHABITING

1. What did you think living together would be like? Was it like what you thought it would be?

2. What chores do you actually do? What chores does your partner actually do?

3. Have there been changes in your relationship with ____ since you moved in together?

4. From your point of view, what are the BEST things about living together?

5. What are the WORST things about living together?

6. How do you think your life would be different if you were **dating** but **not living with** your partner?

7. Who controls the money in your home? Do either of you have veto power over the other one's purchase?

8. How do you think your life would be different if you were **married** to your partner?

9. What does "marriage" mean to you? What does "marriage" mean **for you personally?**

10. Has living together changed the way you think about marriage? HOW SO?

11. Do you feel like you're ready to have children right now? Why or why not? What do you think is the ideal time for having children?

If They Have Children

12. Tell me a little about what happened when you/your partner found out that you were/she was pregnant.

13. Either before or after you/your partner became pregnant, have you/your partner been worried that you were/she was pregnant, or thought you/she might be? Tell me a little about that.

14. Do you feel like you're ready to have more children with your partner? Why or why not? When do you think is the ideal time for having children?

15. Are you and your partner trying to have children now?

For All

16. Many couples in relationships use birth control when they're not sure about having kids. Are either of you using birth control right now? When did you last talk with your partner about birth control? Tell me about that. When did you first talk about birth control? Tell me about that.

17. Even when people use birth control it sometimes fails. If you/your partner got pregnant right now, how do you think you would react? How do you think your partner would react? How would your family react? Have the two of you talked about what you would do?

18. Have you ever been worried that you/your partner were pregnant, or thought you might be? Have you/partner ever been pregnant? Tell me a little bit more about that.

19. Do you think people should be married before having children? Why or why not?

20. What about your partner? What do they think?

21. What do you see as the main differences between cohabitation and marriage?

22. What is marriage for? Does marriage mean different things for women as opposed to men? Why or why not? What does it mean for each?

23. What would have to happen for you two to get married?

Let them know you are reaching the end of the interview.

24. Over the last few months, how have you and your partner covered your living costs? Are you getting any kinds of assistance?

25. How satisfied are you with your relationship right now? WHY?

26. Where do you see your relationship going in the future? Do you think your partner feels the same way?

Do they want to add anything else?

Methods and Sample Information

Data for the qualitative themes unpacked in this book are from semi-structured, in-depth interviews with 30 service-class and 31 middle-class heterosexual couples who were living in a large metropolitan area (Columbus, Ohio) between 2004 and 2006.[1] We conducted these interviews with both members of each couple simultaneously but in different rooms; this enabled us to assess partner similarities and differences in responses. Our project obtained approval from the Institutional Review Board at the university we both were at when we began this project (The Ohio State University's main campus in Columbus, Ohio), and each participant signed a consent form denoting their agreement to participate in our study. We also provided each couple with monetary compensation ($50 per couple) for their participation. Interviews took between one to two and a half hours, were digitally recorded, and transcribed verbatim.[2]

All respondents were between the ages of 18 and 36, the prime family formation years when young adults make key decisions about work, marriage, and fertility. Couples were eligible if they reported sharing a residence for at least three months.[3] Respondents who had another residence in addition to the one with his or her partner were not eligible for the study.[4]

Interviews were held in varying locations. Sharon Sassler often conducted interviews in her rather messy office, but at other times we utilized empty classrooms, borrowed others' offices, and pilfered conference rooms. Most of the individuals we interviewed were engaging and friendly, and enjoyed chatting about their lives. Others were quieter but often revealed information that added profound richness to our knowledge about cohabitors. As with any large group of individuals, a few characters provided some unexpected moments. Several of the male cohabitors hit on their interviewer (despite the presence of their girlfriends in a nearby room) or expressed misogynistic views; one young man revealed his chest, where his girlfriend had written her name in his chest hair using a depilatory (a territorial marker if ever there was one). Some of the women were under the impression that we were social workers and asked us to weigh in on their relationships, a task which we deflected. When one young woman almost cried out her contact lens in discussing her relationship uncertainty, we provided tissues. After their interviews were over, we also offered information regarding school enrollment and funding to some, and advice about how to reduce the nausea that sometimes ensues from taking the birth control pill to others.

In all, we did as much as was ethically responsible to keep the respondents talking. We viewed our job as making the respondents comfortable enough to talk about anything with us. Although both of us were married at the time we conducted our interviews, we removed our wedding rings to avoid having our respondents think we were promoting marriage. Our strategies to encourage respondents to tell us about the most intimate details of their lives seemed to work. Talk they did. The 122 interviews resulted in 4,013 single-spaced pages of transcripts.

DETERMINING COUPLES' SOCIAL CLASS

Educational attainment, occupation, mobility opportunities, and earnings were used to distinguish our two class groups, which for the sake of simplicity we designated as *service class* and *middle class*. Some scholars, such as family demographer and sociologist Andrew Cherlin, utilize the term "moderately educated" to characterize the group we classify as *service class*. Our service-class respondents generally had some college education or less. We initially sought out our service-class sample by posting signs at one of the country's largest community colleges. Research on community college students has found that they come from families with fewer economic resources than those who matriculate immediately into four-year schools, are less likely to have been on an academic track in high school, and have lower rates of attaining a college degree than students who attend a four-year institution.[5] Despite the recruiting locale, fewer than half of our service-class respondents were students, and most of them attended part time or intermittently while working at least part time. Several nonstudents who saw the postings or were told of the study by an acquaintance also contacted us; we limited referrals to one per couple. Data collection for the service-class sample took place from July 2004 to April 2005.

The second stage of data collection targeted middle-class cohabitors, also defined predominantly by their level of educational attainment—a college degree. The 31 middle-class couples were recruited primarily through fliers posted in high-end grocery stores, coffee shops, and restaurants, as well as a posting on an online community bulletin board.[6] In five instances, couples were referred to the project by colleagues, friends, or family members of the researchers. Participants in the middle-class sample were interviewed between April 2005 and June 2006.

Of course, defining social class is a thorny methodological issue. It is rarely captured by a single measure, and it is likely that our respondents might not so identify themselves. Furthermore, some of the service-class respondents attending school may complete their degrees and obtain middle-class status as they age; nonetheless, a considerable number of the students in the service-class sample had been attending school sporadically and working on an associate's degree for several years. While obtaining a bachelor's degree in one's late twenties or thirties may improve job prospects, obtaining a college degree "on time" (in one's early twenties) has a different impact on job trajectories, which may also influence marriage timing and readiness to support a family.

Additionally, because many of the respondents are fairly young, income—another criterion—is also not an optimal measure of social class. Among the service-class sample, couples had to be earning a combined income of greater than $18,000 from a source other than public or familial assistance (though some did receive some form of assistance, most commonly through student loans or "loans" from family).[7] Middle-class couples were required to earn a combined income of at least $25,000 to be included in the sample. This level was purposefully lower than that often suggested by typologies or textbooks, because we wanted to be able to include couples where one partner was enrolled in school or staying home with children.[8] Most, however, had incomes that were significantly higher than this floor.

Our sample includes eight couples where one partner had a bachelor's degree while the other partner had some college education, or less. These couples were classified as "service class" or "middle class" based upon the occupation of the partner who differed from the overall group to which the couple was assigned. Among the four couples placed among the service class, none of the degreed partners were working in occupations that required a college degree; instead they were employed in service occupations such as telemarketing. Of the four couples placed in the middle class, nondegreed partners were either financially established and working in occupations similar to their middle-class peers (such as computer network design or as successful business owners) or, in a single instance, the female partner having less education was from a well-off middle-class family. Married couples increasingly are drawn from those with the same educational attainment; educational dissonance is greater among cohabiting couples.

Demographic characteristics of our full sample are presented in Table 1 (see Chapter 1). Middle-class couples were slightly older than service-class couples, with a mean age of 28.3 for middle-class men versus 26.4 for service-class men, and 25.2 for the middle-class women compared with 24.4 for the service-class women. The modal level of education among the service-class couples is some college for each partner (n = 19) and among middle-class couples is a bachelor's degree for each partner (n = 14). Not surprisingly, income levels are quite a bit higher among the middle-class sample, with an average couple-level income of $67,672 versus $38,971 for the service class. Looking at couples' relative earnings highlights the growing importance of women's labor force participation and suggests some potential avenues for discord. Whereas men earn more in thirteen of the service-class and fourteen of the middle-class couples, women earn more than 60% of their partners in six service-class and three middle-class couples. In the remaining couples, both partners contributed relatively equal amounts (with each providing between 40% and 60% of the household income).

As for other attributes of our sample, the majority of the middle-class couples (n = 24) were racially homogamous, but the service-class sample was more racially and ethnically diverse. Five of the service-class couples were racially homogamous minority couples (four black and one Hispanic), while couples of mixed racial and ethnic background (a black woman with a white man, for example) were far more common among our service-class sample (n = 9). The largest number of couples in both samples contained two never-married partners, though six couples in the service-class sample and four in the middle-class contained at least one partner who had been previously married.[9] Parenthood (of one or both partners) was most common among the service-class couples; a total of fourteen service-class couples contained at least one partner who had a child or was currently pregnant, compared to four middle-class couples. In contrast, twenty-seven of the middle-class couples reported that neither partner was a parent. Among the parents, five of the service-class couples and two of the middle-class couples had children together, though for two of the service-class couples the male partner also has a child from a previous relationship. Of note is that male partners who had fathered children with previous partners seldom had the child living in their household for a major portion of the year.

As for how long the couples we interviewed had lived together, our samples reflect disparate outcomes experienced by couples from different social class backgrounds. The service-class sample contains a larger number of couples that have cohabited for two years or more than is found among the middle-class sample. Eight of our service-class couples had been cohabiting for three or more years, compared with only two of our middle-class couples. At the other end of the spectrum, twelve of our middle-class couples had been living together only for three to six months when interviewed, and another twelve had been cohabiting for between a year and two years. Consistent with national data, our service-class sample, then, is more length-biased—containing couples that have lived together for longer durations—than our middle-class group.

Specific Characteristics
of Cohabiting Couples

TABLE A1   SPECIFIC CHARACTERISTICS OF COHABITING SERVICE-CLASS COUPLES

Couple	Age	Race/ Ethnicity	Education Level	Occupation	Work/School Hours (Full Time, Part Time)	Children	Duration to Cohab	Total Time as Couple	Talk of Marriage (At Time of Interview)
Eugene	22	White	Some college	Telemarketer; Stock clerk	FT work	None	4 months	8 months	Not discussing
Susan	20	White & Native American	Some college	Telemarketer	FT work				
Anthony	21	Hispanic	Some college	Freight worker	PT work	They have 1	1 year, 6 months	3 years, 6 months	Have discussed
Diana	19	White	Some college	Retail; bar	PT work				
Ray	31	White	Some college	Bookkeeper	FT work; PT school	None	4.5 months	7 years, 5 months	Engaged
Julie	30	White	Some college	Nanny	PT work; FT school				
Sam	18	White	Some college	Telemarketer	FT work; PT school	She has 3	4 months	8 months	Not discussing
Rhoda	34	Black	Some college	Administrative assistant	FT work; intermittent school				
Jake	26	White	Some college	Computer support	FT work	None	6 months	1 year	Have discussed
Stephanie	23	White	BA	Telemarketer	FT work				

Name	Age	Race	Education	Occupation	Work/School	Children			
Robert	26	White	Some college	Independent book reseller	FT work	None	1 week	2 years	Not discussing
Vanessa	25	Black	BA	Independent book reseller	FT work; intermittent school			3 years, 3 months	
Harry	32	White	Some college	Unemployed	Neither work nor school	She has 2			Seriously discussing
Marta	28	Hispanic	Some college	Gas station clerk	PT work; PT school		3 months		
Andre	25	Latino	Some college	Mortgage processor	FT work	None	1 year, 5 months		Never intend to marry anyone
Stacy	21	White	Some college	Telemarketing asst. manager	FT			2 years, 1 month	
Stan	31	Black	High school	Orderly	FT	He has 1	6.5 months		Seriously discussing
Keisha	30	Black	Some college	Bookkeeper	PT			3 years, 6.5 months	
Vic	28	White	AA	Acquisitions intern	PT work; FT school	She's Pregnant	2 months		Engaged
Carly	18	White	Some college	Library clerk	PT work			6 months	
Mark	31	White	Some college	Stay-at-home father	Neither work nor school	They have 1 and she's pregnant			Engaged
Tracy	30	White	High school	Coffee shop manager	FT Work		6 months	6 years, 6 months	
Adam	28	White	Some college	Unemployed	No work; intermittent school	Each has 1	7 months	3 years, 1 month	Not discussing
Sheryl	29	White	Some college	Waitress	PT work				

(continued)

TABLE A1 *(continued)*

Couple	Age	Race/ Ethnicity	Education Level	Occupation	Work/School Hours (Full Time, Part Time)	Children	Duration to Cohab	Total Time as Couple	Talk of Marriage (At Time of Interview)
Jerry	27	White	BFA	Retail manager	FT work	None	4 months	10 months	Seriously discussing
Natalie	24	White	Some college	Secretary	FT work				
Josh	22	White	Some college	Library clerk	PT work; PT school	None	7.5 months	1 year, 2 months	Not discussing
Patty	18	White	Some college	Barista	PT work				
Bill	34	White	Some college	Lab assistant	PT work; FT school	He has 1, they have 1 together	6 months	6 years, 6 months	Engaged
Maria	32	Hispanic	Some college	Bookkeeper	FT work				
Max	29	Black	Some college	Secretary, coach	FT work; PT school	He has 1	4 years	6 years, 9 months	Seriously discussing
Tameka	29	Black	Some college	Unemployed	FT school				
Shane	22	White	11th grade	Retail	PT work	None	1 year, 11 months	3 years, 9.5 months	Not discussing
Sandra	21	White	Some college	Restaurant shift manager	FT work				
Mitch	25	White	AA	Chef	FT work	None	5 months	6 years, 5 months	Never intend to marry anyone
Beth	23	White	Some college	Nanny	PT work				
Tyrone	25	Black	GED	Postman	FT work	He has 1	5.5 months	8.5 months	Not discussing
Sherry	21	Black	Some college	Waitress	PT work				

Name	Age	Race	Education	Occupation	Work/School	Children			
Brian	22	White	Some college	Mechanic, waiter	PT work; FT school	None	9.5 months	2 years, 4 months	Never intend to marry anyone
Shelly	28	White	Some college	Waitress	PT work; PT school				
Terrell	23	Black	High school	Freight worker	PT work	He has 1, they have 1 together	2 years, 3.5 months	4 years	Have discussed
Aliyah	20	Some College	Some college	Administrative assistant	PT work; FT school				
Chad	24	White	High school	Telecommunications	FT work	None	3.5 months	1 year, 3.5 months	Not discussing
Jackie	24	White	Some college	Social service paraprofessional	FT work; FT school				
Howard	23	White	Some college	Catering waiter	PT work; FT school	None	11.5 months	2 years, 2 months	Not discussing
Vickie	21	White	Some college	Pharmacy technician	FT work; FT school				
Jorge	22	Hispanic	AA	Mortgage processor	FT work	None	7.5 months	11 months	Seriously discussing
Valencia	22	Hispanic	Some college	Unemployed	Neither work nor school				
Ron	33	White	AA	Mortgage processor	FT work	He has 1	5 months	2 years, 11 months	Not discussing
Crystal	21	White	Some college	Exotic dancer	PT work; FT school				

(continued)

TABLE A1 *(continued)*

Couple	Age	Race/ Ethnicity	Education Level	Occupation	Work/School Hours (Full Time, Part Time)	Children	Duration to Cohab	Total Time as Couple	Talk of Marriage (At Time of Interview)
Randy	35	White	Some college	Mechanic, waiter	FT work; PT school	None	2 years, 2 months	5 years, 1 month	Engaged
Ming	29	Asian	Some college	Bookkeeper	PT work; FT school				
Artie	28	White	BA	Computer repair	FT work	None	1 year, 1 month	4 years, 1 month	Have discussed
Brandi	24	White	High school	Government auditor	PT work; FT school				
Eric	23	White and Pacific Islander	Some college	Security guard	PT work; PT school	None	9.5 months	3 years, 3 months	Have discussed
Dawn	22	White	Some college	Fitness center front desk clerk	PT work; PT school				
Simon	25	White	11th grade	Carpenter	FT work	He has 1	6 months	10.5 months	Seriously discussing
Laura	23	White	High school	Waitress	PT work				
Spencer	29	White	Some college	Sound engineer	FT work	He has 1	1 year, 4.5 months	4 years, 4.5 months	Never intend to marry anyone
Brittany	24	White	Some college	Veterinary assistant	PT work; FT school				

TABLE A2   SPECIFIC CHARACTERISTICS OF COHABITING MIDDLE-CLASS COUPLES

Couple	Age	Race/Ethnicity	Education Level	Occupation	Work/School Hours	Children	Duration to Cohab	Total Time as a Couple	Talk of Marriage (At Time of Interview)
Jared	24	White	BA	Mechanical engineer	FT work	None	1 year, 5 months	1 year, 11 months	Engaged
Alisha	24	White	BA	Pricing analyst	FT work				
Edward	23	Black	Some college	Distribution center order-taker	PT work; PT school	They have 1	2 years, 11 months	4 years, 10 months	Have discussed
Tabitha	23	Black	BA	Customer service	FT work				
Sean	25	White	BA	Art installer, property manager	FT work	None	1 year, 3 months	3 years, 11.5 months	Engaged
Emily	28	White	BA	Pastry chef	FT work				
James	26	White	BA	Health food store manager	FT work	None	11 months	2 years, 10.5 months	Engaged
Monica	26	White	BA	Large-mammal keeper	FT work				
Travis	29	White	BA	Certified public accountant	FT work	None	3 years	4 years, 3 months	Not discussing
Katherine	25	Black and white	BA	Research coordinator	FT work				
Jeremy	29	White	BA	News editor, stringer	FT work; FT school	None	1 year, 4 months	1 year, 7 months	Seriously discussing
Karen	24	White	MS	Research assistant	PT work				

(continued)

TABLE A2   (continued)

Couple	Age	Race/ Ethnicity	Education Level	Occupation	Work/School Hours	Children	Duration to Cohab	Total Time as a Couple	Talk of Marriage (At Time of Interview)
Jeff	32	White	BA	Computer networker	FT work	None	3.5 months	6 months	Not discussing
Sabrina	24	White	Some college	Gourmet grocery clerk	PT work; FT school				
Matthew	30	White	MA	Architect	FT work	None	11 months	1 year, 11 months	Seriously discussing
Kristina	24	White	BA	Architect	FT work				
Martin	31	White	MFA	Textbook editor	FT work	None	1 year	3 years, 3 months	Engaged
Jessica	30	White	MA	Teacher	FT work				
Soliman	31	Arabic	MA	Private investor	FT work	None	2 years, 1 month	3 years, 9.5 months	Not discussing
Naomi	23	White	BA	Freelance translator	FT work				
Jonathan	28	White	Some college	Author	FT work	None	4 months	1 year, 10 months	Engaged
Janelle	33	White	BA	Fitness studio owner	PT work				
Jack	24	White	BA	Financial planner	FT work	None	4 years, 11 months	5 years, 2 months	Have discussed
Audrey	23	White	BA	Graduate student	PT work; FT school				
Nathan	24	White	BA	Purchasing and estimation	FT work	None	2 years, 6.5 months	3 years, 9 months	Engaged
Andrea	25	White	MA	Social worker	FT work				

Name	Age	Race/Ethnicity	Degree	Occupation	Work status	Children			Marriage
Paul	26	White	BA	Political lobbyist	FT work	None	1 year, 8 months	2 years, 2 months	Have discussed
Kate	29	Asian and white	BA	Internship coordinator	FT work				
David	30	White	BS	Retirement planner, realtor	FT work	He has 1	8.5 months	1 year, 10.5 months	Not discussing
Justine	27	White	MS	Graduate student, equine therapist	PT work; FT school				
Brad	29	White	MEd	Graduate student	PT work; FT school	None	3 months	7 months	Not discussing
Carrie	24	White	BA	Teacher	FT work				
Nicholas	29	White	MA	Architect	FT work	None	1 year, 8 months	3 years, 1 month	Seriously discussing
Rachel	24	White	BS	Graduate student	PT work; FT school				
Justin		White	BA	Sales	FT work	None	7.5 months	1 year, .5 months	Have discussed
Lauren	23	White	BA	Political lobbyist	FT work				
Kevin	27	White	BA	Industrial general manager	FT work	None	11.5 months	1 year, 4.5 months	Engaged
Amy	28	White	MA	Respiratory therapist	FT work				
Miguel	27	Hispanic	MA	Graduate student, research assistant	PT work; FT school	None	4.5 months	1 year, .5 months	Seriously discussing
Lisette	26	Hispanic	BA	Graduate student, research assistant	PT work; FT school				

(continued)

TABLE A2 (continued)

Couple	Age	Race/Ethnicity	Education Level	Occupation	Work/School Hours	Children	Duration to Cohab	Total Time as a Couple	Talk of Marriage (At Time of Interview)
Greg	35	White	Some college	Construction company owner	FT work	None	3 months	9 months	Engaged
Natasha	28	White	BA	Fitness center owner	FT work				
Evan	27	White	BA	Salesman	FT work	None	1 year, 1 month	2 years, 1 month	Engaged
Juliana	23	White	MS	Summer camp employee	PT work				
Andrew	27	White	BA	Tennis professional	FT school	None	1 year, 9 months	2 years, .5 months	Not discussing
Rebekah	25	White	BA	Graduate student, bartender	PT work; FT school				
Derek	28	White	BA	Computer programmer	FT work	None	1 year, 11.5 months	9 years, 5.5 months	Never intend to marry anyone
Kathleen	27	White	BA	Midwife apprentice	PT work				
Peter	30	Black	MA	Graduate student, machinist	PT student; FT work	They have 2	8 months	2 years, 9 months	Not discussing
RaShinda	27	Black	MA	Stay-at-home mother					
Drew	35	White and Asian	BA	IT security	FT work	He has 1	1 month	9 months	Seriously discussing
Tara	28	White	BA	Computer programmer	FT work				

Name	Age	Race	Degree	Occupation	Work	Children			Marriage
Caleb	26	White	BA	Musician, pizza delivery	PT work	None	1 year, 6.5 months	2 years, 6.5 months	Have discussed
Sophie	26	White	BA	Parks office employee	FT work				
Taylor	25	White	BA	Computer repair	FT work	None	1 year, 7 months	4 years, 3 months	Engaged
Bree	25	White	BA	Auditor	FT work				
Aaron	35	White	BS	Copy shop manager	FT work	None			Not discussing
Emma	30	White	BA	Photographer, waitress	PT work		9.5 months	2 years, 9 months	
Mason	26	White	BA	Construction worker	FT work	None			Not discussing
Kiersten	24	White	BA	Market research assistant	FT work		4 months	10.5 months	
Dean	36	White	JD	Attorney	FT work	None			Never intend to marry anyone
Lindsey	36	White	PhD	Professor	FT work		2 years	16 years	

Notes

1. NBC News (2013); see also Newser story by Evann Gastaldo (2013). Katie J.M. Baker for *Jezebel* published her story on April 4, 2013, with the title "Living Together Without Getting Married Is the 'New' Norm."

2. Data from the 2010 census are from Kreider (2010). Data from 2000 and 1990 can be found in Simmons and O'Connell (2003).

3. In 1995, 45% of women aged 19 to 44 had ever cohabited, but by 2002 this had increased to 54%, according to a 2008 study by Sheela Kennedy and Larry Bumpass. Serial cohabitation has also increased over time. A 2008 study by Zhenchao Qian and Daniel Lichter found that in 2000, less than 20% of women aged 35 to 44 had lived with multiple cohabiting partners. Daniel Lichter, Richard Turner, and Sharon Sassler (2010) found that rates of serial cohabitation increased nearly 40% between the late 1990s and the early years of the 21st century.

4. Of women married between 2000 and 2004, 68% had cohabited prior to the wedding, while the figure was 67% for those married between 2005 and 2009. See Manning (2013).

5. For example, as of 2000, only 31% of men had attained the traditional benchmarks of reaching adulthood by age 30—leaving home, finishing school, getting married, having a child, and being financially independent. If marriage and parenthood are excluded, the picture looks somewhat better, as 70% of men aged 30 had left home, were financially independent, and had completed their schooling. See Furstenberg et al. (2004); Settersten and Ray (2010).

6. Various scholars have highlighted how childhood social class position is associated with adult outcomes. Annette Lareau's (2003) study of parenting styles distinguished between middle-class parents' strategies to ensure children's educational and economic success, which she termed "concerted cultivation,"

and working class and poor parents' laissez-faire approaches to monitoring childhood development, labeled "natural growth." Jessi Streib (2015) detailed how childhood social class shaped the sensibilities of married couples, revealing the hidden role that class plays in the intimate lives of married couples. These works indicate that childhood social class shapes how individuals think about their lives, plan (or don't) for the future, and organize household labor.

7. The demographic contours of cohabitation are set out in note 3 (above).

8. These statistics were drawn from a study released a year earlier than the one that resulted in the discovery that cohabitation was the new "normal." One key advantage of this report over the later study is that it included information on both men and women. See Copen et al. (2012).

9. For an examination of how transitions differed for women with college degrees and poor women, see Lichter, Qian, and Mellot (2006).

10. The least educated—high school dropouts—have always been the most likely to cohabit. This was the case in 1987, when 43% of women aged 15 to 44 who had not completed high school had ever cohabited, and it remained so as of 2006–2010, when over three-quarters (76.7%) of women lacking a high school diploma had ever cohabited. What has changed in the past two decades is the behavior of moderately educated and college-educated women. In the late 1980s, moderately educated women did not look much different from college-educated women in terms of their likelihood of having ever cohabited. In 1987, less than a third of women aged 19 to 44 who had completed high school had ever lived with a partner—32% of high school graduates, 31% of women who had some postsecondary schooling, and 30% of women who had graduated from college. But the cohabitation experience of groups with different educational experiences diverged in the 1990s and beyond. Between 1995 and 2002, growth in the proportions that had ever cohabited was largest among women who were high school graduates and those with some postsecondary schooling but no degree. From 1987 through 2010 the proportions of women who had ever cohabited more than doubled among high school graduates and grew by over 80% among women with some postsecondary training but no college degree. College-educated women also became more likely to have cohabited, but this growth was much slower.

11. Bumpass, Sweet, and Cherlin (1991).

12. Copen, Daniels, and Mosher (2013).

13. One study of recently formed sexual relationships using data from the 2006–2010 National Survey of Family Growth (NSFG) found that after 12 months, only 23.2% of respondents remained in a dating relationship, whereas 26.8% had moved in with that partner. See Sassler, Michelmore, and Holland (2016).

14. The woman interviewed detailed all of this in her November 29 "Smitten" blog for *Glamour* magazine (Melms, 2012).

15. According to the data from the 2006–2010 NSFG, three years after moving in with a partner, 53% of college-educated women who had cohabited with their partner had gotten married, compared with only 40% of women with some postsecondary schooling, and 39% of women with only a high school degree. See Copen, Daniels, and Mosher (2013).

16. These figures are from Table 8, National Center for Education Statistics (2009).

17. That is due to the rise in credentialism. Education, not occupation, has become the primary marker of social class position; additional schooling ostensibly provides individuals with higher-level skills and an edge in the labor market. See Cherlin (2014).

18. See, for example, Skocpol (2000), Shipler (2004), Newman and Chen (2007), Cherlin (2009).

19. For an excellent rebuttal to Murray's argument, see Lee (2015).

20. Broersma (2008).

21. Before the Great Recession, these rates were still low—4.3% of high school graduates vs. 2% of those with a college degree were unemployed. Between 2001 and 2003, individuals who had graduated from high school had a median duration of unemployment of 2.8 months, compared with 2.3 months for those with at least some college. See U.S. Bureau of Labor Statistics (2006), Gottschalck (2006).

22. Authors' calculations from the 2006–2008 NSFG question on attitudes toward marriage and premarital cohabitation. See also Miller, Sassler, and Kusi-Appouh (2011).

23. College-educated women who became pregnant while cohabiting were far more likely to marry before the birth of their child; the children born after these so-called shotgun marriages would be recorded in vital statistics as marital births. See Lichter, Sassler, and Turner (2014).

24. Among marriage cohorts from the mid-1970s to the 1990s, divorce rates fell among women with a bachelor's degree or more but remained high among women with less than a four-year college degree. This divergence in the dissolution rates of women with more or less education is not explained by recent increases in women's overall educational attainment, the age at first marriage, or premarital childbearing. Researchers suggest that this growing divergence indicates a strengthening of the association between socioeconomic disadvantage and family instability. See Steven P. Martin (2006).

25. The majority of married and unmarried adults say that love (93% vs. 84%), making a lifelong commitment (87% vs. 74%), and companionship (81% vs. 63%) are very important reasons to get married. Less than a third of married and unmarried adults (31% vs. 30%) said that financial stability was a very important reason to get married. Taylor (2010).

26. Jane Austen (1813) introduced *Pride and Prejudice* with a reference to the necessary prerequisite for marriage—money: "It is a truth universally acknowledged that a man in possession of a good fortune *must* be in want of a wife."

27. Differences in asset ownership (possession of cars, bank accounts, and homes) explain a significant portion of race and educational attainment gaps in first marriages. Daniel Schneider (2011) concluded that wealth mattered on the marriage market primarily for its "symbolic value," serving as a marker to potential partners that one had "made it" in the real world and was eligible for marriage.

28. The lack of resources is one reason why cohabitors often say they are not yet ready to get married. See Smock, Manning, and Porter (2005).

29. In recent years, economic markers—educational attainment and earnings—are increasingly predictive of marriage rather than cohabitation, for both men and women. See Sassler and Goldscheider (2004), Sweeney (2002), Addo (2014).

30. In the 1990s, Jeb Bush wrote a book chapter devoted to the challenges associated with single motherhood, in which he suggests marriage as a panacea for poverty. In 2015, Marco Rubio, Florida senator and presidential hopeful, echoed the view that if only poor women would marry, they would no longer be poor. Various think tanks continue to espouse the argument that marriage is the best approach to reducing child poverty. See Rector (2012).

31. See Antonovics and Town (2004). Ron Mincy and colleagues (2009) focused on a sample of new fathers, most of whom were not married to their children's mothers at the birth, and used a variety of strategies to control for selection; they found no evidence that the impact of a transition to marriage among unmarried men on their earnings differed from zero, either for subsamples defined by race-ethnicity or by union status (whether fathers were cohabiting at the child's birth).

Whether marriage is beneficial for women in a causal way is also debatable. Most studies focus on psychological well-being or the experience of domestic abuse. Both childless women and single mothers experience a decline in psychological distress upon marrying, though effects are limited to women whose marriages endure; see Williams, Sassler, and Nicholson (2008). Among single mothers who had a nonmarital birth, marriage is associated with better physical health than remaining unpartnered, but only if they wed the biological father of their child and if the marriage endured; see Williams et al. (2011). These studies have found little effect on the physical health of women who marry. Of note is that studies do not explore whether marriage improves women's earnings, under the presumption that women who marry may reduce their work hours or exit the labor force to engage in role specialization. Furthermore, the proportion of the population to which such gains would be experienced may be rather small and selective. The percent of women who marry following conception (so-called shotgun marriage) has declined, while the share who give birth while cohabiting, or move into shared living during the pregnancy, has increased; see England, Shafer, and Wu (2012). The proportion of women who marry the father of their child after giving birth is small; among women giving birth in the late 1990s, only 28% of couples who were cohabiting at the birth of their child married within the first five years, with another 28% separating; see Carlson and Hognas (2010).

32. For a review of changes affecting marriage and the rise of marriage as a "capstone" event, see Cherlin (2004). See also Gary Lee (2015), who argues that marriage is not a panacea for poverty.

33. From Bernard (1972). Bernard concluded (p. 7) by asserting, "There are two marriages, then, in every marital union, his and hers. And his, is better than hers. The questions, therefore, are these: In what direction will they change in the future? Will one change more than the other? Will they tend to converge or diverge? Will the future continue to favor the husband's marriage? And if the wife's marriage is improved, will it cost the husband's anything, or will his benefit along with hers?"

34. In 1970, close to 90% of couples had conventional earnings arrangements, where the husband was the sole provider or contributed 60% or more of the household earnings; by 2001, husbands were still the sole or major provider in a majority (64%) of couples, but wives shared equally in providing income in 24% of the couples. Fewer studies focus on cohabiting couples, but several have found that the mean ratio of female to male earnings is around 90%. See Brines and Joyner (1999); Raley, Mattingly, and Bianchi (2006); Sassler and McNally (2003).

35. The median annual earnings of men with only a high school degree who worked full time was $37,030, compared to $43,830 for similarly aged men with some postsecondary schooling and $66,930 for men with a bachelor's degree or more. The majority of those 25 and over are assumed to have completed their schooling (or obtained a college degree if they are going to). Digest of Education Statistics (2010).

36. Male high school graduates experienced a 14.5% earnings loss, while those with some postsecondary schooling lost 6% of their earnings over that time period.

37. Over this time period, women's inflation-adjusted earnings grew by 5.3% for those with a high school degree and by 11.1% among women with some postsecondary education.

38. U.S. Bureau of Labor Statistics (2007), Levy (1998), Rubin (1994).

39. Blumberg and Coleman (1989) argued that, at least within marriage, the partner with greater overall economic resources should have the most power within the relationship. They defined this power as the ability to have "greater say-so" in a number of arenas, including fertility, economics, domesticity, sexual fulfillment, and conflict resolution. See also Bloode and Wolfe (1960) for a further discussion of marital power.

40. In 1981, Jessie Bernard published an article that optimistically presaged the transformation of relationships between young adults to one of equality. Women have come a long way in closing the wage gap; in 1970 they earned 62 cents for every 100 a man did, and this narrowed to 82 cents by 2011. But women continue to earn less than men for comparable work at all levels of educational attainment. See Hegewisch, Williams, and Henderson (2010); U.S. Bureau of Labor Statistics (2012); Luscombe (2010).

41. See, for example, Ferree (1990) and Lorber (1994). West and Zimmerman (1987) explained that individuals "do gender" as a way of displaying their gendered selves to others. Everyday interactions thus reinforce perceptions of what men and women do. Furthermore, as individuals are positively or negatively sanctioned for "doing gender" correctly or incorrectly, behavioral norms are reinforced. If individuals "do gender" inappropriately, they may be stigmatized, but they don't force institutional arrangements to be questioned. See also Martin (2004) and Risman (2004).

42. See Clarkberg, Stolzenberg, and Waite (1995).

43. Sociologist Kathleen Gerson (2009) revealed just how distant men's and women's expectations were in her analysis of young adults who were the first generation to grow up during a time when parental divorce was common, the proportion of mothers working in the paid labor force increased, and family

roles were often in flux. In her interviews with young adults in the late 1990s she found that young women desired to be economically self-reliant, should an equal marriage not be possible. Young men had a different fallback plan should their idealized egalitarian relationships fail to materialize; most believed in a neotraditional view of family responsibility, where their work was prioritized over their partners' careers. They presumed that women would continue to work but would also bear the brunt of reproductive labor (domestic work and child care). In short, a gender divide has emerged. Young women say they would rather be alone than in an unequal relationship, and young men expect a relationship that actually puts more of a burden on their female partners than they would experience were they stay-at-home mothers. Despite their professions, though, many of the individuals Gerson interviewed were already married or cohabiting, or had relationships that had foundered and ended.

44. See, for example, Collins (1993, 1990).

45. The 1960 census provided the first official count of unmarried partners of the opposite sex, which came to be known as POSSLQ (Persons of the Opposite Sex Sharing Living Quarters), who numbered 439,000; by 1970, they numbered 523,000, and 1.589 million by 1990. For a review of how data on cohabitation was gathered, see Hayford and Morgan (2008). For a discussion of estimates utilized to indirectly assess the numbers and characteristics of cohabitors from 1977 to 1997, see Casper and Cohen (2000).

46. Gwartney-Gibbs (1986).

47. Nearly one-half (47%) of cohabiting respondents in the 1987 National Survey of Families and Households reported having definite plans to marry their partner, while another 27% thought they would marry eventually (Bumpass and Sweet, 1989). Looking at couple responses and repairing data for sample attrition and missing responses, Sassler and McNally (2003) found that only 32.1% of couples concurred that they had definite plans for marriage. Over one-quarter (26.9%) consisted of couples where one partner had definite plans to wed while the other partner thought they would marry eventually, and another 10.8% of couples agreed that they would marry eventually. Combining couples who reported definite plans to marry and those who believed they would eventually marry yielded about the same percentages but suggests far less certainty regarding the future outcome of the relationship.

48. In her 2000 *Annual Review of Sociology* article, Pamela Smock explained three possible roles that cohabitation served: as an alternative to marriage, a precursor to marriage, or an alternative to being single. She concluded that the function of cohabitation frequently differed by race and ethnicity; cohabitation more often served as a precursor to marriage for white women, but as an alternative to marriage for black and Latina women.

49. See Rindfuss and VandenHeuval (1990), Schoen (1989).

50. See Sassler (2004).

51. In European countries where cohabitation has many of the same legal protection as marriage, long-term permanently cohabiting unions are far more stable. See Perelli-Harris et al. (2010), Musick and Michelmore (2015).

52. Previously, some prominent Americans expressed the belief that because not all couples in the United States can wed they should stand in solidarity with

them. Such was the expressed view of several of the cohabitors we interviewed for our study. Same-sex marriage was not legalized in the United States until 2015.

53. A *New York Times* article commenting on the rise of nonmarital childbearing to women under the age of 30 asserted that "motherhood without marriage has settled deeply into middle America" (DeParle and Tavernise, 2012). Among women giving birth in the ten years prior to 2006–2010, the majority of nonmarital births were to cohabiting women. See Lichter, Sassler, and Turner (2014).

54. Musick (2007) finds that for Hispanic partners, cohabitation seems to serve as an alternative to marriage. Other qualitative studies have found that many cohabitors are not actually intending to become parents but, if they become pregnant, do not believe that that is sufficient reason to wed. See Sassler and Cunningham (2008); Sassler, Miller, and Favinger (2009); Reed (2006).

55. Only 5% thought that marriage someday was not important. Women were more likely than men to view marriage someday as very important (53% vs. 47%). See Scott et al. (2009).

56. Community college students come from families with fewer economic resources than those who matriculate immediately into four-year schools, are less likely to have been on an academic track in high school, and have lower rates of attaining a college degree than students who attend a four-year institution. See Goldrick-Rab (2006).

57. See figure 3 in Copen, Daniels, and Mosher (2013).

CHAPTER TWO. IN THE BEGINNING

1. In 2008, $957 million in revenue were generated in the United States from online dating services, according to Mitchell (2009). In Arlie Hochschild's *The Commercialization of Intimate Life: Notes from Home and Work* (2003) and *The Outsourced Self: Intimate Life in Market Times* (2012), the author explored the ways that people create the emotional terms of engagement they rely on when they pay others to perform work that used to be the responsibility of family, friends, or community members, such as paying an internet dating site to screen out potentially unsuitable mates and identify only the most appropriate partners.

2. Sullivan (2009). Despite the claims of online dating establishments, nationally representative surveys of American adults interviewed in 2005 found few who reported having utilized internet dating sites. Similar proportions met online as had met at church—only 3% each—which suggests that internet dating was highly selective. In the ensuing decade, acceptance of internet dating has clearly grown. A 2015 Pew report on internet dating found that in 2005 only 44% of those surveyed believed that online dating was a good way to meet people. By 2013 that proportion had increased to 59%. In fact, over one in five adults aged 25 to 34 years old (22%) had used online dating as of 2013. Still, only 5% of Americans who were married or in a committed relationship reported having met their significant other online. While the internet has become a popular way to meet people, it has not replaced all other forms of meeting romantic partners.

See Madden and Lenhart (2006); Sautter, Tippett and Morgan (2010); Smith and Anderson (2015).

3. This was due to the distance that often separated families from one another in Colonial America as well as limitations in living space. The couple was expected to remain clothed, sometimes "bundled" into additional layers, and often had a board placed between them. Nonetheless, approximately one-third of couples engaged in premarital sexual relationships. Later, in the 19th century, a young woman (or her mother) might invite a suitor to call upon a young woman in the afternoon. If the two became exclusive, he may have been permitted to "keep company," meaning to stay late into the evening, long after her parents had retired to bed. Again, sexual relationships were not infrequent. See Ingoldsby (2002, 2003) and Whyte (1992).

4. Fass (1977) and Rothman (1984).

5. Bailey (1988). See also Fass (1977) and Rothman (1984).

6. The current existence of a sexual double standard has been widely debated by researchers. See Lyons et al. (2011). The sexual double standard is a system of social values and norms that reward young men for engaging in sexual activity (especially with multiple partners) while sanctioning young women for similar behaviors. Still, there is an expectation that young women will reciprocate for a paid date through affection and sexual intimacy. See Firminger (2013) and Sprecher (1985).

7. The U.S. Census Bureau has tracked the median age at first marriage since 1890; see Table MS-2, "Estimated Median Age at First Marriage, by Sex: 1890 to the Present."

8. Data from the National Center for Health Statistics (NCHS) demonstrates shifts over time in divorce rates. The annual divorce rate for married women increased dramatically between 1970 and 1975, rising from 15 to 20 divorces per 1,000 married women as divorce laws were undergoing change. The divorce rate per 1,000 married women leveled off in the mid-1970s and remained at about 20 per 1,000 women through the mid-1990s. Current divorce rates are similar to those from the end of the 1960s, as more marriages are surviving to their tenth anniversary (and hopefully beyond). As evidence that marriage has stabilized and divorce rates declined, the proportion of women reaching their tenth wedding anniversary between 1990 to 1994 was significantly greater than for women married between 1980 to 1984, 74.5% versus 71.1%, respectively. See Kreider and Ellis (2011); see also U.S. Census Bureau (2002, table 117), Stevenson and Wolfers (2007).

Philip Blumstein and Pepper Schwartz's (1983) book *American Couples,* with its review of married, cohabiting, gay, and lesbian couples, offers a window into how relationships played out in the 1980s.

9. In fact, many young adults express such concern about high divorce rates that they are unwilling to marry until they are totally sure that their marriage will not founder. The specter of divorce therefore further delays marriage. See Miller, Sassler, and Kusi-Appouh (2011).

10. Instead of their 1995 advice, "Wait at least four hours to call him back," Ellen Fein and Sherrie Schneider's newest version (2013) suggests that women "wait at least four hours to text him back."

11. See Gilbert et al. (1999).

12. An article reviewing the top-selling dating advice books, as well as articles on dating and courtship, found during a 35-year period that heterosexual dating among young adults in the United States remains highly gender-typed in terms of cultural scripts, such as who initiates dates or pays. See Eaton and Rose (2011). Though some variability was observed in interpersonal behaviors aimed at signaling a partner, in terms of occasional initiation of dates by women, such behaviors were not utilized enough to challenge the dominant script. See also Laner and Ventrone (1998), Rose and Frieze (1989). In her 1998 book, *Gender Vertigo: American Families in Transition,* Barbara Risman finds that socially learned choices (such as which partner initiates a date) often seem "natural" and "logical" because they are so engrained. As a result, many of us lead lives that are conventionally gendered, even if that is not our intent.

13. At least that was the case for early cohorts of cohabitors. See Clarkberg, Stolzenberg, and Waite (1995).

14. Studies of the lives of college-educated women, for example, focus on the challenges of balancing work lives and family, particularly motherhood. See, for example, Blair-Loy (2003), Hewlett (2002), Stone (2007). Alternately, a new genre explores sexual exploration on college campuses but asserts that these are not about establishing intimate relationships. See Stepp (2007) or Boggle (2008). New research, however, has begun to explore the consequences of the hook-up culture and how the ramifications differ for women from more and less privileged backgrounds. See Armstrong and Hamilton (2013).

15. Paula England (2010) has referenced the stalled gender revolution, while Sharon Sassler and Amanda J. Miller (2011) have studied how adherence to normative gender roles continues to disadvantage moderately educated women.

16. Of course, that may well be a function of our sample, whether because women are less likely than men to pursue someone who does not reciprocate their interest for very long, or because such couples were more likely to break up or marry.

CHAPER THREE. SHACKING UP, LIVING IN SIN, SAVING ON RENT?

1. Cohabitation is, in the words of family demographer Andrew Cherlin, "uninstitutionalized." See Cherlin (2004).

2. Individuals may be reluctant to leave a relationship if they perceive that they may not be considered attractive by others looking for mates or if they feel that alternative partners are not as attractive as their current partner. The mechanisms binding partners together may include things such as joint investments or bank accounts, shared children, or economic need. See Stanley and Markman (1992).

3. The chief proponent of this view, Scott Stanley, has an extensive body of literature on how cohabitation undermines commitment. According to Stanley, cohabitors pose the ideal unit with which to assess constraints, as compared to those dating; cohabitors have more factors that may bind partners together (such as shared housing) and make leaving the relationship more difficult, without necessarily experiencing increased dedication (via formal marriage). Stanley

and Markman (1992); Stanley, Rhoades, and Markman (2006); Rhoades, Stanley, and Markman (2009).

4. One episode of *Girls* (2013) featured a character, Shoshana, coming to a surprising realization that since her boyfriend no longer had a place to live and had been staying over every night, they had moved in together without discussing it. In Sassler's 2004 article, the author described a young woman whose friends had to convince her she was cohabiting, as she was reluctant to acknowledge it herself.

5. While Stanley, Rhoades, and Markman (2006) report that cohabiting unions are often formed rapidly, without much deliberation about the future, they never directly address the concept of time.

6. Social psychologist Catherine Surra has suggested the existence of two types of processes relating to the deepening of commitment: relationship-driven and event-driven. In relationship-driven processes, beliefs about the future of the relationship were attributed to increased closeness, resulting from time spent together, joint activities, and growing disclosure between partners. These factors were associated with moderate and gradual shifts in commitment over relatively long periods of time, as well as higher levels of subsequent marital happiness and union stability. But commitment can also be driven by circumstances external to the relationship, such as job loss or economic exigencies. Event-driven commitments are associated with greater relationship volatility and lower levels of happiness among couples who marry, and may also be a function of time in the relationship. See Surra, Arizzi, and Asmussen (1988); Surra (1987); Surra and Hughes (1997).

7. See Birtchnell and Kennard (1984); Cate and Lloyd (1988); Grover et al. (1985); Surra, Arizzi, and Asmussen (1988).

8. See Sassler (2004).

9. Whereas we asked about the first date, the National Survey of Family Growth is a fertility study and therefore provides information on the date of first sexual intercourse, the date of moving in together, and other relevant dates—marriages, conceptions, births. Despite these differences, a recent quantitative study also found that substantial numbers of recent sexual relationships transitioned rapidly into cohabiting unions. In fact, transitions into cohabiting unions were highest in the very early months after initiating a sexual relationship, and the longer one remained involved without moving in with a partner the lower the likelihood of doing so. See Sassler, Michelmore, and Holland (2016).

10. Some respondents had one primary reason for moving in with their partners, but most of our cohabitors gave two reasons, and nearly half of our respondents provided three or more factors that shaped their decisions.

11. Of note is that there are social class differences in the number of reasons reported, as the middle class provided more reasons than the service class (155 vs. 138); middle-class women also mentioned more reasons than middle-class men (83 vs. 78).

12. Nearly a quarter of the college-educated respondents stated that moving in made day-to-day life easier when explaining their decisions to cohabit; middle-class respondents who moved in together within six months of the start of their relationships were most likely to mention convenience as a motivator.

Among the service class, convenience was also mentioned frequently, both among those who moved in within six months and those who deferred cohabitation beyond the first year of their relationships.

13. Our categories differ from those used by Rhoades and colleagues in their research on reasons for cohabiting; they grouped convenience, economic rationality, and financial necessity into one measure of "convenience." We argue that it is important to disentangle these reasons, paying special attention to the financial necessity category, as there are salient social class differences in why cohabitors move in together. College-educated respondents were less likely to mention fiscal necessity and also take considerably longer to enter into shared living. See Rhoades, Stanley, and Markman (2009); Sassler (2004).

14. Middle-class cohabitors who mentioned moving in because it was the economically rational thing to do generally had dated for over a year before making the transition to shared living.

15. Two-thirds of those who mentioned economic difficulties were from the service class.

16. In 2006, the median household income for Ohio was $45,900, with a standard deviation of $633. See U.S. Census Bureau, Table H-8: "Median Household Income by State: 1984 to 2011."

17. They also lived with his sibling and a nephew, making for a very full house.

18. While other respondents in our sample also became pregnant, they tended to be older and were already cohabiting at the time they conceived.

19. Only four men and one woman among the service class, and two men and one woman among the middle class, described their relationship progressions as slow.

CHAPTER FOUR. "I LIKE HUGS, I LIKE KISSES"

1. According to a Pew Research Center poll (posted July 18, 2007), sharing household chores was one of the top three issues associated with a successful marriage, with 62% of respondents indicating that it was very important, up 15 percentage points from 1990. The study also found virtually no difference in the proportion of men and women attributing great importance to sharing household tasks.

2. In 2006, for example, when we completed our interviews, 71% of respondents who participated in a Roper Center poll disagreed with the statement, "It is much better for everyone if the man is the achiever outside the home and the woman takes care of the home and family." Not surprisingly, women are somewhat more likely than men to disagree with this statement, but over two-thirds of male respondents do not express support for separate spheres.

3. In 1992, 74.6% of women between the ages of 25 and 54 were employed in the civilian labor force. This proportion increased slightly, to 75.9%, by 2002 but has since declined somewhat in the aftermath of the Great Recession. See Hegewisch, Williams, and Henderson (2011).

4. For a review of how attitudes toward family issues and gender roles have changed in the four decades from 1960 to 2000, see Thornton and

Young-DeMarco (2001). Gender attitudes have continued to change in the early years of the 21st century.

5. For an excellent review of the relationship between time and work, see Epstein and Kallenberg (2006). A great paradox of the modern American workplace is that those who most often need to work additional hours in order to survive (the working class) often struggle to find full-time employment; in contrast, white collar workers find themselves working far more hours than they desire. Further, the workplace punishes, rather than rewards, behaviors which do not conform to conventional ideas of gender roles, such as men taking paternity leave or women working long hours for pay. See Blair-Loy (2003).

6. One of the first jobs that the first author, Sassler, had as a teenager was conducting market research in a large mall. One memorable survey she recruited for required her to approach shoppers and ask them what products they used to get their toilet bowls sparkling fresh and clean. She was then to ask willing participants to rate their familiarity with various cleaning products; the actual interview did not involve any actual cleaning of toilets. Nonetheless, refusal rates for participating in this survey were high, and participants were disproportionately women; it was exceedingly difficult to fill the quota set for men to be interviewed. This experience dissuaded the author from desiring more involvement in market research, though it may have spurred her interest in gender inequality.

7. An extensive body of literature details the roles played by immigrant and minority women in performing domestic work in American households. See, for example, Pierette Hondagneu-Sotelo's *Domestica: Immigrant Workers Cleaning and Caring in the Shadows of Affluence* (2001) and Mary Romero's *Maid in the U.S.A.* (1992).

8. Jessie Bernard's ovular 1981 article, "The Good Provider Role: Its Rise and Fall," describes the establishment of "separate spheres," with women engaged in the private realm of the home while men entered into the paid labor force, which excused men from having to engage in labor in the home, including child care or cleaning.

9. Robert Orrange (2002) reported similar expectations regarding how work and family would play out in his study of adults pursuing graduate degrees in law and business, while Miller, Sassler, and Kusi-Appouh (2011) found that cohabiting working-class women feared that marriage would elevate their partner's expectations that they would assume the bulk of domestic responsibilities.

10. Using time-diary data from the 1960s through the 1990s, Suzanne Bianchi and her colleagues (2000) showed that the number of overall hours spent on domestic labor (excluding child care and shopping) declined steadily since 1965, mainly due to dramatic declines in the hours women spent in housework. About half of the decline was accounted for by women's increased labor force participation, fertility declines, and marital delay. Men's housework has increased during this same time period, nearly doubling (so that men were responsible for about a third of the housework in the 1990s) from 4.9 hours in 1965 to 10 hours by 1995. There has been little change in the number of hours both women and men spend in housework over the past two decades, though men's performance of childcare has increased. For recent estimates, see Liana Sayer (2015).

11. In the United States, of those interviewed in the American Time Use Survey in the early 21st century, only 35.63% of married individuals were childless, compared with 69.94% of cohabitors. Cohabiting women were somewhat more likely than married women to be employed, 75.2% vs. 70.56%, respectively, while cohabiting men were slightly less likely than their married counterparts to be employed (87.57% vs. 92.23%). These differences help account for the findings of a recent study of the amount of time married and cohabiting couples spent in paid work and domestic work in the United States, Italy, and France. The ratio of men's to women's time in paid work was always higher in marriages than in cohabitations, suggesting that specialization was greater in formal marriages. See Bianchi et al. (2014).

12. Married men in the United States averaged about 56% as much time as married women in domestic labor, while cohabiting men averaged about 62% as much as their cohabiting women in domestic work. See Bianchi et al. (2014).

13. Sanjiv Gupta (1999) found that never-married men reduced the time they spent doing what he classified as "female chores" (such as preparing meals, washing dishes, housecleaning, washing and ironing, shopping) by 2.9 hours when they entered into a cohabitation, and by 3.5 hours when they married. The housework time of never-married women, on the other hand, increased by 6.6 hours when they moved into a cohabiting union, and by 3.3 hours when they married. On the basis of these findings, Gupta concluded that men benefitted more in terms of how domestic labor was performed than did women when relationships advance.

14. Resistance to creating egalitarian households has been frequently studied among those interested in new roles for men. In his book *Family Man: Fatherhood, Housework, and Gender Equity,* Scott Coltrane (1996) wrote about the challenges men who sought to be egalitarian partners and parents faced, often from unexpected sources. More recent studies of "new men" find that those fathers who make the trade-offs necessary to be equal fathers often face a difficult time in the labor market. See Kaufman (2013). Women also face pressure from family members to maintain traditional gender norms, even if they and their spouse are eager to pursue more egalitarian practices. The second author, Miller, recalled how shortly after she was first married, an older female relative visited and noted assorted manly clothing Amanda's husband had left around the living room, including three pair of size 11 shoes under the coffee table, and an XXL t-shirt hanging on the chair. Amanda's relative went back home and relayed, "Amanda is a terrible housekeeper," assigning to her the role of putting away what were obviously the man's clothes.

15. Pepper Schwartz's (1995) *Love Between Equals: How Peer Marriage Really Works* revealed both negative and positive aspects of egalitarian relationships.

16. As dual-career couples become more normative, and gender attitudes liberalize, sharing household labor more equitably is less detrimental to relationship satisfaction. One such study, using data collected in 2006, found that couples where both partners shared domestic work had greater levels of sexual frequency, and were more satisfied with sexual frequency and the quality of the sexual relationship, than couples who had a conventional division of domestic labor. See Carlson et al. (2016).

17. Yoav Lavee and Ruth Katz (2002) refer to couples where at least one partner adheres to a gender ideology that is neither strictly conventional nor strictly egalitarian as "transitional couples." They suggest that when at least one partner's gender ideology ranges between strongly conventional and strongly egalitarian, such couples are likely to experience a great deal of relationship strain, because failing to follow clear social scripts may result in greater uncertainty. Others have also found that changes in normative gender roles can discomfit either couples or individuals, as new social norms often require more frequent negotiation of everyday pursuits. See Deutsch (1999), Hochschild with Machung (1989), Tichenor (2005).

18. For more on this topic, see Lillian Rubin's 1976 and 1994 classics on working class families.

19. There is generally an association between higher levels of schooling and more tolerant attitudes toward female employment and political leadership (Myers and Booth, 2002) as well as agreement on a need to address structural inequalities affecting women and minorities (Petola, Milkie, and Presser, 2004).

20. Jessie Bernard (1981) discussed how men who were "good providers" were not expected to contribute in other ways to the family. But even in the early 2000s, men who expected to be the primary provider anticipated that their partners would pick up the bulk of the domestic labor and childcare (Gerson, 2009; Orrange, 2002).

21. Women have surpassed men in the receipt of bachelor's and advanced degrees. By the early 1980s, more women than men were earning bachelor's degrees, and women have increased their share of bachelor's degrees in every year since then. By 1987, women earned the majority of master's degrees, and by 2006, more women than men earned doctoral degrees (see U.S. Department of Education, 2012). The meaning of women gaining more education than their husbands has changed as well, as women's educational advantage is no longer associated with higher risks of divorce (Schwartz and Han 2014).

22. Women generally do a smaller share of the housework and/or outsource the household labor to lower-class women when at least one member of the couple has a relatively high level of income or education. For studies of how couples outsource domestic work, see De Ruijter, Treas, and Cohen (2005).

23. In fact, only two of the men in our college-educated sample did not work full-time; one was finishing up a graduate degree.

24. Amanda Miller and Daniel Carlson (2016) argue that having no expectations for sharing household chores is an expectation that things will default to a conventional model. Others have found that when men think about equality, it is more in the realm of labor force participation than domestic labor. In her study of professional women who left the labor force to take care of children and the home, Pamela Stone (2007) found that husbands were comfortable with wives working, even in demanding professional jobs, as long as the women were also able to handle housework and childcare without assistance from them. Overall, men have accepted women's labor force participation to a much greater extent than men have embraced performing domestic labor.

25. See Miller and Sassler (2010).

26. In most of these couples, regardless of their class status, the man's job was privileged over the woman's. These women anticipated building their jobs around the needs of their partners and considered his work more important or deserving of sacrifice on their part. Anthony was attending college in hopes of becoming an architect and working part time, while his partner, Diana, worked several jobs and cared for their two-year-old daughter. When asked where he saw family fitting in with his career plans, Anthony noted, "They're coming along for the ride." Diana agreed, explaining when asked about her own job goals, "Well, I'm waiting for Anthony to graduate (*laughs*)." Although she currently worked, her career goals were hazy, and their energies were focused on the protracted schooling that Anthony needed to obtain his professional desires. Though the middle-class women in our sample had completed their degrees, and a few were even working on master's degrees, many also assigned primacy to their partner's careers. Juliana, who worked as an athletic trainer, was looking for a friendly and fun work environment, rather than one that offered advancement opportunity. She noted about her desired job, "I don't mind traveling a little bit, but I'm very much a homebody. I don't want to have to travel all the time with the teams." Whether these pairings reflect a certain amount of selection of compatible couples, or whether work orientations of the women had shifted over time in response to the realities of their relationship or their partners' behaviors, cannot be determined with our data. In general, however, the women with conventional housework expectations expressed desires for more flexible work, fewer hours, less travel, or voiced greater uncertainty about what their job goals were than their male partners.

27. Among the service-class couples where women worked, the proportion of what women earned relative to their male partners was 79.1%, whereas the ratio was not quite so high among the middle class (70.0%), even though more of the college-educated women were working.

28. In her 2010 book, *Reshaping the Work-Family Debate: Why Men and Class Matter,* Joan Williams argues that the need for working class men to constantly prove their masculinity to their coworkers leads blue collar men to not only reinforce one another's relatively conservative views of manhood, but also reduces women's bargaining power within the relationship as these men then feel less comfortable taking time off to tend to sick children or household responsibilities, lest they be viewed as emasculated.

29. According to Aafke Komter's (1989) article, "manifest power" is the ability to get another to bend to one's will. She found that wives desired more change in the division of labor than their husbands did, but their attempts at getting men to take on more housework were largely ineffectual, the result of men's manifest power. Komter found that latent or covert power, the ability to attain one's end without conflict due to fear of destabilizing the relationship or because of previous failed attempts or anticipating the wishes of the more powerful member, was more evident among the upper class than the lower or middle class, whereas we observe covert power operating more clearly among the service class. Times have clearly changed. College-educated women are better able to exert convincing power, and their college-educated partners are more amenable to contributing to equality. See Miller and Carlson (2016).

30. A study utilizing data gathered in 2006 from low- to moderate-income couples with a minor child in the house found that men performed 65% or more of the domestic labor in only 5% of the couples. See Carlson et al. (2016).

31. In fact, there are tacit hints among our sample women who do more housework to "make up for" their partners' higher incomes that societal expectations about what men and women should do reinforce service-class men's preferences more than they overturn such expectations. One of our service-class women, Dawn, expressed the idea that traditional gender roles were to be expected. "You know, we see all these ads in papers of how we should look and society puts such a role on you," she explained. "I mean, you're kind of brought up that way. Plus, I mean, I hate to say it but you still want to please the guy. We're still kind of in that homemaker kind of phase of cleaning and taking care of the kids and stuff. So really in the long run, the women [are] working just as much as the men, getting paid less, doing all of the housework, taking care of the kids, while the men are sitting on their butts, watching the football game."

32. Such a conclusion was pointed out by Arlie Hochschild (1989) in *The Second Shift,* over a quarter-century ago.

33. This is a concern expressed by service-class women as a reason to eschew marriage. See Miller, Sassler, and Kusi-Appouh (2011).

CHAPTER FIVE. FAMILY PLANNING OR FAILING TO PLAN?

1. For statistics on changing patterns of births to unmarried women, see Ventura (2009).

2. Among women aged 20 to 29 who conceived between 1990 and 1994 only 23% who were unmarried at conception had wed prior to the birth of the child. See Basu (1999, reference 7).

3. See Gibson-Davis and Rackin (2014).

4. Studies of contraceptive failure in the 1990s found that cohabiting women experienced a contraceptive failure rate of 16.5% in the first year of contraceptive use, compared with only 9% among married women and 13.3% among unmarried noncohabiting women. See Fu et al. (1999).

5. The 1972 Eisenstadt v. Baird Supreme Court ruling expanded access to birth control to unmarried couples, extending the 1965 Supreme Court ruling in Griswold v. Connecticut that gave contraceptive access to married couples. In 2001, 70% of cohabiting women's pregnancies were unintended, with 54% ending in abortion. See Finer and Zolna (2011).

6. Women who do not foresee a future with the presumed father are particularly likely to terminate the pregnancy. See Zabin et al. (2000); see also Bouchard (2005) and Finer and Henshaw (2006).

7. Such decisions are detailed by Kathryn Edin and Maria Kefalas (2005) and further elaborated upon in studies utilizing the "fragile families" data (Edin et al., 2007).

8. In their qualitative study of cohabitors living in the metropolitan New York area, Sassler and Cunningham (2008) found that upwardly mobile cohabiting women said they would marry before childbearing were they to become pregnant, whereas those who were less careerist more often saw no real difference

between living together and marriage when it came to parenting. See Ellwood and Jencks (2004).

9. The majority of treatments of men's roles in nonmarital fertility have focused on men in inner city neighborhoods and low-income minority men, like Elijah Anderson's (1990) ethnographic *Streetwise: Race, Class, and Change in an Urban Community*. In *My Baby's Father: Unmarried Parents and Paternal Responsibilities* (2002), Maureen Waller explores how couples explain unmarried father's obligations to their children, drawing on interviews with both men and women. For a more recent treatment, see Kathryn Edin and Timothy Nelson's *Doing the Best I Can: Fatherhood in the Inner City* (2013).

10. In her study of college-educated heterosexual couples, Julie Fennell (2011) finds that a substantial minority of men were highly committed contraceptors, though even these men were reluctant to discuss contraception with their partners. Amanda Miller (2012) also finds that even though men would like to provide input into fertility decisions, most were not involved in deciding outcomes when pregnancies occurred.

11. Paula England and colleagues (2016) conceptualize efficacy as "(1) being planful enough to organize action in the service of a goal, (2) having sufficient self-regulation to 'make oneself' do things that are onerous now but necessary to realize a goal, (3) being assertive with others when it is necessary to realize a goal, and (4) believing that one can take action and that it is likely to bring about a desired goal."

12. High usage failure of even the most effective contraception, hormonal methods, highlights the challenges of being an efficacious user among certain populations. During the first 12 months of use, 16.9% of cohabiting women aged 20 to 24 who had incomes below 200 percent of the poverty level experienced contraceptive failure. But inconsistent use varies widely by marital status and income, as only 9.7% of similarly aged, married low-income women experienced a contraceptive failure. See Fu et al. (1999); see also England, McClintock, and Shafer, (2011). England and colleagues (2016) also find that individuals with high efficacy in other areas of their life, for example in educational pursuits, have high contraceptive efficacy. Furthermore, women who experienced an unintended first birth are significantly more likely than women with an intended first birth to have an unintended second birth, further highlighting the role of efficacy. See Guzzo and Hayford (2011).

13. See Sassler, Miller, and Favinger (2009); Zabin et al. (2000).

14. See England, McClintock, and Shafer (2011); Finer and Henshaw (2006); Longmore et al. (2003); Sweeney (2010).

15. See England et al. (2016); England, McClintock, and Shafer (2011).

16. It is likely much easier for the middle class to be "planners" than it is for their service-class peers, because they have more resources and reason to believe that their plans will be successful. In contrast, for the service class, attaining the future they want is farther out of reach than ever before (Silva, 2013). Our work suggests that some service-class men echo the sentiments of low-income individuals when it comes to childbearing. Edin and Kefalas (2005) find that among the low income, children are strongly desired, even when young adults were not economically ready for them.

17. For a discussion of the effectiveness of various methods, see Trussell (2007) or go to the Bedsider website of the National Campaign to Prevent Teen and Unplanned Pregnancy.

18. Our findings and other qualitative studies suggest that certain populations—moderately educated cohabitors whose access to health insurance may be spotty as well as homeless women and women who have been incarcerated—do perceive affordability as an issue. See Silverman, Torres, and Forress (1987); Wenzel et al. (2001); LaRochelle et al. (2012).

19. England and colleagues (2016) include being assertive under their omnibus concept of efficacy, arguing that sometimes women need to persist in order to ensure contraceptive compliance.

20. Trussell (2011).

21. In several instances, one partner reported an actual conception that the other partner reported as a scare. Men were more likely to report that their partner was pregnant, while the woman described the very same episode as a scare. Abortions are notoriously underreported in surveys, and it is possible that men were not always aware of when partners were pregnant; several of our respondents said they would not have told their partners if they had obtained an abortion. Underreporting is more common among racial or ethnic minorities and low-income women. See Jones and Kost (2007).

22. Peter described how he and RaShida, who both had master's degrees at the time of their interview, talked about how their first daughter, who they described as "a surprise," would be lonely without a sibling; he was not startled when RaShida got pregnant again, within a year of having their daughter.

23. According to Barrett and Wellings (2002) a "planned" pregnancy includes four components: (1) the couple was intending to become pregnant, (2) they stopped using contraception, (3) both partners agreed they were trying to conceive, and (4) partners felt that they had reached the right point in their lives for childbearing. Most of the couples in our sample who became pregnant only satisfied the second criterion, but generally not with the intention of conceiving.

24. While some men were categorically opposed to abortion, others felt that only women should be able to decide the outcome of an unexpected pregnancy, in large part because it was women who had to carry an unexpected pregnancy. Miller (2012) found that cohabiting men's preferences depended both upon their own emotional and financial readiness for fatherhood and whether they felt that their relationship with their partners were stable enough to coparent with.

25. Unintended pregnancies are associated with higher rates of union dissolution, an increased likelihood of experiencing additional unintended pregnancies, harsh parenting and parental regret, and lower levels of human capital accumulation among women. Furthermore, children whose births were unintended experience poorer cognitive development and health in childhood, and lower levels of educational attainment. See Guzzo and Hayford (2012, 2011); East, Chien, and Barber (2012); Johnson and Schoeni (2011).

26. This is, in fact, what various studies utilizing nationally representative data have shown. As a result, even as the proportion of college-educated

cohabitors has increased, the proportion giving birth while cohabiting has remained relatively flat. See Lichter, Sassler, and Turner (2014).

27. This is the topic of Jennifer Silva's (2013) book.

CHAPTER SIX. FOR BETTER OR FOR WORSE?

1. Wang and Parker (2014).

2. See, for example, Focus on the Family (2014) and Heritage Foundation (2014).

3. According to the Pew Research Center, only 12% of 18- to 25-year-olds said that they probably or definitely will not ever marry; a full 85% of those currently unmarried plan to do so in the future. And, despite complaints that these young adults spend too much time pursuing casual hookups, their generation clearly values love, commitment, and fidelity. See Pew Research Center (2007a).

4. Gubernskya (2011).

5. Authors' calculations from the 2006–2008 National Survey of Family Growth's questions on attitudes toward marriage and premarital cohabitation. See also Miller, Sassler, and Kusi-Appouh (2011). For a contrast, see Gubernskya (2011), who finds that some family attitudes appear to differ by both sex and social class. She finds that women and those who have higher levels of education hold less traditional views about family than men and those who are less educated, using a composite measure which asks individuals to rate their agreement with three statements: "Married people are generally happier than unmarried people," "People who want children ought to get married," and "People who have never had children lead empty lives."

6. Research on changing attitudes toward divorce finds that the growing proportion of those with some college or four-year degrees does not explain the change in divorce attitudes. See Martin and Parashar (2006).

7. Men's poor economic circumstances have long been strongly associated with lower marriage rates. Studies of cohabiting women have found that men's economic disadvantage reduced their partner's marital expectations. See Manning and Smock (2002); Edin and Reed (2006); Sassler, Roy, and Stasny (2014).

8. That living together would enable couples to determine whether they should marry was one of the major reasons given by cohabiting respondents, especially those concerned about high rates of divorce. See Miller, Sassler, and Kusi-Appouh (2011).

9. Wright and Guzzo (2015). See also Lichter, Sassler, and Turner (2014).

10. Wright and Guzzo (2015) find that acceptance of unmarried childbearing rose just 4% between 1994 and 2012, from 16.4% to 20.1%.

11. Almost half (47%) of high school graduates, compared with 43% of those with some college education and 40% with at least a bachelor's degree, believe that unmarried women having children is "always or almost always wrong." Nonetheless, the less educated are far more likely to experience nonmarital births than are college-educated women. Today, over 87% of college-educated women experience their first birth within marriage, compared to

40.4% of women with some college, and 16.6% of women with a high school diploma or less. See Pew Research Trends (2009); Lichter, Sassler, and Turner (2014).

12. See Brown (2000); see also Sassler and Schoen (1999).

13. Similar to the findings of Huang and colleagues (2011), among our sample, middle-class men more often mentioned that the loss of freedom was a disadvantage of moving in together than did middle-class women. However, this sentiment was far more common among our service-class respondents, who showed no such gender difference in this attitude.

14. Only one middle-class individual raised the concern that moving in together had hurt him financially. Miguel and Lisette were both graduate students at the time they moved in together, but because he was earning a larger scholarship and university stipend than she was, he explained that moving in together had actually decreased his standard of living.

15. While service-class men more often express the financial downside of moving in together, the gender difference that exists is interesting. Of service-class women who say that one negative of moving in together is that they are worse off financially than when they were first dating, all but one is the primary earner in their household. In contrast, about half of the service-class men who expressed this sentiment actually earn significantly less than do their partners.

16. Scott Stanley and colleagues (2006) have argued that moving in without a clear picture of what the future holds imposes additional constraints on relationships that would not have happened had the couple maintained separate residences. Sharing an apartment makes leaving more difficult, even if couples are poorly matched, which the Stanley, Rhoades, and Markman study suggests may be one of the reasons why marriages preceded by cohabiting unions may be more likely to break up than marriages where couples had not cohabited first.

17. Perhaps because of their more precarious economic situations, service-class individuals more often discussed the financial advantages that marriage offered as compared to cohabiting.

18. Both Haire and McGeorge (2012) and DeJean, McGeorge, and Carlson (2012) found that stigma is higher for single mothers than it is for single fathers. Further, negative attitudes toward single mothers tend to be very personal judgments about the women themselves, while negative attitudes about single fatherhood tend to be more situational.

19. Of the eight middle-class men who did not feel that marriage prior to parenting was important, one already had a child with his partner outside of marriage, and two never wanted to marry but were amenable to being parents if their partner agreed with that arrangement.

20. See Lichter, Sassler, and Turner (2014).

21. Our service-class sample was, on average, younger than our middle-class one, with an overrepresentation of 18- to 21-year-old cohabitors in our less educated group, while more of the college-educated couples were in their late twenties. Yet we do not believe that it is their older age alone that makes the middle class more ready for marriage. In fact, the most common age range for our middle-class individuals to get engaged was in their early twenties (between 22 and 25).

CHAPTER SEVEN. WAITING TO BE ASKED?

1. New research has highlighted the difficulties of overturning traditional gender roles, even among couples expressing egalitarian preferences. Some scholars argue that men use egalitarian narratives as a form of identity work, but such narratives allow men to dismiss inequalities within their own emerging romantic relationships (Lamont, 2015). Other research suggests that women's narratives of choice, individualism, and personal autonomy cloud women's abilities to engage in egalitarian behaviors during an important stage of the courtship process, and therefore maintain gender inequality (Lamont, 2014); Lamont's work (2014, 2015) focused on older, college-educated respondents.

2. Sassler (2004) found that, among a sample of cohabitors in the New York metropolitan area, only around a third discussed future goals for their relationships before moving in together.

3. Lichter, Sassler, and Turner (2014).

4. Komter (1989) described how couples often ceded to what she termed men's "hidden power," thereby demonstrating adherence to the belief that gender roles are natural and inevitable.

5. In "A 'Real Man's Ring': Gender and the Invention of Tradition," Vicki Howard (2003) traces the history of a failed experiment by jewelers in the 1920s to popularize an engagement ring for men. She argues that because this trend did not resonate with traditional ideas of courtship, the public never adopted the practice.

6. For an excellent article explaining changes in marriage timing, see Oppenheimer (1988). The belief that men have more power in their relationships because of their greater economic contributions is well established in the research literature. See Becker (1974). For an early study of how couples made purchasing decisions, see Blood and Wolfe (1960).

7. This includes families in which husbands have no earnings from work. For data on this, see U.S. Bureau of Labor Statistics (2009, table 25). For another study of how persistent this earnings balance is, see Winkler, McBrode, and Andrews (2005). Cohabiting women are even more likely to outearn their partners than are married women. See Fields (2004).

8. Miller, Sassler, and Kusi-Appouh (2011) find that some service-class women in this sample are reluctant to marry because they envision themselves working the "second shift" as described by Hochschild with Machung (1989)—working a full day for pay, then coming how and doing nearly all of the household chores and childcare.

9. A recent Pew study found that most of those marriages formalized following the Great Recession were concentrated among the college educated. See Fry (2014). Research evidence continues to show that college-educated men are more likely to marry than men with less education, as are men who are stably employed and in professional occupations. See Sassler and Goldscheider (2004), Oppenheimer (2003).

10. These are the three forms of power described by Komter (1989) in her analysis of hidden power in marriage. The first type, manifest power, is the ability to get others to do as you wish. One partner may request (or order) the other to empty the dishwasher, for example. A second type of power, latent power, is

the ability to get someone to desist from pursuing what they want. Your partner may stop complaining that you never unload the dishwasher, for example, because they realize you do not like hearing them complain, because their complaints in the past have gone unheeded, or because they do not want to risk destabilizing the relationship with yet another fight about housework. A third type of power, hidden (or invisible) power, results from social norms, particularly with regard to gender roles. If you and your partner believe that women are "naturally" better at particular types of chores or that men are best able to make decision about serious matters, then female partners will be more resigned to unloading the dishwasher, regardless of personal preferences, while both women and men will believe that it is up to men to propose marriage, even if a female partner is more impatient to take such a step.

11. This proportion is well below the estimates provided by surveys that ask cohabitors about their plans upon moving in together. In a study of cohabitors and those who had cohabited prior to marriage gathered in 2002, Karen Guzzo reported that almost half of first cohabitations began with intentions to marry. That is, respondents reported being engaged or planning to be at the time they moved in with their partner. The proportions engaged declined somewhat by the next survey wave, from 2006 to 2010. See Guzzo (2014).

12. Lynne Casper and Suzanne Bianchi also found that only around 10% of American cohabiting couples fell within the definition of "alternative to marriage" cohabitors, in that they intended to remain permanently nonmarried. Their findings were drawn from data gathered from cohabitors in the late 1980s who were under the age of 45; over the past three decades, as cohabitation has become more normative, even among seniors, and more couples are living together for extended periods of time without marrying, this group may have grown. The proportion of "alternative to marriage" cohabitors in our sample, however, is about 10%—six of 61 couples. See Casper and Bianchi (2002); Brown, Bulanda, and Lee (2012); Vespa (2012).

13. Her use of power, however, is more consistent with women's traditional usage, which is often limited to the realm of breaking up rather than persisting. See England and Kilbourne (1990).

14. This is consistent with other research on low-income and working-class cohabitors, who have, in the words of one article, high hopes (for marriage) but even higher expectations of what needs to be in place first. See Gibson- Davis, Edin, and McLanahan (2005); Smock, Manning, and Porter (2005).

15. "Putz" is a Yiddish term, with various meanings. It is sometimes used to describe a person who lacks social skills, though others translate it as referring to a man who is something of a jerk. But in this usage, it seems to mean someone who dawdled, as in, "Stop putzing around."

16. There was also one middle-class couple that had planned much of the wedding, including having a dress purchased and a site for the reception, though Jeremy had not yet formally proposed.

17. It was also clear that they had already had a serious discussion about this contribution on Emily's part. Sean's interviewer suggested that making the wedding cake was perhaps an overly optimistic endeavor, given the amount of

pressure there would be around the time of the wedding. To that, Sean replied, "She said she can make it [the wedding cake] weeks in advance."

18. Sara McLanahan's discussion of "diverging destinies" (2004) hinges on the premise that the children of low-income mothers are more often born outside of marriage, to mothers with low levels of employment and father involvement, than those born to more advantaged women; today, the service class increasingly looks more similar to low-income women than to their college-educated counterparts.

CHAPTER EIGHT. COHABITATION NATION

1. Nonetheless, even if cohabitation had not become more acceptable, we believe that the increasing emphasis on economic prerequisites for marriage would still have reduced the number of those married among our less educated respondents, and the marriages that ensued (the counterfactual) would look much like the often low-quality working-class marriages of the 1960s and 1970s, with high rates of instability. See Rubin (1976, 1994).

2. Women do more housework than men, regardless of marital status; single women with no children, for example, report doing almost twice as much cooking, cleaning, and laundry as single men with no children. But married mothers do nearly four times as much domestic work as married fathers, with much of that time spent on laundry and cleaning (Sayer, 2015). The presence of children, especially those born early on in romantic relationships, also reduces relationship quality. One recent study (Trillingsgaard, Baucom, and Heyman, 2014) found that those who had been involved for shorter periods of time at conception and with poorer communication experienced declines in satisfaction from pregnancy through 30 months postpartum. Another study, based on data gathered in Norway, where the majority of births were to cohabiting women, found that cohabiting and married women experienced similar negative change in relationship satisfaction during the transition to parenthood. However, cohabiting women started off and stayed less satisfied throughout the transition period, suggesting the presence of a negative cohabitation effect that remained even after controlling for a variety of background characteristics. See Mortensen et al. (2012).

3. Our middle-class respondents were generally from more advantaged families than our service-class youth, and their stronger financial foundation no doubt facilitated their completion of college degrees. Nationally, over three-quarters (77%) of young adults whose parents earned in the top quartile of income completed a bachelor's degree by age 24, compared to 34% of those in the third quartile, 17% of those in the second quartile, and 9% of those whose parents were among the poorest Americans. See Cahalan and Perna (2015).

4. Drawing from Swidler's (1986) toolkit theory, we argue that the skill sets that young adults from middle- and service-class backgrounds draw on when negotiating romantic relationships differ, due to upbringing and norms, as well as resources. Annette Lareau's (2003) study of the educational outcomes of children from middle-class versus working-class or poor families suggested how

young adults learned different strategies of action; we extend these to behaviors that subsequently influence romantic relationship formation. Lareau depicted different parenting styles that shaped how children interacted with teachers, peers, and institutions and their subsequent educational trajectories. Middle-class parents engaged in "concerted cultivation," where parents provided structured intellectual experiences and interactions that prepared children for educational achievement and future employment. Working-class and poor families, in contrast, engaged in "natural growth," with less structure and future orientation, and where obedience and compliance with authority were encouraged. As a result, working-class and poor children were less prepared to navigate the educational system than their middle-class counterparts. But as we show, similar skills—the ability to ask questions, present one's own viewpoint, and negotiate differences—are necessary in navigating romantic relationships. Frank Furstenberg (2015) also discusses how social class differentiates the experiences of young adults from more and less privileged backgrounds.

5. Guides for those seeking to invest in skills sought by employers often emphasize what are often called "soft skills," or the traits, attitudes, and actions that allow workers to get along with coworkers and supervisors, leadership talents that emphasize persuasive abilities and, sometimes, the capacity to compromise, as well as problem solving skills and flexibility. See AARP's "What Skills are Employers Looking For?"

6. Paula England and her colleagues (2016) refer to assertiveness, or consistently asking for what one wants, as one leg of efficacy.

7. Although they focused on women's behaviors, England and colleagues (2016) would classify self-regulation behavior among middle-class men as a second element of efficacy: the ability to engage in sometimes undesirable pursuits that help achieve a larger goal.

8. The higher levels of education and earnings of college-educated women gave them more options on the marriage market than those of their service-class counterparts. They were also better able to maintain independent living, and so could be more selective about the partners or could defer moving in with that partner.

9. Relying on strong ties as intermediaries in one's love life may also facilitate relationship progression, as couples feel greater social support for their unions. See Coleman (1988) and Granovetter (1973). Among our sample, those who met through friends and family often reported receiving a good deal of social and economic support for their relationships. See Sassler and Miller (2015).

10. Individuals involved in interracial relationships or relationships that began online frequently report receiving less support from family members, and often feel unsupported by family and friends as well as less satisfied with the quality of their relationships. See Madden and Lenhart (2006); Vacquera and Kao (2005); McPherson, Smith-Lovin, and Cook (2001).

11. These discussions are consistent with the trends. College-educated adults are considerably more likely to be married now than those without a college degree. Among adults who were aged 25 and older in 2014, 65% of those with a college degree or more were married, compared with only 53% of adults with less education. The marriages of the college educated last longer, as well. An

estimated 78% of college-educated women who married for the first time between 2006 and 2010 could expect their marriages to last at least 20 years. But among women with some college schooling less than half (49%) could expect such marital stability. See Wang (2015).

12. It has historically been the woman's family that fronts most of the wedding costs. That our college-educated men's parents mention a willingness to contribute suggests not only that they desire to push forward a wedding, but that their sons may have benefitted from the lessons their *parents* learned as they navigated changes in women's roles.

13. Quite a few service-class individuals claimed that marriage would ruin their relationship, mentioning couples that had successfully lived together for long periods of time, only to break up after getting married. See Miller, Sassler, and Kusi-Appouh (2011). The belief that one can successfully attain his or her desired goal, which the service class lack here, is the third element of England and colleagues' (2016) definition of efficacy.

14. Planfulness, or the organizational skills needed to work toward a goal, is the fourth leg in England and colleagues' (2016) definition of efficacy.

15. Yet another example of how college-educated women plan the events in their lives can be found in an episode of *Friends* (which was the hit show during the formative years of our interview respondents), where one of the lead characters hits an age milestone. The episode is titled "The One Where They All Turn 30." After having a meltdown at her birthday party, Rachel says, "You know, I realized it was stupid to get upset over not having a husband and kids. All I really needed was a plan. See, I want to have three kids. I should probably have the first of the three kids by the time I'm 35, right, which gives me five years! I love this plan! I want to marry this plan. So if I want to have a kid when I'm 35, I don't have to get pregnant until I'm 34 which gives Prada four years to start making maternity clothes. Oh, wait, but I do want to be married for a year before I get pregnant. So I don't have to get married until I'm 33! That's three whole years. Oh wait a minute, though. I'll need a year and a half to plan the wedding, and I'd like to know the guy for like a year, year and a half before we get engaged which means I need to meet the guy by the time I'm 30 . . ." She concludes, "According to my plan, I should already be with the guy I'm going to marry!"

16. Murray (2012).

17. Murray also attributes the difficult situations facing moderately educated young adults to a lack of parental guidance. We saw plenty of evidence in our interviews of ways that the parents of our service-class respondents attempted to guide children. Their preferences, however, were often rejected or ignored. Patty, our youngest respondent at 18, refused to abide by the curfews set by her parents, and later her sister, instead moving in with Josh. The fathers of two service-class women, Tracy and Carly, who became pregnant early on in their cohabiting unions were very religious and did not approve of either cohabiting or nonmarital childbearing. We frequently heard from our service-class respondents, such as Susan, that their parents did not approve of cohabiting. Brandi indicated that Artie's mother was very displeased that her son was cohabiting, which cast a pall over their relationship, and Dawn referenced tensions with her father that arose over her decision to move out of the parental home, though at

the time of her interview they had reconciled. We heard far less about parents providing economic support—paying for apartments or schooling—among our service-class respondents compared to their middle-class counterparts.

18. There is an extensive literature on privilege—white privilege, male privilege—that seeks to highlight the ways that invisible factors contribute to the advantages that many take for granted. See McIntosh (1989).

19. Both Sean and Travis mentioned that while they had not played a role in their high school girlfriend's ultimate decision, the girlfriend's mother had. This is also a form of parental guidance, one that Murray does not address.

20. In fact, many of our respondents experienced what Thornberry and colleagues (2016) refer to as "cumulative disadvantage."

21. See, for example, Mullainathan and Shafir (2013), Silva (2013).

22. See Campbell and Horowitz (2016).

23. Myers and Booth (2002) find that young adults who are college educated are more likely to be "gender forerunners" (that is, those whose gendered attitudes are at least one standard deviation less traditional than the mean). This effect is multiplied if they have parents who have nonconventional attitudes toward gender as well.

24. The likelihood of graduating from college is diminished for those from single parent households, and this disadvantage holds even if one controls for household income while growing up. For example, Ziol-Guest, Duncan, and Kalil (2015) find that living in a single-parent household from ages 14–16 decreased the odds of completing college by 16.6% compared to those who were living in a two-parent household at that time.

25. See Conley (2008).

26. Over the past decade, the loss of male-typed blue collar occupations heavily impacted those with only a high school degree. Jobs such as fork-lift driver, once readily available, have been disappearing, replaced (or not) by lower wage, service-sector jobs. The housing crisis not only impacted rates of homeownership among those on the margins, but also impacted jobs associated with housing. At the time of their interviews, three of our 30 service-class men worked in mortgage processing. Given the increased difficulty of obtaining home loans, it is likely that mortgage processing jobs have become scarcer. At the same time that jobs have been lost, the cost of rent has gone up. A CNN Money report announced that between 2001 and 2014, household incomes declined 9% but rents went up 7%, and rental housing supplies are down. The national vacancy rate is the lowest that it has been in 30 years. Finally, unexpected pregnancy may be pushing more adults into cohabitation. While historically most common among women with less than a high school degree, the largest increases recently in out-of-wedlock childbearing have been to the moderately educated. Many of those individuals will choose to live together if they are not already doing so at the time of conception; by 2013, 59% of all out-of-wedlock births were to cohabitors. Of those with some postsecondary schooling but no four-year degree, a quarter of all births between 2009 and 2013 were to cohabiting women, compared to 15% of all births between 1997 and 2001. See Sum, Khatiwada, and Palma (2011); Vasel (2015a); Shah (2015).

27. See Denmark, Shaw, and Ciali (1985); Shelton and John (1993); South and Spitze (1994).

28. Cotter, Hermsen, and Vanneman (2011).

29. See Miller, Sassler, and Kusi-Appouh (2011). The woman who profiled her cohabitation and subsequent engagement in her "Smitten" column for Glamour.com explained that cohabiting was a way to make sure she and her partner were ready for the daily rewards and challenges of marriage, and added that most of the young women she knew felt the same way. In fact, not cohabiting would have raised eyebrows. "I think it would be weird to me to have a friend who would wait to move in together until after they got married," the *Glamour* blogger said. See also Aleccia (2013).

30. For years, *Glamour* magazine has offered a recipe for "Engagement Chicken." It is advertised as "the meal that will make your boyfriend propose." The chicken recipe has purportedly been so successful that it is a regular feature on their blog, with pictures of soon-to-be brides flashing their engagement rings and showing off the chicken they cooked to get their men to propose. As we were finishing up our book, we even found a story about how the *man* had cooked the engagement chicken before proposing. We may be grasping at straws, but we view this as a tentative movement toward greater gender equality!

31. See Bernstein (2004). For an example of differences between the U.S. minimum wage policy and Denmark's living wage focus, see Liz Alderman and Steven Greenhouse's October 27, 2014, *New York Times* article.

32. But many of our service-class respondents were not necessarily working a full forty-hour a week job (though many were working more), in part because they were also attending school or could not get full-time hours at their jobs.

33. See Jon Gertner's January 15, 2006, *New York Times* article and Bernstein (2004).

34. The gap in yearly earnings between those earning a living wage and a minimum wage, if they worked full time for a full year, was sizable—the living wage estimate was over $3,500 greater. For the 2014 estimates of the difference between the living wage and the minimum wage, for Columbus, Ohio, go to http://livingwage.mit.edu/metros/18140. See Misra (2015), Ashkenas (2014).

35. See Sherman (2016).

36. McKinley (2015).

37. See, for example, Schwartz and Wilson (2008). Numerous cost-of-living calculators suggest limiting the amount spent on housing to 30% of your take home (post-tax) pay. One particularly funny example can be found at http://www.apartmenttherapy.com/how-much-rent-you-can-really-afford-renters-solutions-186462, which explains that someone with a yearly income of $72,000 should pay no more than $1,800 a month for rent and utilities. In fact, that yearly income is well above the median household income for a family of four in the U.S. as of 2006 and also far exceeds the majority of what our respondents earned.

38. See http://www.deptofnumbers.com/rent/ohio/columbus/, citing the U.S. Census Bureau's American Community survey.

39. None of our respondents mentioned receiving government housing assistance, such as Section 8 vouchers.

40. In November 2015, the *New York Times* reported that leasing had begun for the first "micro-apartments" in the city. The builder of these small abodes had special permission to create apartments that, at 260 to 360 square feet, were smaller than the 400-square-foot city ordinance required. Apparently, size was not an impediment for many potential renters, as the paper reported that over 60,000 people had applied for the fourteen available apartments (Kaysen, 2015). The real estate bust in 2008, and high rates of foreclosure among young families that had overextended themselves to purchase housing, altered many young adults' orientations toward buying. Today's 18 to 34 year olds often prefer to rent rather than purchase a home because, in part, they view doing so as more affordable. See Lutz (2015). The great irony of this is that, in doing so, they may actually be driving up rental costs because there are fewer vacant properties on the rental market. See Vasel (2015b).

41. Fertility rates among 20 to 24 year olds were 11% lower in 2011 than predicted were LARCs not available, and the abortion rate for that age group decreased 18% from 2009 to 2012. See Ricketts, Klinger, and Schwalberg (2014).

42. During the 2008–2013 period, the mean annual rates of pregnancy, birth, and abortion among women participating in the CHOICE program were 34.0, 19.4, and 9.7 per 1,000 teens. National comparisons were much higher, with rates of pregnancy, birth, and abortion among sexually experienced U.S. teens in 2008 that were 158.5, 94.0, and 41.5 per 1,000. See Secura et al. (2010, 2014).

43. Guttmacher Institute (2016).

44. A total of 17 of the service-class women earned less than 138% of the poverty threshold (about $15,000 as of 2013). Somewhat fewer would have qualified if the 2006 poverty threshold multiplied by 138 was utilized. But many of the service-class women who qualified were already mothers. In our view, preventing pregnancies of childless women with incomes closer to 150% of the poverty level should be a priority, especially as none of the women at this earning level were hoping to conceive but were not always acting on their preferences.

APPENDIX B

1. It was not always possible for both Sharon Sassler and Amanda Miller to arrange to be present at an interview, especially as Sharon became a mother during the early stages of this project. In addition to the authors, a third interviewer, Sarah Favinger, was instrumental in our collection of the data. Amanda conducted 61 interviews, Sarah 38, and Sharon 24 interviews.

2. Rather than outsource transcribing, two members of the original study team were responsible for all of the transcription. This ensured that the words and meanings of the respondents were accurately captured, enabled us to document pauses and other responses (laughter, tears), and facilitated coding.

3. We followed the precedent established by Bracher and Santow (1998), in an early study of cohabiting unions in Sweden. They argued that it can be misleading to give equal weight to very short-lived unions (which may not be consistently reported) and those of longer duration, and therefore they omitted cohabiting unions that lasted for fewer than three months.

4. This specification is not one used by many surveys that include questions on cohabitation. The questionnaire utilized by the National Survey of Family Growth (NSFG) to determine if a respondent has cohabited with a sexual partner, for example, defines living together as having a sexual relationship while sharing the same usual residence. In contrast, another survey frequently utilized to assess the experiences of young adults, the National Longitudinal Study of Adolescent Health (Add Health), simply asks respondents if they had ever lived with any of the sexual and romantic partners they list, with no residence specification. As a result, estimates of the proportion of current cohabitors aged 18 to 24 drawn from Add Health are higher than those drawn from NSFG, perhaps because Add Health respondents who spent considerable time with sexual partners may have classified these relationships as cohabitation. See Sassler and Joyner (2011).

5. See, for example, the work of Goldrick-Rab (2006).

6. Although online recruitment in general may result in a higher income, more educated sample (Hamilton and Bowers 2006), in this instance (where middle-class participants were the desired respondents) it was an effective way of reaching the target sample. See Hamilton and Bowers (2006).

7. We interviewed an additional seven couples who passed our initial screener, but later decided not to utilize their interviews as we learned at the end of their interviews that their sources of income were primarily from public assistance or parents, meaning that they were not among the service or middle class. We then set income floors that we utilized to screen our couples. We also interviewed one woman whose partner had planned to participate in the study but changed his mind; we therefore excluded her interview from our sample.

8. Some studies of the American class structure set the lower threshold for middle-class family income at around $40,000 and the working (service) class family income lower threshold at around $25,000 per year, making our income floors well below those requirements. The national median household income in inflation adjusted dollars in 2006 was $48,451, though in Ohio it was only $44,532. We believe the relative youth of our sample justifies our thresholds, though the majority of our couples earned considerably more than these limits. See Gilbert (2002). Median household income for the United States and Ohio are from Webster and Bishaw (2007).

Because we were interviewing in a university town, excluding those pursuing degrees would have seriously limited our pool of eligible respondents. There is no "natural" place to recruit cohabiting couples. No organizations represent them, and while there are associations whose goal is to increase the rights available to unmarried couples, such as the Alternatives to Marriage Project (see http://www.unmarried.org), recruiting from such locations might result in a selective group of respondents—both those who may have been marriage rejecters as well as those who were more privileged, having access to the internet.

9. In fact, at least one of our previously married service-class women had never finalized her divorce, and technically was not eligible to marry again. She had been separated from her husband for over nine years at the time of her interview. Another, who thought for over a decade that she was married, discovered that their marriage had never been registered with the state.

Bibliography

AARP Foundation. "What Skills Are Employers Looking For?" Accessed 8/2016 (http://www.aarpworksearch.org/Inside/Pages/HowEmployableAmI.aspx).

Addo, Fenaba R. 2014. "Debt, Cohabitation, and Marriage in Young Adulthood." *Demography* 51:1677–1701.

Alderman, Liz and Steven Greenhouse. 2014. "Fast Food in Denmark Serves Something Atypical: Living Wages." *New York Times,* October 27.

Aleccia, J. 2013. Health News, April 4 (http://www.nbcnews.com/health/new-normal-cohabitation-rise-study-finds-1C9208429).

Anderson, Elijah. 1990. *Streetwise: Race, Class, and Change in an Urban Community.* Chicago: University of Chicago Press.

Antonovics, Kate and Robert Town. 2004. "Are All the Good Men Married? Uncovering the Sources of the Marital Wage Premium." *American Economic Review* 94:317–321.

Armstrong, Elizabeth A. and Laura T. Hamilton. 2013. *Paying for the Party: How College Maintains Inequality.* Cambridge: Harvard University Press.

———. 2009. "Gendered Sexuality in Young Adulthood: Double Binds and Flawed Options." *Gender & Society* 23:589–616.

Armstrong, Elizabeth A., Laura Hamilton, and Paula England. 2010. "Is Hooking Up Bad for Young Women?" *Contexts* 9:22–27.

Ashkenas, Jeremy. 2014. "Can You Live on the Minimum Wage?" *New York Times,* June 8. (http://www.nytimes.com/interactive/2014/02/09/opinion/minimum-wage.html?_r = 0).

Baker, Katie J.M. 2013. "Living Together Without Getting Married Is the 'New' Norm." Posted April 4 (http://jezebel.com/5993610/living-together-without-getting-married-is-the-new-normal).

Bailey, Beth. 1988. *From Front Porch to Back Seat.* Baltimore: The Johns Hopkins University Press.

Barrett, Geraldine and Kaye Wellings. 2002. "What Is a 'Planned Pregnancy'? Empirical Data from a British Study." *Social Science and Medicine* 55:545–557. doi: 10.1016/S0277-9536(01)00187-3.

Basu, Amara. 1999. "Trends in Premarital Childbearing: 1930 to 1994." *Current Population Reports,* pp. 23–197. Washington, DC: U.S. Census Bureau.

Becker, Gary. 1974. *Economics of the Family: Marriage, Children, and Human Capital.* Chicago: University of Chicago Press.

Bernstein, Jared. 2004. "The Living Wage Movement. What Is It, Why Is It, and What's Known about Its Impact." In *Emerging Labor Market Institutions for the Twenty-First Century,* edited by Richard B. Freeman, Joni Hersch, and Lawrence Mishel. Chicago: University of Chicago Press.

Bernard, Jessie. 1981. "The Good Provider Role: Its Rise and Fall." *American Psychologist* 36:1–12.

———. 1972. *The Future of Marriage.* New York: Penguin Books.

Bianchi, Suzanne, Laurent Lesnard, Tiziano Nazio, and Sara Raley. 2014. "Gender and Time Allocation of Cohabiting and Married Women and Men in France, Italy, and the United States." *Demographic Research* 31(8):183–216.

Bianchi, Suzanne M., Melissa A. Milkie, Liana C. Sayer, and John P. Robinson. 2000. "Is Anyone Doing the Housework? Trends in the Gender Division of Household Labor." *Social Forces* 79(1):191–228.

Birtchnell, John and J. Kennard. 1984. "Early and Current Factors Associated with Poor Quality Marriages." *Social Psychiatry* 19:31–40.

Blair-Loy, Mary. 2003. *Competing Devotions: Career and Family among Women Executives.* Cambridge: Harvard University Press.

Blood, Robert Oscar and Donald MacCreery Wolfe. 1960. *Husbands and Wives: The Dynamics of Married Living.* Glencoe, IL: Free Press.

Blumberg, Rae Lesser and Marion Tolbert Coleman. 1989. "A Theoretical Look at the Gender Balance of Power in the American Couple." *Journal of Family Issues* 10:225–250.

Blumstein, Philip and Pepper Schwartz. 1983. *American Couples: Money, Work, Sex.* New York: William Morrow.

Boggle, Kathleen A. 2008. *Hooking Up: Sex, Dating and Relationships on College Campuses.* New York: New York University Press.

Bouchard, G. 2005. "Adult Couples Facing a Planned or an Unplanned Pregnancy: Two Realities." *Journal of Family Issues,* 26:619–637

Bracher, Michael and Gigi Santow. 1998. "Economic Independence and Union Formation in Sweden." *Population Studies* 52:275–295.

Brines, Julie and Kara Joyner. 1999. "The Ties that Bind: Principles of Cohesion in Cohabitation and Marriage." *American Sociological Review* 64:333–355.

Broersma, Lourens. 2008. "Differences in Unemployment by Educational Attainment in the U.S. and Europe: What Role for Skill-Bias Technological Change and Institutions?" EU KELMS project, Paper 20 (www.euklems.net /pub/no20.pdf).

Brown, Susan L. 2000. "Union Transitions among Cohabitors: The Significance of Relationship Assessments and Expectations." *Journal of Marriage and the Family* 62(3):833–846.

Brown, Susan L., Jennifer Roebuck Bulanda, and Gary R. Lee. 2012. "Transitions into and out of Cohabitation in Later Life." *Journal of Marriage and Family* 74(4):774–793

Bumpass, Larry L. and James A. Sweet. 1989. "National Estimates of Cohabitation." *Demography* 26:615–625.

Bumpass, Larry L., James A. Sweet, and Andrew Cherlin. 1991. "The Role of Cohabitation in Declining Rates of Marriage." *Journal of Marriage and Family* 53(4):913–927.

Bush, Jeb and Brian Yablonski. 1995. *Profiles in Character*. Tallahassee: Foundation for Florida's Future.

Cahalan, Margaret and Laura Perna. 2015. "Indicators of Higher Education Equity in the U.S." The Pell Institute, Washington, D.C. (http://www.pellinstitute.org/downloads/publications. Indicators_of_Higher_Education_Equity_in_the_US_45_Year_Trend_Report.pdf).

Campbell, Colin and Jonathan Horowitz. 2016. "Does College Influence Sociopolitical Attitudes?" *Sociology of Education* 89(1):40–58.

Carlson, Daniel, Amanda Miller, Sharon Sassler, and Sarah Hanson. 2016. "The Gendered Division of Housework and Couples' Sexual Relationships: A Re-Examination." *Journal of Marriage and Family* 78:975–995.

Carlson, Marcy J. and Robin Hognas. 2010. *Coparenting in Fragile Families*. Working Paper WP09–13–55. Princeton, NJ: Center for Research on Child Well-Being (http://crcw.princeton.edu/workingpapers/WP03–13-FF.pdf).

Casper, Lynne M. and Suzanne M. Bianchi. 2002. *Continuity and Change in the American Family*. Thousand Oaks, CA: Sage Publications.

Casper, Lynne M. and Philip N. Cohen. 2000. "How does POSSLQ Measure Up? Historical Estimates of Cohabitation." *Demography* 37(2):237–245.

Cate, Rodney M. and Sally A. Lloyd. 1988. "Courtship." Pp. 409–427 in *Handbook of Personal Relationships,* edited by S. Duck. New York: Wiley.

Cherlin, Andrew J. 2004. "The Deinstitutionalization of American Marriage." *Journal of Marriage and Family* 66:848–861.

———. 2009. *The Marriage Go Round: The State of Marriage and the Family in America Today*. New York: Vintage Books.

———. 2014. *Labor's Love Lost: The Rise and Fall of the Working-Class Family in America*. New York: Russell Sage Foundation.

Clarkberg, Marin, Ross Stolzenberg, and Linda Waite. 1995. "Attitudes, Values, and Entrance into Cohabitational Versus Marital Unions." *Social Forces* 74:609–626.

Coleman, James S. 1988. "Social Capital in the Creation of Human Capital." *American Journal of Sociology,* 94:S95-S120.

Collins, Patricia Hill. 1993. "Toward a New Vision: Race, Class, and Gender as Categories of Analysis and Connection." *Race, Sex, and Class* 1:25–45.

———. 1990. "Black Feminist Thought in the Matrix of Domination." Pp. 221–238 in *Black Feminist Thought: Knowledge, Consciousness, and the Politics of Empowerment*. New York: Routledge.

Coltrane, Scott. 1996. *Family Man: Fatherhood, Housework, and Gender Equity*. New York: Oxford University Press.

Conley, Dalton T. 2008. "Rethinking College Readiness." *New Directions for Higher Education* 144:3–13.

Copen, Casey E., Kimberly Daniels, and William Mosher. 2013. *First Premarital Cohabitation in the U.S: 2006–2010 National Survey of Family Growth.* National Health Statistics Reports, #64, Table 2. Hyattsville, MD: National Center for Health Statistics.

Copen, Casey, Kimberly Daniels, Jonathan Vespa, and William D. Mosher. 2012. *First Marriages in the United States: Data from the 2006–2010 National Survey of Family Growth.* National Health Statistics Reports, #49. Hyattsville, MD: National Center for Health Statistics.

Cotter, David A., Joan M. Hermsen, and Reeve Vanneman. 2004. "Gender Inequality at Work." In *The American People: Census 2000,* edited by Reynolds Farley and John Haaga. New York: Russell Sage Foundation.

———. 2011. "The End of the Gender Revolution? Gender Role Attitudes from 1977 to 2008." *American Journal of Sociology* 117(1):259–289.

DeJean, Sarah L., Christi R. McGeorge, and Thomas Stone Carlson. 2012. "Attitudes toward Never-Married Single Mothers and Fathers: Does Gender Matter?" *Journal of Feminist Family Therapy* 24:121–138.

Denmark, Florence L., Jeffrey S. Shaw, and Samuel D. Ciali. 1985. "The Relationship among Sex Roles, Living Arrangements, and the Division of Household Responsibilities." *Sex Roles* 12:617–625.

DeParle, Jason and Sabrina Tavernise. 2012. "For Women Under 30, Most Births Occur Outside Marriage." *New York Times,* February 17.

Department of Numbers. 2014. Columbus, Ohio, Residential Rent and Rental Statistics (http://www.deptofnumbers.com/rent/ohio/columbus/).

De Ruijter, Esther, Judith K. Treas, and Philip N. Cohen. 2005. "Outsourcing the Gender Factory: Living Arrangements and Service Expenditures on Female and Male Tasks." *Social Forces* 84(1):305–322.

Deutsch, Francine. 1999. *Halving it All: How Equally Shared Parenting Works.* Cambridge: Harvard University Press.

Digest of Education Statistics. 2010. Chapter 5: "Outcomes of Education, Educational Characteristics of Workers," Table 391 (*https://nces.ed.gov/pubs2011/2011015.pdf*).

East, Patricia L., Nina C. Chien, and Jennifer S. Barber. 2012. "Adolescents' Pregnancy Intentions, Wantedness, and Regret: Cross-Lagged Relations with Mental Health and Parenting." *Journal of Marriage and Family* 74(1):167–185.

Eaton, Asia Anna and Suzanna Rose. 2011. "Has Dating Become More Egalitarian? A 35-year Review Using Sex Roles." *Sex Roles* 64:843–862.

Edin, Kathryn, Paula England, Emily F. Shafer, and Joanna Reed. 2007. "Forming Fragile Families: Was the Baby Planned, Unplanned, or In Between?" Pp. 25–54 in *Unmarried Couples with Children,* edited by P. England and K. Edin. New York: Russell Sage Foundation.

Edin, Kathryn and Maria Kefalas. 2005. *Promises I Can Keep: Why Poor Women Put Motherhood before Marriage.* Oakland: University of California Press.

Edin, Kathryn and Timothy Nelson. 2013. *Doing the Best I Can: Fatherhood in the Inner City*. Oakland: University of California Press.

Edin, Kathryn and Joanna M. Reed. 2006. "Why Don't They Just Get Married? Barriers to Marriage among the Disadvantaged." *The Future of Children* 15.2:117–137.

Ellwood, David T. and Christopher Jencks. 2004. "The Uneven Spread of Single Parent Families: What Do We Know? Where Do We Look for Answers?" Pp. 3–77 in *Social Inequality*, edited by K. Neckerman. New York: Russell Sage Foundation.

England, Paula. 2010. "The Gender Revolution: Uneven and Stalled." *Gender & Society* 24(2):149–166.

England, Paula, Monica L. Caudillo, Krystale Littlejohn, Brooke C. Bass, and Joanna Reed. 2016. "Why Do Young, Unmarried Women Who Do Not Want to Get Pregnant Contracept Inconsistently? Mixed-method Evidence for the Role of Efficacy." *Socius* 2:1–15.

England, Paula and Barbara S. Kilbourne. 1990. "Markets, Marriages, and Other Mates: The Problem of Power." Pp. 163–188 in *Beyond the Marketplace*, edited by R. Friedland and A. F. Robertson. New York: Aldine de Gruyer.

England, Paula, Elizabeth A. McClintock, and Emily F. Shafer. 2011. "Birth Control Use and Early, Unintended Births." Pp. 21–49 in *Social Class and Changing Families in an Unequal America*, edited by M. J. Carlson and P. England. Stanford: Stanford University Press.

England, Paula, Emily F. Shafer, and Lawrence L. Wu. 2012. "Premarital Conceptions, Postconception ('Shotgun') Marriages, and Premarital First Births: Education Gradients in U.S. Cohorts of White and Black Women Born 1925–1959." *Demographic Research* 27:153–166.

Epstein, Cynthia Fuchs and Arne L. Kalleberg. 2006. *Fighting for Time: Shifting Boundaries of Work and Social Life*. New York: Russell Sage Foundation.

Fass, Paula. 1977. *The Damned and the Beautiful: American Youth in the 1920's*. New York: Oxford University Press.

Fein, Ellen and Sherrie Schneider. 2013. *Not Your Mother's Rules: The New Secrets for Dating*. New York: Grand Central Publishing.

———. 1995. *The Rules: Time-Tested Secrets for Capturing the Heart of Mr. Right*. New York: Warner Books.

Fennell, Julie L. 2011. "Men Bring Condoms, Women Take Pills: Men's and Women's Roles in Contraceptive Decision Making." *Gender & Society*, 25:496–521.

Ferree, Martha Marx. 1990. "Beyond Separate Spheres: Feminism and Family Research." *Journal of Marriage and the Family* 52:866–884.

Fields, Jason. 2004. "America's Families and Living Arrangements: 2003." In *Current Population Reports*, pp. 20–553. Washington, DC: U.S. Census Bureau.

Finer, Lawrence and Stanley Henshaw. 2006. "Disparities in Rates of Unintended Pregnancy in the United States, 1994 and 2001." *Perspectives on Sexual and Reproductive Health* 38:90–96.

Finer, Lawrence B. and Mia R. Zolna. 2011. "Unintended Pregnancy in the United States: Incidence and Disparities, 2006." *Contraception* 84:478–485.

Firminger, Kirsten B. 2014. "Is He Boyfriend Material? Representations of Males in Teenage Girls' Magazines." In *The Kaleidoscope of Gender: Prisms, Patterns, and Possibilities,* edited by Joan Z. Spade and Catherine G. Valentine. 4th ed. Los Angeles: Sage Publications.

Focus on the Family. 2014. "What You Need to Know about Marriage: Questions and Answers Driving the Debate" (http://media.focusonthefamily.com /fotf/pdf/channels/social-issues/marriage-ebook-download2014.pdf?_ga = 1 .102761730.324225966.1442850355).

Friends. 2001. "The One Where They All Turn 30," Season 7, Episode 14. Directed by Ben Weiss. Originally aired February 8.

Fry, Richard. 2014. "New Census Data Show More Americans Are Tying the Knot, But Mostly It's the College Educated." Fact Tank: Pew Research Center (http://www.pewresearch.org/fact-tank/2014/02/06/new-census-data-show-more-americans-are-tying-the-knot-but-mostly-its-the-college-educated/).

Fu, Haishan, Jacqueline E. Darroch, Taylor Haas, and Nalini Ranjit. 1999. "Contraceptive Failure Rates: New Estimates from the 1995 NSFG." *Family Planning Perspectives* 31:56–63, table 3.

Furstenberg, Frank, F. 2015. "Diverging Development: The Not-So-Invisible Hand of Social Class in the United States." In *Families as They Really Are,* edited by B. J. Risman and V. Rutter. 2nd ed. New York: W. W. Norton.

Furstenberg, Frank F., Sheela Kennedy, Vonnie C. McLoyd, Ruben G. Rumbaut, and Richard A. Settersten, Jr. 2004. "Growing Up Is Harder to Do." *Contexts* 3(3):33–41.

Gastaldo, Evann. 2013. "The New Normal: Cohabitation." Posted April 4 (http://www.newser.com/story/165647/the-new-normal-cohabitation.html).

Gerson, Kathleen. 2009. *The Unfinished Revolution: Coming of Age in a New Era of Gender, Work, and Family.* New York: Oxford University Press.

Gertner, Jon. 2006. "What Is a Living Wage?" New York Times, January 15.

Gibson-Davis, Christina, Katherine Edin, and Sara McLanahan. 2005. "High Hopes but Even Higher Expectations: The Retreat from Marriage among Low-Income Couples." *Journal of Marriage and Family* 67:1301–1312.

Gibson-Davis, Christina and Heather Rackin. 2014. "Marriage or Carriage? Trends in Union Context and Birth Type by Education." *Journal of Marriage and Family* 76(3):506–519.

Gilbert, Dennis. 2002. *The American Class Structure: In An Age of Growing Inequality.* 7th ed. Thousand Oaks, CA: Pine Forge Press.

Gilbert, Lucia A., Sarah J. Walker, Sherry McKinney, and Jessica L. Snell. 1999. "Challenging Discourse Themes Reproducing Gender Inequality in Heterosexual Dating: An Analog Study." *Sex Roles,* 41:753–775.

Girls. 2013. "It's a Shame About Ray," Season 2, Episode 4. Produced by Lena Dunham, Judd Aptow, and Jenni Konner. Originally aired February 2.

Glamour Magazine. "Engagement Chicken" (http://www.glamour.com/about /engagement-chicken).

Goldrick-Rab, Sara. 2006. "Following Their Every Move: An Investigation of Social-Class Differences in College Pathways." *Sociology of Education,* 79:61–79.

Gottschalck, Alfred O. 2006. "Dynamics of Economic Well-Being: Spells of Unemployment 2001–2003." *Household Economic Studies,* pp. 70–105.

Washington, DC: U.S. Census Bureau (http://www.census.gov/prod/2006pubs /p70–105.pdf).

Granovetter, Mark S. 1973. "The Strength of Weak Ties." *American Journal of Sociology* 78:1360–1380.

Grover, Kelly J., Candace S. Russell, Walter R. Schumm, and Louis A. Paff-Bergen. 1985. "Mate Selection Processes and Marital Satisfaction." *Family Relations* 34:383–386.

Gubernskya, Zoya. 2011. "Changing Attitudes toward Marriage and Children in Six Countries." *Sociological Perspectives* 63:179–200.

Gupta, Sanjiv. 1999. "The Effects of Transitions in Marital Status on Men's Performance of Housework." *Journal of Marriage and the Family* 61(3):700–711.

Guttmacher Institute. 2016. "Fact on Publicly Funded Family Planning Services: Ohio." State Center (http://www.guttmacher.org/statecenter/family-planning /OH.html).

Guzzo, Karen Benjamin. 2014. "Trends in Cohabitation Outcomes: Compositional Changes and Engagement among Never Married Young Adults." *Journal of Marriage and Family* 76(4):826–842.

Guzzo, Karen B. and Sarah R. Hayford. 2012. "Unintended Fertility and the Stability of Coresidential Relationships." *Social Science Research* 41(5):1138–1151.

———. 2011. "Fertility Following an Unintended First Birth." *Demography* 48(4):1439–1516.

Gwartney-Gibbs, Patricia A. 1986. "The Institutionalization of Premarital Cohabitation: Estimates from Marriage License Applications, 1970 and 1980." *Journal of Marriage and the Family* 48(2):423–434.

Haire, Amanda R. and Christi R. McGeorge. 2012. "Negative Perceptions of Never-Married Custodial Single Mothers and Fathers: Applications of a Gender Analysis for Family Therapists." *Journal of Feminist Family Therapy* 24:24–51.

Hamilton, Rebekah and Barbara Bowers. 2006. "Internet Recruitment and Email Interviews in Qualitative Studies." *Qualitative Health Research* 16:821–835.

Hayford, Sarah R. and S. Philip Morgan. 2008. "The Quality of Retrospective Data on Cohabitation." *Demography* 45(1):129–141.

Hegewisch, Ariane, Claudia Williams, and Amber Henderson. 2010. "Fact Sheet: The Gender Wage Gap 2010." Institute of Women's Policy Research (http://www.iwpr.org/publications/pubs/the-gender-wage-gap-2010-up-dated-march-2011).

The Heritage Foundation. 2014. "Promoting Health Marriage." (http://www .heritage.org/issues/family-and-marriage/promoting-healthy-marriage).

Hewlett, Sylvia Ann. 2002. *Creating a Life: Professional Women and the Quest for Children*. New York: Miramax Books.

Hochschild, Arlie. 2012. *The Outsourced Self: Intimate Life in Market Times*. New York: Metropolitan Books.

———. 2003. *The Commercialization of Intimate Lives: Notes from Home and Work*. Oakland: University of California Press.

Hochschild, Arlie with Anne Machung. 1989. *The Second Shift: Working Parents and the Revolution at Home*. New York: Penguin Books.

Hondagneu-Sotelo, Pierrette. 2001. *Domestica: Immigrant Workers Cleaning and Caring in the Shadows of Affluence.* Oakland: University of California Press.

Howard, Vicki. 2003. "A 'Real Man's Ring': Gender and the Invention of Tradition." *Journal of Social History* 36:837–856.

Huang, Penelope, M., Pamela J. Smock, Wendy D. Manning, and Cara A. Bergstrom-Lynch. 2011. "He Says, She Says: Gender and Cohabitation." *Journal of Family Issues* 32(7):876–905.

Hymowitz, Kay S. 2012. *Manning Up: How the Rise of Women Has Turned Men into Boys.* New York: Basic Books.

Ingoldsby, Bron B. 2003. "The Mate Selection Process in the United States." In *Mate Selection Across Cultures,* edited by Raeann R. Hamon and Bron B. Ingoldsby. Thousand Oaks, CA: Sage Publications.

———. 2002. "Bundling." In *International Encyclopedia of Marriage and Family Relationships.* 2nd ed. New York: Macmillan.

Johnson, Rucker C. and Robert F. Schoeni. 2011. "The Influence of Early-Life Events on Human Capital, Health Status, and Labor Market Outcomes over the Life Course." *Journal of Economic Analysis and Policy* 11(3): Article 3.

Jones, Rachel, and Kathryn Kost. 2007. "Underreporting of Induced and Spontaneous Abortion in the United States: An Analysis of the 2002 National Survey of Family Growth." *Studies in Family Planning* 3:187–197.

Kaysen, Ronda. 2015. "Leasing Begins for New York's First Micro-Apartments." *New York Times,* November 20, RE1.

Kaufman, Gayle. 2013. *Superdads: How Fathers Balance Work and Family in the 21st Century.* New York: New York University Press.

Kennedy, Sheela and Larry Bumpass. 2008. "Cohabitation and Children's Living Arrangements: New Estimates from the United States." *Demographic Research* 19:1663–1692.

Komarovsky, Mirra. 1964. *Blue Collar Marriage.* New York: Random House.

Komter, Aafke. 1989. "Hidden Power in Marriage." *Gender & Society* 3:187–216.

Kreider, Rose M. 2010. "Housing and Household Economic Statistics Division Working Paper," U.S. Census Bureau, Table 6. Released 9/15/2010 (http://www.census.gov/population/www/socdemo/Inc-Opp-sex-2009-to-2010.pdf).

Kreider, Rose M. and Renee Ellis. 2011. "Number, Timing, and Duration of Marriages and Divorces: 2009." *Current Population Reports,* pp. 70–125. Washington, DC: U.S. Census Bureau.

Lamont, Ellen. 2015. "The Limited Construction of an Egalitarian Masculinity: College-Educated Men's Dating and Relationship Narratives." *Men and Masculinities* 18(3):271–292.

———. 2014. "Negotiating Courtship: Reconciling Egalitarian Ideals with Traditional Gender Norms." *Gender & Society* 28(2):189–211.

Laner, Mary and Nicole Ventrone. 1998. "Egalitarian Daters/Traditionalist Dates." *Journal of Family Issues* 19: 468–477.

Lareau, Annette. 2003. *Unequal Childhoods: Class, Race, and Family Life.* Oakland: University of California Press.

LaRochelle, Flynn, Cynthia Castro, Joe Goldenson, Jacqueline P. Tulsky, Deborah L. Cohan, Paul D. Blumenthal, and Carolyn B. Sulfrin. 2012. "Contraceptive Use and Barriers to Access among Newly Arrested Women." *Journal of Correctional Health Care* 18:111–119.

Lavee, Yoav and Ruth Katz. 2002. "Division of Labor, Perceived Fairness, and Marital Quality: The Effect of Gender Ideology." *Journal of Marriage and Family* 64: 27–39.

Lee, Gary R. 2015. *The Limits of Marriage: Why Getting Everyone Married Won't Solve All Our Problems*. Lanham, MD: Lexington Books.

Levy, Frank. 1998. *The New Dollars and Dreams*. New York: Russell Sage Foundation.

Lichter, Daniel T., Zhenchao Qian, and Leanna Mellot. 2006. "Marriage or Dissolution? Union Transitions among Poor Cohabiting Women." *Demography* 43:223–250.

Lichter, Daniel T., Sharon Sassler, and Richard N. Turner. 2014. "Cohabitation, Post-Conception Unions, and the Rise in Nonmarital Fertility." *Social Science Research* 47:134–147.

Lichter, Daniel T., Richard N. Turner, and Sharon Sassler. 2010. "National Estimates of the Rise in Serial Cohabitation." *Social Science Research* 39:754–765.

Longmore, Monica A., Wendy D. Manning, Peggy Giordano, and J. L. Rudolph. 2003. "Contraceptive Self-Efficacy: Does It Influence Adolescents' Contraceptive Use?" *Journal of Health and Social Behavior* 44:45–60.

Lorber, Judith. 1994. *Paradoxes of Gender*. New Haven: Yale University Press.

Luscombe, Belinda. 2010. "Workplace Salaries: At Last, Women on Top." *Time* Magazine, September 1 (http://www.time.com/time/business/article/o,8599,2015274,00.html).

Lutz, Ashley. 2015. "Millennials Don't Care about Owning and It's Destroying Traditional Retail." *Business Insider* (http://www.businessinsider.com/millennials-are-renting-instead-of-buying-2015-5).

Lyons, Heidi, Peggy C. Giordano, Wendy D. Manning, and Monica A. Longmore. 2011. "Identity, Peer Relationships, and Adolescent Girls' Sexual Behavior: An Exploration of the Contemporary Double Standard." *Journal of Sex Research* 48(5):437–449.

Madden, Mary and Amanda Lenhart. 2006. "Online Dating." Pew Internet and American Life Project (http://www.pewinternet.org/2013/10/21/online-dating-relationships/).

Manning, Wendy D. 2013. *Trends in Cohabitation: Over Twenty Years of Change, 1987–2010*. Family Profile-13-12, National Center for Family and Marriage Research, Bowling Green, OH (http://ncfmr.bgsu.edu/pdf/family_profiles/file130944.pdf).

Manning, Wendy D. and Pamela J. Smock. 2002. "First Comes Cohabitation and Then Comes Marriage? A Research Note." *Journal of Family Issues* 23:1065–1087.

Martin, Patricia Yancey. 2004. "Gender as a Social Institution." *Social Forces* 82:1249–1273.

Martin, Steven P. 2006. "Trends in Marital Dissolution by Women's Education in the United States." *Demographic Research* 15:537–559.

Martin, Steven P. and Sangeeta Parashar. 2006. "Women's Changing Attitudes toward Divorce, 1974–2002: Evidence for an Educational Crossover." *Journal of Marriage and Family* 68:29–40.

McIntosh, Peggy. 1989. "White Privilege: Unpacking the Invisible Knapsack." *Peace and Freedom Magazine* July/August, pp. 10–12.

McKinley, Jesse. 2015. "Cuomo to Raise Minimum Wage to $15 for All New York State Employees." *New York Times,* November 10, A1.

McLanahan, Sara. 2004. "Diverging Destinies: How Children Are Faring under the Second Demographic Transition." *Demography* 41(4):607–627.

McPherson, Miller, Lynn Smith-Lovin, and James M. Cook. 2001. "Birds of a Feather: Homophily in Social Networks." *Annual Review of Sociology* 27:415–444.

Melms, Melissa. 2012. "The 7 things You Learn Your First Year of Living with a Guy." *Glamour Smitten,* November 29 (*http://www.glamour.com/sex-love-life/blogs/smitten/2012/11/the-7-things-you-learn-your-fi*).

Miller, Amanda. J. 2012. "Cohabiting Men's Preferences for and Roles in Determining the Outcomes of Unexpected Pregnancies." *Sociological Forum* 27:708–731.

Miller, Amanda J. and Daniel Carlson. 2016. "Great Expectations? Cohabitors' Preferred and Actual Divisions of Labor." *Journal of Marriage and Family* 78:346–363.

Miller, Amanda J. and Sharon Sassler. 2010. "Stability and Change in the Division of Labor among Cohabiting Couples." *Sociological Forum* 25(4):677–702.

Miller, Amanda, Sharon Sassler, and Dela Kusi-Appouh. 2011. "The Specter of Divorce: Views from Working- and Middle-Class Cohabitors, *Family Relations* 60:602–616.

Mincy, Ronald, Jennifer Hill, and Marilyn Sinkewicz. 2009. "Marriage: Cause or Mere Indicator of Future Earnings Growth?" *Journal of Policy Analysis & Management* 28(3):417–439.

Misra, Tanvi. 2015. "Mapping the Difference between Minimum Wage and Cost of Living." *Citylab,* September 10 (http://www.citylab.com/work/2015/09/mapping-the-difference-between-minimum-wage-and-cost-of-living/404644/).

Mitchell, Robert L. 2009. "Online Dating: It's Bigger than Porn." *Computerworld.* Accessed 10/30/2013 (http://blogs.computerworld.com/online_dating_its_bigger_than_porn).

Mortensen, Øystein, Torbjør Torsheim, Øle Melkevik, and Frode Thuen. 2012. "Adding a Baby to the Equation: Married and Cohabiting Women's Relationship Satisfaction in the Transition to Parenthood." *Family Process* 51:122–139.

Mullainathan, Sendhil and Elder Shafir. 2013. *Scarcity: Why Having Too Little Means So Much.* New York: Times Books.

Murray, Charles. 2012. *Coming Apart: The State of White America, 1960–2010.* New York: Crown Forum.

Musick, Kelly. 2007. "Cohabitation, Nonmarital Childbearing, and the Marriage Process." *Demographic Research* 16:249–285.

Musick, Kelly and Katherine Michelmore. 2015. "Cross-National Comparisons of Union Stability in Cohabiting and Married Families with Children." Presented at the 2016 Annual Meeting of the Population Association of America, Washington, DC.

Myers, Scott and Alan Booth. 2002. "Forerunners of Change in Nontraditional Gender Ideology." *Social Psychology Quarterly* 65:18–37.

National Center for Education Statistics, 2009. "Percentage of Persons Age 25 and Over, by Race/Eethnicity, Years of School Completed and Sex." *Digest of Education Statistics,* Table 8 (http://nces.ed.gov/programs/digest/09/d09/tables/dt09_008.asp).

NBC News. 2013. "'The New Normal': Cohabitation on the Rise, Study Finds." (http://www.nbcnews.com/health/new-normal-cohabitation-rise-study-finds-1C9208429).

Newman, Katherine and Victor Tan Chen. 2007. *The Missing Class: Portraits of the Near Poor in America.* New York: Beacon Press.

Oppenheimer, Valerie K. 1988. "A Theory of Marriage Timing." *American Journal of Sociology* 94:563–591.

———. 2003. "Cohabiting and Marriage during Young Men's Career-Development." *Demography* 40:127–149.

Orenstein, Peggy. 2001. "Parasites in Pret-a-Porter," *New York Times Magazine,* July 1, pp. 31–35.

Orrange, Robert. 2002. "Aspiring Law and Business Professionals' Orientations to Work and Family Life." *Journal of Family Issues* 23(2):287–317.

Perelli-Harris, Brienna, Wendy Sigle-Rushton, Michaela Kreyenfeld, Trude Lappegård, Renske Keizer, and Caroline Berghammer. 2010. "The Education Gradient of Childbearing within Cohabitation in Europe." *Population Development and Review* 36(4):775–801.

Petola, Pia, Melissa Milkie, and Stanley Presser. 2004. "The 'Feminist' Mystique: Feminist Identity in Three Generations of Women." *Gender & Society* 18:122–144.

Pew Research Center. 2007a. "How Young People View Their Lives, Futures, and Politics: A Portrait of the 'Generation Next.'" Pew Research Center for the People and the Press. Posted January 9 (*http://www.people-press.org/files/legacy-pdf/300.pdf*).

———. 2007b. "Modern Marriage." Posted July 18 (http://www.pewsocialtrends.org/2007/07/18/modern-marriage/).

Pew Research Trends. 2009. "Public Has Split Verdict on Increased Level of Unmarried Motherhood." Pew Research Center Social and Demographic Trends Project. Posted March 19 (http://www.pewsocialtrends.org/2009/03/19/public-has-split-verdict-on-increased-level-of-unmarried-motherhood/)

Piotrkowski, Chaya. 1979. *Work and the Family System: A Naturalistic Study of Working-Class and Lower-Middle-Class Families.* New York: The Free Press.

Purnell, Caroline. 2013. "How Much Rent Can You Really Afford" (http://www.apartmenttherapy.com/how-much-rent-you-can-really-afford-renters-solutions-186462).

Qian, Zhenchao and Daniel T. Lichter. 2008. "Serial Cohabitation and the Marital Life Course." *Journal of Marriage and Family* 70:861–878.

Raley, Sara B., Marybeth J. Mattingly, and Suzanne M. Bianchi. 2006. "How Dual Are Dual-Income Couples? Documenting Change from 1970 to 2001." *Journal of Marriage and Family* 68(1):11–28.

Rector, Robert. 2012. "Marriage: America's Greatest Weapon against Child Poverty." The Heritage Foundation, Special Report #117 on Poverty and Inequality (http://www.heritage.org/research/reports/2012/09/marriage-americas-greatest-weapon-against-child-poverty).

Reed, Joanna M. 2006. "Not Crossing the 'Extra Line': How Cohabitors with Children View their Unions." *Journal of Marriage and Family* 68(5):1117–1131.

Rhoades, G., S. Stanley, and H. Markman. 2009. "Couples' Reasons for Cohabitation: Associations with Individual Well-Being and Relationship Quality." *Journal of Family Issues* 30:233–258.

Ricketts, Sue, Greta Klinger, and Renee Schwalberg. 2014. "Game Change in Colorado: Widespread Use of Long-Acting Reversible Contraceptives and Rapid Decline in Births Among Young, Low-Income Women." *Perspectives on Reproductive and Sexual Health* 46(3): 125–132.

Rindfuss, Ronald D. and Audrey VandenHeuval. 1990. "Cohabitation: A Precursor to Marriage or an Alternative to Being Single?" *Population and Development Review* 16(4):703–726.

Risman, Barbara. 2004. "Gender as a Social Structure: Theory Wrestling with Action." *Gender & Society* 18:429–450.

———. 1998. *Gender Vertigo: American Families in Transition*. New Haven: Yale University Press.

Romero, Mary. 1992. *Maid in the U.S.A.* New York: Routledge Press.

Roper Center. Accessed 4/21/2014 (http://ropercenter.cornell.edu/the-changing-role-of-women.html).

Rose, Suzanna and Irene H. Frieze. 1989. "Young Single's Scripts for a First Date." *Gender & Society,* 3:258–268.

Ross, Louise, and A. Clarke Davis. 1996. "Black-White College Student Attitudes and Expectations in Paying for Dates." *Sex Roles,* 35:43–56.

Rothman, Ellen K. 1984. *Hands and Hearts: A History of Courtship in America*. Cambridge: Harvard University Press.

Rubin, Lillian B. 1994. *Families on the Fault Line: America's Working Class Speaks about the Family, the Economy, Race, and Ethnicity*. New York: Harper Collins.

———. 1976. *Worlds of Pain: Life in the Working-Class Family*. New York: Basic Books.

Sassler, Sharon. 2004. "The Process of Entering into Cohabiting Unions." *Journal of Marriage and Family* 66:491–505.

Sassler, Sharon and Anna Cunningham. 2008. "How Cohabitors View Childbearing." *Sociological Perspectives* 51:3–28.

Sassler, Sharon and Frances Goldscheider. 2004. "Revisiting Jane Austen's Theory of Marriage Timing: Union Formation among American Men in the Late 20th Century." *Journal of Family Issues* 25(2):139–166.

Sassler, Sharon and Kara Joyner. 2011. Social Exchange and the Progression of Sexual Relationships in Emerging Adulthood. *Social Forces* 90:223–245.

Sassler, Sharon and James McNally. 2003. "Cohabiting Couples' Economic Circumstances and Union Transitions: A Re-Examination Using Multiple Imputation Techniques." *Social Science Research* 32:553–578.

Sassler, Sharon, Katherine Michelmore, and Jennifer Holland. 2016. "The Progression of Sexual Relationships." *Journal of Marriage and Family.* 73: 587–97.

Sassler, Sharon and Amanda J. Miller. 2015. "The Ecology of Relationships: Meeting Locations and Cohabitors' Relationship Perceptions." *Journal of Social and Personal Relationships* 32:141–160.

———. 2011. "Waiting to Be Asked: Gender, Power, and Relationship Progression among Cohabiting Couples." *Journal of Family Issues* 32(4):482–506.

Sassler, Sharon, Amanda Miller, and Sarah Favinger. 2009. "Planned Parenthood? Fertility Intentions and Experiences among Cohabiting Couples." *Journal of Family Issues.* 30:206–232.

Sassler, Sharon, Soma Roy, and Elizabeth Stasny. 2014. "Men's Economic Status and Marital Transitions of Fragile Families." *Demographic Research* 30(3):71–110.

Sassler, Sharon and Robert Schoen. 1999. "The Effect of Attitudes and Economic Activity on Marriage." *Journal of Marriage and the Family* 61(1): 147–159.

Sautter, Jessica, Rebecca M. Tippett, and S. Philip Morgan. 2010. "The Social Demography of Internet Dating in the United States." *Social Science Quarterly* 91(2): 554–575.

Sayer, Liana. 2015. "The Complexities of Interpreting Changing Household Patterns." *CCF Online Symposium on Housework, Gender, and Parenthood* (https://contemporaryfamilies.org/complexities-brief-report/).

Schneider, Daniel. 2011. "Wealth and the Marital Divide." *American Journal of Sociology* 117: 627–667.

Schoen, Robert. 1989. "Whither the Family?" *Contemporary Sociology* 18(4): 618–620.

Schwartz, Christine R. and Hongyun Han. 2014. "The Reversal of the Gender Gap in Education and Trends in Marital Dissolution." *American Sociological Review* 79(4): 605–629.

Schwartz, Christine and Robert D. Mare. 2005. "Trends in Educational Assortative Marriage from 1940 to 2003." *Demography* 42:621.646.

Schwartz, Mary and Ellen Wilson. 2008. "Who Can Afford to Live in a Home? A Look at Data from the 2006 American Community Survey." Washington, DC: U.S. Census Bureau (http://www.census.gov/housing/census/publications/who-can-afford.pdf).

Schwartz, Pepper. 1995. *Love Between Equals: How Peer Marriage Really Works.* New York: Touchstone Books.

Scott, Mindy E., Erin Schelar, Jennifer Manlove, and Carol Cui. 2009. "Young Adult Attitudes about Relationships and Marriage: Times May Have Changed, but Expectations Remain High." *Trends Research Brief,* 2009–30.

Secura, Gina M., Jenifer E. Allsworth, Tessa Madden, Jennifer L. Mullersman, and Jeffrey F. Peipert. 2010. "The Contraceptive CHOICE Project: Reducing

Barriers to Long-Acting Reversible Contraception." *American Journal of Obstetric Gynecology* 203(2):115.e1–115.e7.

Secura, Gina M., Tessa Madden, C. McNicholas, Jennifer L. Mullersman, C. M. Buckel, Q. Zhao, and Jeffrey F. Piepert. 2014. "Provision of No-Cost, Long-Acting Contraception and Teenage Pregnancy." *New England Journal of Medicine* 371(14):1316–23.

Settersten, Richard A., Jr. and Barbara Ray. 2010. "What's Going On with Young People Today? The Long and Twisting Path to Adulthood." *Future of Children* 20(1):19–41.

Shah, Neil. 2015. "U.S. Sees Rise in Unmarried Parents." *Wall Street Journal,* March 10 (http://www.wsj.com/articles/cohabiting-parents-at-record-high-1426010894).

Shelton, Beth A., and Daphne John. 1993. "Does Marital Status Make a Difference? Housework among Married and Cohabiting Men and Women." *Journal of Family Issues* 14:401–420.

Sherman, Erik. 2016. "Seattle Food Jobs Soar After $11 Minimum Wage Starts." *Forbes,* January 8, Personal Finance (http://www.forbes.com/sites/eriksherman/2016/01/08/seattle-food-jobs-soar-after-11-minimum-wage-starts/).

Shipler, David K. 2004. *The Working Poor: Invisible in America.* New York: Alfred A. Knopf.

Shostak, Arthur B. 1969. *Blue-Collar Life.* New York: Random House.

Silva, Jennifer M. 2013. *Coming Up Short: Service-Class Adulthood in an Age of Uncertainty.* New York: Oxford University Press.

Silverman, Jane, Aida Torres, and Jacqueline D. Forrest. 1987. "Barriers to Contraceptive Services." *Family Planning Perspectives* 19:94–97.

Simmons, Tavia and Martin O'Connell. 2003. "Married-Couple and Unmarried-Partner Households: 2000," Census 2000 Special Reports, CENSR-5, U.S. Census Bureau. Accessed 3/18/2013 (http://www.census.gov/prod/2003pubs/censr-5.pdf).

Skocpol, Theda. 2000. *The Missing Middle: Working Families and the Future of American Social Policy.* New York: W.W. Norton.

Smith, Aaron and Monica Anderson. 2015. "5 Facts about Online Dating." Pew Research Center, Fact Tank. April 20 (http://www.pewresearch.org/fact-tank/2015/04/20/5-facts-about-online-dating/).

Smock, Pamela J. 2000. "Cohabitation in the United States: An Appraisal of Research Themes, Findings, and Implications." *Annual Review of Sociology* 26:1–20.

Smock, Pamela J., Wendy D. Manning, and Meredith Porter. 2005. "Everything's There Except Money: How Money Shapes Decisions to Marry among Cohabitors." *Journal of Marriage and Family* 67:680–696.

South, Scott J. and Glenna Spitze. 1994. "Housework in Marital and Non-marital Households." *American Sociological Review* 59(3):327–347.

Sprecher, Susan. 1985. "Sex Differences in Bases of Power in Dating Relationships." *Sex Roles,* 12(3–4):449–462.

Stanley, Scott M. and Howard J. Markman. 1992. "Assessing Commitment in Personal Relationships." *Journal of Marriage and the Family* 54:595–608.

Stanley, Scott M., Galeana K. Rhoades, and H. J. Markman. 2006. "Sliding versus Deciding: Inertia and the Premarital Cohabitation Effect." *Family Relations* 55(4):499–509.

Stepp, Laura Sessions. 2007. *Unhooked: How Young Women Pursue Sex, Delay Love, and Lose at Both.* New York: Riverhead Books.

Stevenson, Betsey and Justin Wolfers. 2007. "Marriage and Divorce: Changes and Their Driving Forces." *Journal of Economic Perspectives* 21(2):27–52.

Stone, Pamela. 2007. *Opting Out? Why Women Really Quit Careers and Head Home.* Oakland: University of California Press.

Streib, Jessi. 2015. *The Power of the Past: Understanding Cross-Class Marriages.* New York: Oxford University Press.

Sullivan, J. Courtney. 2009. "Let's Say You Want to Date a Hog Farmer." *New York Times*, April 27, Fashion and Style Section.

Sum, Andrew, Ishwar Khatiwada, Joseph McLaughlin, and Sheila Palma. 2011. "No Country for Young Men: Declining Labor Market Prospects for Low-skilled Men in the United States." *The Annals of the American Academy of Political and Social Science* 635(1):24–55.

Surra, Catherine A. 1987. "Reasons for Changes in Commitment: Variations by Courtship Type." *Journal of Social and Personal Relationships* 4:17–33.

Surra, Catherine A., Peggy Arizzi, and Linda Asmussen. 1988. "The Association between Reasons for Commitment and the Development and Outcome of Marital Relationships." *Journal of Social and Personal Relationship* 5:74–63.

Surra, Catherine A. and Christine R. Gray. 2000. "A Typology of the Processes of Commitment in Marriage: Why Do Partners Commit to Problematic Relationships?" Pp. 253–280 in *The Ties that Bind: Perspectives on Marriage and Cohabitation,* edited by L. J. Waite. New York: Aldine de Gruyter.

Surra, Catherine A. and Deborah K. Hughes. 1997. "Commitment Processes: Accounts of the Development of Premarital Relationships." *Journal of Marriage and the Family* 59:5–21.

Sweeney, Megan M. 2010. "The Reproductive Context of Cohabitation in the U.S.: Recent Change and Variation in Contraceptive Use." *Journal of Marriage and Family* 72:1155–1170.

———. 2002. "Two Decades of Family Change: The Shifting Economic Foundations of Marriage." *American Sociological Review* 67(1):132–147.

Swidler, Ann. 1986. "Culture in Action: Symbols and Strategies." *American Sociological Review* 51:273–286.

Taylor, Paul, ed. 2010. "The Decline of Marriage and Rise of New Families." Pew Research Center. Released 11/18/2010, accessed 2/5/2013 (http://www.pewsocialtrends.org/files/2010/11/pew-social-trends-2010-families.pdf).

Thornberry, Terence P., Marvin D. Krohn, Megan B. Augusty, Molly Buchanan, and Sarah J. Greenman. 2016. "The impact of adolescent risk behavior on partner relationships." *Advances in Life Course Research* 28:6–21.

Thornton, Arland and Linda Young-Demarco. 2001. "Four Decades of Trends in Attitudes toward Family Issues in the United States: The 1960s through the 1990s." *Journal of Marriage and Family* 63:1009–1037.

Tichenor, Veronica. 2005. "Maintaining Men's Dominance: Negotiating Identity and Power When She Earns More." *Sex Roles* 53(3/4):191–205.

Trillingsgaard, Tea, Katherine J.W. Baucom, and Richard E. Heyman. 2014. "Predictors of Change in Relationship Satisfaction during the Transition to Parenthood." *Family Relations* 63:667–679.

Trussell, James. 2011. "Contraceptive Failure in the United States," *Contraception* 83:397–404.

———. 2007. "Contraceptive efficacy." Pp. 747–826 in *Contraceptive Technology*, edited by R.A. Hatcher, J. Trussell, A.L. Nelson, W. Cates, Jr., F.H. Stewart, and D. Kowal. 19th rev. ed. New York: Ardent Media. See also http://bedsider.org/.

U.S. Bureau of Labor Statistics. 2012. "Women in the Labor Force: A Databook." (http://www.bls.gov/cps/wlf-databook-2012.pdf).

———. 2009. "Women in the Labor Force: A Databook." Report 1018, Table 25 (http://www.bls.gov/cps/wlf-databook2008.htm).

———. 2007. "Highlights of Women's Earnings in 2006." Report 1000, Table 14 (http://www.bls.gov/cps/cpswom2006.pdf).

———. 2006. "Employment Status of the Civilian Non-institutional Population 25 Years and Over by Educational Attainment, Sex, Race, and Hispanic or Latino Ethnicity" (http://www.bls.gov/cps/cps_aa2006.htm).

U.S. Census Bureau. Table MS-2: "Estimated Median Age at First Marriage, by Sex: 1890 to the present." Accessed 10/20/2014 (*https://www.census.gov /population/socdemo/hh-fam/ms2.xls*).

———. Table H-8: "Median Household Income by State: 1984 to 2011." Accessed 3/22/2013 (*http://www.census.gov/data/tables/time-series/demo/income-poverty/historical-income-households.html*).

———. 2002. *Statistical Abstract of the United States: 2001* (121st edition). Table 117 (222.census.gov/prod/2002pubs/01statab/vitstat.pdf).

U.S. Department of Education. 2012. *Earned Degrees Conferred, 1869–70 through 1964–65; Projections of Education Statistics to 2021.* Table 310: "Degrees Conferred by Degree-granting Institutions, by Level of Degree and Sex of Student." National Center for Education Statistics. Accessed 7/23/2014 (http://nces.ed.gov/programs/digest/d12/tables/dt12_310.asp).

Vacquera, Elizabeth and Grace Kao. 2005. "Private and Public Displays of Affection among Interracial and Interracial Adolescence Couples." *Social Science Quarterly* 86:485–508.

Vasel, Kathryn. 2015a. "Half of All Renters Can't Afford the Rent." *CNN Money,* December 9 (http://money.cnn.com/2015/12/09/real_estate/renters-cant-afford-rent/).

———. 2015b. "Why Your Rent Check Just Keeps Going Up." *CNN Money,* June 2. (http://money.cnn.com/2015/06/02/real_estate/rising-rent-prices/).

Ventura, Stephanie. 2009. "Changing Patterns of Nonmarital Childbearing in the United States." NCHS Data Brief No. 18. Accessed 2/15/2013 (http://www.cdc.gov/nchs/data/databriefs/db18.pdf).

Vespa, Jonathan. 2012. "Union Formation in Later Life: Economic Determinants of Cohabitation and Remarriage among Older Adults." *Demography* 49(3):1103–1125.

Waller, Maureen. 2002. *My Baby's Father: Unmarried Parents and Paternal Responsibilities.* Ithaca, NY: Cornell University Press.

Wang, Wendy. 2015. "The Link between a College Education and a Lasting Marriage." Pew Research Center Fact Tank (http://www.pewresearch.org /fact-tank/2015/12/04/education-and-marriage/).

Wang, Wendy and Kim Parker. 2014. "Record Share of Americans Have Never Married as Values, Economics, and Gender Patterns Change." Washington, DC: Pew Research Center Social and Demographic Trends Project.

Webster, Bruce H. and Alemayehu Bishaw. 2007. *Income, Earnings, and Poverty Data from the 2006 American Community Survey.* U.S. Census Bureau, American Community Survey Reports, ACS-08. Washington, DC: U.S. Government Printing Office.

Wenzel, Suzanne L., Barbara D. Leake, Ronald M. Andersen, and Lillian Gelberg. 2001. "Utilization of Birth Control Services among Homeless Women." *American Behavioral Scientist* 45(1):14–34.

West, Candice and Don Zimmerman. 1987. "Doing Gender." *Gender & Society* 2:125–151.

Whyte, Martin King. 1992. "Choosing Mates—the American Way." *Society* 29(3):71–77.

Williams, Joan. 2010. *Reshaping the Work-Family Debate: Why Men and Class Matter.* Cambridge: Harvard University Press.

Williams, Kristi, Sharon Sassler, Adrianne Frech, Fenaba Addo, and Elizabeth Cooksey. 2011. "Single Mothers, Union History, and Health at Midlife." *American Sociological Review* 76(3):465–486.

Williams, Kristi, Sharon Sassler, and Lisa M. Nicholson. 2008. "For Better or For Worse? The Consequences of Marriage and Cohabitation for Single Mothers." *Social Forces* 86:1481–1511.

Winkler, Ann E., Timothy D. McBride, and Courtney Andrews. 2005. "Wives Who Outearn Their Husbands: A Transitory or Persistent Phenomenon for Couples?" *Demography* 42:523–535.

Wright, Matthew and Karen Benjamin Guzzo. 2015. "Trends in Nonmarital Birth Rates and Approval of Nonmarital Childbearing in Western Countries." Poster presented at the 2015 annual meeting of the Population Association of America, San Diego, CA.

Zabin, Laurie, G.R. Huggins, Mark R. Emerson, and V.E. Cullins. 2000. "Partner Effects on a Woman's Intention to Conceive: 'Not with this partner.'" *Family Planning Perspectives* 32:39–45.

Ziol-Guest, Kathleen, Greg J. Duncan, and Ariel Kalil. 2015. "One-Parent Students Leave School Earlier: Education Attainment Gap Widens." *Education Next* 15:36–41.

Index

abode choice, 35

abortion: childbearing and, 184; cohabitation and, 93, 111, 230n5; educational attainment and, 184; LARC (long-acting reversible contraception) and, 190, 242n41; men and, 112–13, 115, 117, 232n24; middle-class couples and, 114–16, 119–120; race and, 232n21; service-class couples and, 110, 112–13, 114–16; St. Louis CHOICE Project and, 190, 242n42; underreporting and, 232n21; unintended pregnancies and, 111–12, 115–16; women and, 112–13, 115, 117, 120

adoption, 96

Affordable Care Act (ACA), 190–91

affordable housing, 189, 242n40. *See also* housing

age, 1, 4–5, 16, 17*table,* 22, 100–101, 204–8*table,* 209–13*table,* 234n21

Alderman, Liz, 241n31

alternatives to marriage, 3, 12–13, 123, 186, 187, 193, 220n48, 236n12, 243n8

Alternatives to Marriage Project, 243n8

American Couples (Blumstein and Schwartz), 222n8

Americans: cohabitation and, 127; dating and, 221n2; domestic labor/work and, 226n7, 227n11; educational attainment and, 6; employment and, 226n5, 227n11; gender norms/roles and, 10–11, 23, 223n12; household income and, 243n8; inequality and, 2; marriage and, 3, 8, 126–27, 191–93; men and, 9; middle class and, 7–8; nonmarital births and, 128; same-sex marriage and, 220n52; social class and, 243n8; working class and, 6

American Time Use Survey, 227n11

Annual Review of Sociology, 220n48

anxiety/hesitation, 25, 32–34

Asians, 14

Bailey, Beth, 21–22

Barrett, G., 232n23

barrier methods, 103, 104, 105, 107–8, 109, 110, 116

becoming a couple, 20, 21, 24–31

Bernard, Jessie, 9, 218n33, 219n40, 226n8, 228n20

Bianchi, Suzanne, 226n10, 236n12

birth control. *See* contraception; contraception methods; contraceptive efficacy; contraceptive utilization

births, 190, 242n42. *See also* childbearing; nonmarital births; nonmarital childbearing

Bishaw, Alemayehu, 243n8

blacks, 14, 220n48

Blumberg, Rae Lesser, 219n39

Booth, Alan, 240n23